The Last Neighborhood Cops

Critical Issues in Crime and Society

Raymond J. Michalowski, Series Editor

Critical Issues in Crime and Society is oriented toward critical analysis of contemporary problems in crime and justice. The series is open to a broad range of topics including specific types of crime, wrongful behavior by economically or politically powerful actors, controversies over justice system practices, and issues related to the intersection of identity, crime, and justice. It is committed to offering thoughtful works that will be accessible to scholars and professional criminologists, general readers, and students.

For a list of titles in the series, see the last page of the book.

The Last Neighborhood Cops

The Rise and Fall of Community Policing in New York Public Housing

FRITZ UMBACH

RUTGERS UNIVERSITY PRESS
NEW BRUNSWICK, NEW JERSEY, AND LONDON

LIBRARY OF CONGRESS CATALOGING-IN-PUBLICATION DATA

Umbach, Gregory Holcomb.
The last neighborhood cops : the rise and fall of community policing in New York public housing / Fritz Umbach.
p. cm. — (Critical issues in crime and society)
Includes bibliographical references and index.
ISBN 978-0-8135-4906-4 (hardcover : alk. paper)
1. Community policing—New York (State)—New York. 2. Public housing—New York (State)—New York. I. Title.
HV7936.C83U43 2011
363.2'32—dc22

A British Cataloging-in-Publication record for this book is available from the British Library.

Visit our Web site: http://rutgerspress.rutgers.edu

Manufactured in the United States of America

For Amanda and Buck, who made it all worthwhile; the inspiring residents of the Housing Authority, who made it all possible; and the Housing Police, who didn't always get thanked

CONTENTS

ACKNOWLEDGMENTS

Early in my research for this book, one of the Housing Authority residents who generously sat for several interviews gestured to the neighbor-filled playground in front of her development and said—riffing off the African proverb popularized by Hillary Clinton's 1996 book—"It takes a courtyard to raise a kid right." The same, I've learned, goes for writing a book right. And I've had the best of courtyards, filled with colleagues whose generosity bordered on the absurd at times. Betsy Gitter, Gerry Markowitz, and Carol Groneman read far more drafts—and corrected far more gaffes—than friendship calls for in this life. Ellen Noonan at the American Social History Project brought order to my chaotic prose when it was needed—and it often was.

But the assistance started long before I wrote the book's first line. At the La Guardia and Wagner Archives, Steve Levine and Douglas DiCarlo largely tolerated my expansive and noisy research style and, far more importantly, shared their encyclopedic knowledge of New York City history and the quirks of the archives' vast holdings. Richard Lieberman, without whom there would no archive and so no book, deserves special thanks. The anonymous readers at Rutgers University Press proved how inaccurate the poor reputation of readers' reports among some academics can be. The readers' probing criticisms nudged the text just where it needed to go. Thank you.

Evan Mason, Kate Wood, and Arlene Simon at Landmark West! added immensely to this project with their dedication to preserving the Amsterdam Houses for their residents. New York is a far better place because of such community activists who leverage shoestring budgets to achieve neighborhood miracles. At various junctures, John Jay College freed me from other responsibilities—a generosity without which this book might never have been written. A grant from the City University of New York's Professional Staff Congress helped defray the cost of transcribing oral histories at a critical stage in the research, underscoring the key role a faculty union can play in the scholarship of its members. Eli Faber and Allison Kavey provided ample doses of firm chiding and good cheer when I needed it most. Ed Paulino shared beers in Santo Domingo, conducted oral histories in Brooklyn, and helped me think about public housing and Latinos in New York in ways that have powerfully shaped this book. Zaire Dinzey-Flores, similarly, generously shared her insightful research into security and public housing in Puerto Rico. Dara Byrne was an inspiring and dedicated teaching partner as I was wrapping this book up. Pat Sinatra and Jane Bowers pioneered the service-learning course that helped launch this book; they represent the best of the City University of New York and in the process taught me what sort of colleague I want to be. My biggest debts at John Jay, however, are to its students. Sheyla Celin was the model of a diligent and thoughtful research assistant—any graduate school would be lucky to get her. Maria Jimenez, Melissa Lopez, Maria Figueroa, Christian Nunez, Brittany McGee, Agrona Selimaj, Rasheda Denny, and Caswell Mclean all helped the residents of the Amsterdam Houses tell their stories in ways I might never have been able to. And every semester, John Jay students—with their humanity and independent spark—make me a better a historian.

Writing this book required gathering the perspectives of a number of impressive police officials. Former Housing Authority Police Department assistant chief of department Joe Keeney, who quietly undermines the many stereotypes of police chiefs that circulate outside the law enforcement community, often took calls at odd hours to respond to questions only he could love or answer. Former Housing PBA president Joe Balzano generously shared his deep knowledge of a police force he loyally shepherded through some dark years. Gary Nash of FOP Lodge 997 helped make possible interviews with former housing officers at the Florida HAPD reunions. Chief Joanne Jaffe of the Housing Bureau granted me several interviews and could probably give even hardened critics hope for the future of policing in urban America.

I've accumulated a lot of debts among NYCHA residents and HAPD officers; Rutgers University Press's preference that I keep my informants' names confidential prevents me from properly thanking them all here. I can only hope that I've done justice to the experiences they shared. Their inspiring stories of creative tenacity pushed me to write even when the project seemed stalled.

My parents, who had a firm policy of borrowing or occasionally buying just about any book that intrigued me when I was a child, are probably more responsible for *The Last Neighborhood Cops* than I'd like to admit. They also extended unconditional understanding when I came home to Idaho for the holidays, only to squirrel myself away to work. No expression of gratitude is enough, however, to thank Amanda, to whom this book dedicated. Without her love and support neither my life nor the writing here would be as good.

The Last Neighborhood Cops

FIGURE I.1 Publicity photograph of Housing Officer Cynthia Brown with children. Photograph courtesy of the New York Housing Authority and La Guardia Community College, CUNY Photograph © New York Housing Authority.

Introduction

The "Last Neighborhood Cops," Community Policing, and the History of Law Enforcement in Urban America

Mary Alfson paused, hunting for the right phrase. She was trying to capture for her grandson, Nicholas, how she and her neighbors in her South Bronx public housing development had viewed the police at the explosive close of the 1960s. Recalling the Housing Police who had patrolled the projects in those years, she settled on a simile to express her emotions, still forceful after four decades, about law enforcement in a neighborhood that had once epitomized bleak urban realities. "The officers," she pronounced, leaning in for emphasis, "were like family."[1]

This nostalgia may surprise many today, particularly against the backdrop of countless popular and scholarly depictions of hostility between nonwhite residents and the police as a fact of big city life. But memories such as Mary Alfson's resonate broadly with those who still recall the New York City Housing Authority Police Department (HAPD), an autonomous police force that, between 1952 and 1995, served the roughly one out of ten New Yorkers who made public housing their home.[2] At a time when black and Latino communities elsewhere in United States increasingly saw the police as oppressive, those living in New York City Housing Authority (NYCHA) complexes not only consistently supported their police but also, from the 1950s onward, regularly called for *more,* not fewer, officers. Ask older NYCHA residents and former Housing officers to explain this seeming exception to received urban truths and you will likely get an earful about the HAPD's thirty-year experiment with crime-fighting strategies that would later be called "community policing."

Although the Housing Authority Police Department's remarkable history of innovations is little known outside of New York's public housing complexes, the idea of community policing itself, and the publicity it has received, have changed the way Americans now talk about law enforcement. Indeed, few developments in police science loom larger in both the public imagination and academic writing than the "Blue Revolution" ushered in by community policing. The rhetorical and financial support for community policing in the last two decades has been so pervasive that it has transformed this social science hypothesis into a commonsense principle embraced by the public and, to a lesser degree, by the police themselves.[3]

This widespread acceptance of community policing as both socially progressive and tactically effective has developed without the benefit of any significant study of the Housing Authority Police Department experience.[4] Yet scholars and practitioners have much to learn from that forty-three-year history, which survives in the little-known but voluminous records of the HAPD as well as in the memories of public housing's residents and officers. *The Last Neighborhood Cops* draws upon both of these sources: the traditional paper trails historians follow when writing institutional histories—intra-agency missives and internal memoranda—and the personal voices of individual NYCHA residents and officers who recall the years of NYCHA's police force. Each source is remarkable. Amid the police scandals of the 1970s, the New York City Police Department (NYPD) destroyed nearly all of its precinct-level records, leaving those created by the Housing Police the only surviving documents that detail law enforcement in postwar New York City.[5] Fortuitously preserved when NYCHA transferred custodianship of its papers to the La Guardia and Wagner Archives in 1984, the hundreds of thousands of pages of HAPD documents have received scant attention from historians of policing. They provide a rare glimpse into the daily operation of a police department across a half-century of change. The tenants and officers who participated in the early years of community policing in public housing are an important—though vanishing—resource for scholars, as people who lived this history are now a rapidly aging group. Indeed, two officers interviewed for this book had already died by the time it was being prepared for publication.

Including these more personal perspectives shifts our historical view to the people on the ground in public housing, providing fresh discoveries and raising new questions about community policing that differ from those usually addressed by policy scholars. Their rich work has chronicled the roles of enlightened public opinion and government officials in the emergence of community policing as an urban policy innovation and supplies valuable snapshots of police efforts to implement the strategy in specific cities at particular times.[6] Such scholarship, however, has done less to document the day-to-day incidents, practices, and perceptions that over a sustained period ultimately make policing policies succeed or fail. Reconstructing the history of the HAPD makes possible what reading think tank white papers or department mission statements cannot: a consideration of community policing firmly based in the lived experiences of both the police and the public they serve. Telling the story of the HAPD in this way places the principal actors—tenants and officers—at center stage;

following it over decades reveals social and political intricacies that surface only with time, underscoring the complex role that context plays in community policing.

In contemplating the "Blue Revolution," scholars of all stripes have generally proceeded on the assumption that no big-city police force in the postwar period offered an example of community policing worth investigating. But for decades before the term "community policing" was coined and popularized in the 1980s, the HAPD pioneered policies that we would now hail as typical of community policing.[7] The Housing Police worked not only to integrate officers into communities in an effort to solve problems (rather than merely responding to emergency calls) but also, to a degree that is surprising today, collaborated with community leaders to define the department's priorities and allocation of resources.[8] Because the HAPD's experience in community policing spanned an impressive number of years in a not-so-distant past, it provides a unique look at the unexpected challenges and real-world consequences of the strategy.

By the late 1980s, urban progressives had come to believe in community policing as a prescription for improving city life, granting it a place of honor in their aspirations for urban reform alongside community gardens, neighborhood organizations, and pedestrian malls. Despite the role of community policing in this tableau of urban positivism, the long-term experience of New York's public housing complicates any such easy faith in the strategy. Although the HAPD had impressive success with community policing through the 1970s, by the early 1990s NYCHA officials privately admitted that as a daily practice, community policing was "dead" in the projects, mourned by few of the Housing Authority's tenants or their police department's officers.[9] That America's longest experiment in community policing was abandoned by both the community and the police suggests sobering lessons for a crime-fighting paradigm embraced (to varying degrees) by three-quarters of the nation's police departments, supported by $8.8 billion in federal grant dollars since 1995, and, more recently, offered as the best tool for fighting terrorism.[10]

This history also has particular relevance—even urgency—at a time of repeated calls, by both detractors and defenders of the police, to expand community policing in public housing. Such appeals echo across the ideological spectrum, appearing in publications as diverse as the polemical *Search and Destroy: African-American Males in the Criminal Justice System* and buttoned-down journals such as *Public Management*.[11]

Finally, as a number of criminologists have observed, public housing offers a useful setting in which to implement and study community policing, because it can help to counter a key criticism lobbed at both the strategy itself and assessments of its effectiveness: the fuzziness of "community" as a concept.[12] If the identity of the "police" in "community policing" is rarely in doubt, it is far from obvious, critics argue, who actually makes up the "community" whose interests those police are to protect. There are no clear answers to the questions of who has the power to speak for the community or define its membership. In addition, detractors note, if community means a settlement held together by thick social ties that join individuals together into a shared order, not many places in modern America now seem to fit the bill. These critics draw attention to scholarship asserting that changing patterns of work and family associated first with urbanization and later with suburbanization long ago rendered the notion of community obsolete. In short, community policing, to its opponents, is an impossible return trip to television's Mayberry, where a pie-fueled sheriff resolved the hamlet's problems during ambling talks with the locals.[13]

Public housing, however, may present a special case. Identifying a meaningful community in public housing is frequently more than an act of nostalgia, for reasons grounded in both the architectural and social character of such locations. NYCHA's complexes, for example, nearly always have a broadly understood boundary, and thus a clear geographic identity. Likewise, they often have distinct tenant organizations, chosen through elections that have reasonably high rates of participation.[14] Wesley Skogan, a prominent supporter of community policing, has lamented that "beats don't elect leaders," but for much of the HAPD's half-century, "beats"—in the form of individual NYCHA developments—did exactly that and continue to do so, lending a sense of political identity to the buildings officers patrolled.[15] Dorothy Shields, the tenant association president for the past thirty-three years for Brooklyn's Red Hook Houses (2,545 units), for example, describes herself as the "mayor" of her complex.[16] Since community in public housing can assume unusually precise physical and social dimensions, taking the measure of community policing through the HAPD's long experience offers an unusual opportunity to study this strategy with some degree of certainty over the particulars of neighborhood borders and identity.

Anticrime Activism and the History of Civil Rights

More broadly, charting the HAPD's history—and community policing's rise and eventual fall within NYCHA—documents the influence of the poor and working class on law enforcement, adding to a growing list of public policies (including the New Deal and the War on Poverty) that scholars now recognize as having been powerfully shaped by such groups.[17] Comprehending the complex political chemistry that has shaped policing in America's postwar cities calls for a more panoramic view of who "makes" law enforcement policy and practice. This broader perspective requires considering the political actions of communities *as well as* the police, of rank-and-file officers *as well as* police commissioners, of public housing residents *as well as* public housing administrators—even while acknowledging the very real power differentials separating such groups.

The decades-long battle by NYCHA tenants for a life both dignified and safe challenges a number of the simplistic and stereotypical views of crime that have persistently animated national discussions about poverty and disorder for nearly fifty years. Many of the residents whose stories are recounted here spent their entire lives in the kinds of neighborhoods that social scientists, starting in the early 1960s, claimed gave birth to an unprecedented culture of poverty and social disintegration. As theorists of the "urban crisis" explained it at the time, the inhabitants of this world had become estranged from the regular habits of work and steadying bonds of marriage to a degree that dulled their personal aspirations and collective spirit. The era's interpreters of inner-city maladies—social scientists, media pundits, and policy makers—depicted communities too bereft of male exemplars and too beset by cultural pathologies to summon the collective mettle necessary for combating the growing crime in their midst. And yet NYCHA residents—despite their difficult circumstances and notwithstanding the pessimism of experts—have an impressive history of anticrime grassroots activism, which endured from the 1950s to the 1980s.[18]

With the ascendancy of neoconservative thinkers in the 1980s, popular and scholarly conversations about "the underclass" and their environment tilted away from damaged psyches and toward damaging government policies. In this decade, critics of the welfare state achieved wide credibility and influence by insisting that the machinery of the welfare state, including public housing, had deepened the woes of the urban poor by undermining personal responsibility. NYCHA archives and tenant oral histories, however, reveal a more complex reality. For decades, New York's public housing residents often maintained a hard-won, if incomplete, order in their communities through informal control, tenant patrols, and collaborations with the HAPD. And so, the evidence gathered in *The Last Neighborhood Cops* points toward a more nuanced way of seeing New York's instantly recognizable public housing developments. NYCHA's sprawling red brick complexes were neither the dysfunctional wastelands imagined by social scientists of the 1960s and 1970s nor the hulking ruins of failed social engineering invoked more recently by neoconservatives. Instead, "the PJs," as NYCHA tenants frequently called their homes, often served as largely unheralded—though decidedly imperfect—sites of community mobilization.[19]

Recovering the story of anticrime activism in New York's public housing contributes to a growing body of scholarship that broadens our understanding of the civil rights movement by calling attention to the significance of local grassroots efforts across the country. As historian Robert Self has observed, earlier accounts of black postwar politics often "elevated" the southern movement—with its narrow focus on civil rights and principled adherence to nonviolence—as the model by which other African American political and social campaigns were to be understood and evaluated.[20] According to this influential narrative, the civil rights movement before 1965 represented a liberal triumph against southern backwardness. As the cause journeyed north, however, it lost its way, derailed by the ghetto's nihilistic anger. More recent scholarship challenges this version of African American political engagement by redefining the "black freedom struggle" to include not only the well-publicized activities of prominent organizations but also a national constellation of lesser-known local efforts, each pursuing its own aims and strategies and each contributing to the larger struggle for black empowerment. As the scholars Jeanne Theoharis and Komozi Woodward have observed, adding to the story of celebrated civil rights organizations by documenting the experience of grassroots activists who toiled outside the flashbulb's glare does more than simply enlarge the cast of characters. It transforms the saga itself, by discovering new beginnings and endings for overly neat chronologies of civil rights and Black Power ideologies, by identifying female leaders in a historical record previously dominated by men, and by unearthing struggles for goals more immediate and often less attainable than equal access to public accommodations and the southern franchise.[21]

Anticrime organizing by public housing residents in New York City was in many ways representative of the kinds of unheralded grassroots activism that took place around the country after World War II. The community organizing in NYCHA's developments was neither an imperfect imitation of the fabled southern struggle nor the spontaneous and aimless product of fiery Black Power radicals. Rather, it was a homegrown mobilization, born of local circumstances and neighborhood wisdom. The activists, most of whom were women, understood their efforts in terms of civil rights. They believed that securing their fair share of municipal services, including police protection, was a fundamental right and that working for safer buildings and courtyards was a chapter in the long history of working-class self-help movements. In retrospect, it is perhaps not surprising that the media's preference for television-worthy reports meant that the indelible popular image of urban protest in the late 1960s would be black men sporting bandoliers and preaching revolution rather than female tenant leaders holding police accountable for improving local conditions. But it was often precisely such patient efforts, frequently waged in cooperation with the HAPD officers who policed the developments, that helped sustained New York's public housing through some of its darkest hours of fiscal crisis and national indifference. The survival of New York's public housing system, at a time when other cities such as Chicago and St. Louis saw theirs tumble into chaos, is arguably one of the more enduring legacies of black and Latino activism in New York.

In detailing the ways that NYCHA residents collectively tended to the shared order of their communities, *The Last Neighborhood Cops* builds upon and extends the insights of pathbreaking studies of public housing activism that have reshaped historical understandings of both the "urban crisis" and the War on Poverty. These studies show that in many northern cities, housing developments, for all their shortcomings, did far more than put a roof over residents' heads.

Public housing's scruffy courtyards and crowded hallways often turned out to be rich training grounds for a generation of mostly female activists. In *The Politics of Public Housing: Black Women's Struggles against Urban Inequality*, historian Rhonda Williams reveals how the creation of public housing in Baltimore gave rise to political awakening and class mobility among black women that belied their popular characterization as mired in entrenched dependency. Likewise, Roberta M. Feldman and Susan Stall document what they call *The Dignity of Resistance* among public housing residents in Chicago, whose identities as African American women and struggling mothers shaped their battles against growing government disinvestment in their communities. Lisa Levenstein uncovers in Philadelphia's public housing the history of a *Movement without Marches*. Black women, she argues, challenged the postwar city's racial and gender inequalities by seeking a variety of resources from government programs. These resources, including subsidized housing, provided badly needed leverage in their relations with employers and with men—even as such public programs subjected their largely African American beneficiaries to intensive surveillance and public humiliation.[22]

The Last Neighborhood Cops charts public housing's contradictory impact on the poor. NYCHA provided a place of residence as well as a site of resistance; it eased the daily burdens of poverty even as it imposed conditions of tenancy that limited residents' choices about whom to live with and how to earn a living. In contrast to existing scholarship, however, *The Last Neighborhood Cops* explores at length how public housing residents confronted what they frequently saw as the most threatening consequence of their own economic and political vulnerability: growing lawlessness in their communities. Crucially, recovering the full story of tenants' often overlooked anticrime activism also reveals how the shifting social texture and political context of such struggles put many tenant leaders at odds with New York City's prevailing brand of urban liberalism.

The Fall of Community Policing in New York Public Housing and the Trajectory of Urban Liberalism

The history of community policing in New York's public housing contains the makings of a cautionary tale as well as of a policy success story. Well into the 1990s, NYCHA continued to celebrate its police as the nation's last "neighborhood cops," but as early as the 1970s a careful inside observer might have noticed that community policing in the Authority's complexes had begun to unravel as both the community and the police took steps that frayed the tacit agreements essential to the strategy.[23] Ironically, both groups would break faith with community policing not because it failed but precisely because it had, in fact, worked. HAPD officers *did* come to know the neighborhoods they served, but that familiarity began to trouble many residents who, as the hard times of the 1970s wore on, increasingly depended on an informal economy that they preferred the Housing Authority know little about. NYCHA's tenants *did* come to see the HAPD as integral to their communities, but that embrace grew to unsettle officers who sought, in an era of potent municipal unions, to identify with the city's politically powerful police rather than its economically poorest residents. Public housing residents *did* use their newfound political voice to reshape law enforcement policy in their developments but watched with dismay the unintended consequences of their calls for greater police visibility.

Reconstructing the history of crime-fighting policies in New York's public housing is not merely an exercise in documenting unintended consequences but also an opportunity to examine local and national politics of urban reform in the post–World War II era. In particular, the eventual failure of community policing in New York's public housing lays bare internal contradictions within urban liberalism and so sheds light on two of the most interesting developments in the political landscapes of both New York and the country at large: the rise of neoconservative policies in a city often believed to be a liberal redoubt, and the "punitive turn" in the nation's system of criminal justice. The history of policing in New York's public housing suggests that African American and Latino communities were more active in both of these developments than is commonly believed. Indeed, conventional wisdom rarely gives these communities active roles in the oft-told tale of liberalism's disarray, other than as radical provocateurs who alienated their erstwhile white allies.

Analyses of liberalism have tended to wrestle with the question of who first tugged at the threads that "unraveled" the New Deal coalition, the famed alignment of interest groups and voting blocs that nourished a generation-long Democratic Party majority from FDR to LBJ. Much conventional wisdom points to the defection of white voters alarmed by the "excesses" of 1960s liberalism in general and black militancy in particular.[24] More recent historical research, however, has documented the ways in which white backlash was well underway long before the racial conflicts of the 1960s and 1970s: before controversies over busing, before the "long hot summer" of 1967 and its urban riots, and even before the first flak catcher met the first mau-mau'er.[25] Indeed, some scholars trace the demise of the New Deal coalition to an internal tension encoded within its own electoral DNA. The promise of full citizenship for African Americans (a key voting bloc in northern cities) inevitably collided with the New Deal's social contract, which blue-collar whites (another central constituency) believed assured them segregated neighborhoods and workplace privileges. And so, as recent historical studies have persuasively demonstrated, the assault on liberalism started not with the Great Society of the 1960s but rather with the Great Migration of the 1940s, when large numbers of African Americans fled southern racism and economic stagnation for new opportunities in northern cities. Whites attempting to defend their racial privileges then drive the story of liberalism's internal struggles in these years.[26]

Surprisingly, however, even in accounts of urban liberalism's growing troubles after 1970, African Americans and Latinos continue to play only a walk-on role, despite their emerging political influence in many cities. It was white suburban populists, historians argue, who sealed the fate of liberalism. A recent "Sun Belt synthesis" sees the rise of modern conservatism as propelled less by Republican leaders' "southern strategy" of appealing to white supremacy and more by New South suburbanites' embrace of a "free-market meritocracy." This putatively race-neutral political language rejected "massive resistance" while still managing to justify the residential segregation and property-owner entitlements the expanding suburban communities enjoyed. The Republican Party achieved its late-twentieth-century majority by offering white southern suburbanites a politically palatable means to limit their financial and moral commitments to solve the problems of the cities they had fled. It was in the suburbs, some scholars insist, where modern conservatism was born and the New Deal coalition met its end.[27]

Despite the convincing insights and important corrections offered by this new scholarship, these arguments have, by focusing on the actions and rhetoric of the white majority, overlooked the ways in which many urban minorities also defected from key aspects of liberalism as a philosophy of governance, even as they remained loyal to the Democratic Party in electoral politics. White ethnics and suburban homeowners did not have a monopoly on disillusionment with urban liberalism and its seeming inability to respond effectively to crime.

By "urban liberalism" I mean here the coherent collection of policy tendencies promoted by mayoral administrations and elite organizations in many northern cities from the 1960s through the early 1990s. As sociologist Alex Vitale argues, urban liberalism blended "entrepreneurial economic development strategies, personal rehabilitation and social work philosophies, and a tolerance of social differences in the form of broad support for civil liberties." Urban liberals pursued different aims in different cities in ways that could depart from a national liberal agenda—energetically challenging deindustrialization in Philadelphia, for example—but their policy goals and tools frequently included an emphasis upon freeing individuals from state constraints. The broad consensus on this score by activists and policy makers was no coincidence. After 1965, federal funding and support for a new form of legal advocacy helped expand individual rights in relation to state institutions, from public schools to public housing. But urban liberalism's stress upon social freedoms did not always jibe with many NYCHA residents' long-standing traditions of community uplift and self-determination.[28]

For example, as I will discuss in detail in chapter 4, many NYCHA residents bitterly resented and ultimately, through elected tenant representatives, legally contested the expansion of tenants' procedural rights in eviction cases—a move consistent with urban liberalism's key principles, but one that tenants believed sapped their efforts with the HAPD to maintain the daily order of their world. In the late 1960s, as part of a larger strategy to use the law as an instrument of social change, attorneys working for agencies funded by the Great Society's Office of Economic Opportunity won court cases that enlarged legal protections for NYCHA tenants fighting eviction for violations of either law or NYCHA's own rules of tenancy. In theory, these legal decisions merely redefined public housing residency as a form of property that, under the Fourteenth Amendment, owners could not be deprived of without due process. In practice, the resulting 1971 consent decree (*Escalera v. NYCHA*) made evictions for even serious crimes nearly impossible.[29] Many tenant leaders, whose constituents experienced this change chiefly as a weakening of their community's safety rather than as an enrichment of individual liberty, protested to the Authority almost immediately. Defeated in the courts, however, NYCHA officials could often only sympathize with residents' complaints of having to live next to what one observer called "Wal-Mart-sized drug dens."[30]

Tenant pressure, however, would help remake the legal landscape of public housing. Although popular memory credits New York Mayor Rudolph Giuliani with the city's shift to strong-arm policing strategies, in one of the earliest instances of such practices—the use of asset-forfeiture laws in public housing drug cases—tenant activists and NYCHA's management had to pressure Giuliani, then U.S. attorney for the Southern District of New York, into adopting this more aggressive and punitive legal strategy (an issue explored in depth in chapter 4). When later legal developments in the 1990s encouraged NYCHA to return to court seeking to modify *Escalera* to combat crack cocaine's ravages, elected tenant leaders hired their own attorneys to side with the Authority *against* the Legal Aid lawyers who, under the consent decree, theoretically represented them.[31] Although certainly not a full-blown backlash, such tenant activism did successfully push back against the legal legacy of liberalism's heyday in ways that have been largely overlooked.[32]

Similarly, while civil libertarians opposed the growing police use of video surveillance in public housing and elsewhere under Mayor Giuliani, some NYCHA residents have a tradition of seeing such security equipment as an extension, not violation, of their civil rights: proof of their social dignity, not political frailty.[33] Indeed, residents have scraped together their own scarce savings to acquire surveillance equipment. As one tenant advocate, Mae Miller, proudly said in 1977 when her African Liberation Center purchased security cameras for her complex, "now we've got the same kind of system they've got in luxury buildings."[34]

If the role of conservative groups in promoting law-and-order politics is well documented, the efforts of non-elite groups like public housing activists to mobilize around crime in ways that also challenged some of urban liberalism's ideals is often left unexamined. As the political scientist Marie Gottschalk reminds us, the rise of the "carceral state" after 1970 depended on the sometimes unexpected workings of America's interest-group politics.[35]

Gottschalk explores the role of the victims' movement, the women's movement, the prisoners' rights movement, and opponents of the death penalty in facilitating—if largely unwittingly—the abandonment of a rehabilitative model of criminal justice in favor of a punitive state. *The Last Neighborhood Cops* adds public housing activists to that list—with some important qualifications. First, tenant leaders nearly always organized in highly constrained circumstances. Individual poverty, municipal austerity, and a growing national antagonism toward public housing all meant that tenant activists held few strong cards in their hand. Second, tracing the ways such activists contributed to law-and-order politics beginning in the 1970s is not the same thing as holding them responsible for its current form. Recognizing, for example, the role tenant leaders played in modifying *Escalera* does not require overlooking the documented abuses of the evictions process today.

How are we to understand those aspects of black and Latino anticrime activism in public housing that, at first glance, seem to dovetail so readily with the punitive criminal justice policies championed by conservative politicians? To dismiss tenant leaders' support for strong-arm strategies as merely reflexive panic in response to crime or subservient acquiescence to the Housing Authority would be to underestimate their insight. In truth, tenant anticrime activism often reflected many public housing residents' tempered reckoning of their own political situation. By the middle of the 1970s, many public housing tenants believed that living in the house that liberalism built meant experiencing firsthand the consequences of that political project's expansion of individual rights at the expense of the shared standards that sustained their own communities. An analysis of residents' support for fast-track evictions and strict enforcement of housing regulations, understood in the context of tenants' decades of neighborhood activism, makes clear that such positions were, in fact, continuations of the residents' seasoned philosophy of locating both strength and rights in their own communities.

Community Policing and the History of Urban Law Enforcement in America

The Last Neighborhood Cops interprets the experience of the Housing Police as a way to explore the larger story of law enforcement in America, in particular the strategy known as community policing. These goals require a somewhat extended discussion of community policing itself. The proponents of community policing argue that it reorganizes the aims, tactics, and sources of legitimacy of modern policing. In doing so, the approach explicitly rests upon a particular reading of the history of law enforcement. The new strategy, its adherents argue, reaches back to a better era in order to apply to today's streets the wisdom of a time when cops still walked a beat. In recovering a tradition of police patrol that supposedly flourished a century ago, advocates claim that community policing can set right the policy blunders of subsequent decades, which have magnified the social distance between officers and the public. But this "usable past" of knowledgeable patrolmen walking steady beats in grateful neighborhoods has been the subject of some debate. Historians of policing have reminded us that the good old days weren't that good: foot patrols were hopelessly inefficient, patrolmen enjoyed scant legitimacy, and corruption and brutality reigned. And so, as historian Samuel Walker has expressed it, "there is no viable older tradition to restore."[36]

Both of these contrasting accounts, however, contribute to our understanding of the history of the HAPD. The first version exposes the sometimes unspoken assumptions behind community policing and helps explain why it emerged as a concept in the 1980s. The story of police history narrated by community policing advocates, for example, reveals and intentionally bolsters the strategy's assumptions that communities possess the ability and desire for social control—and that wise police practices can spark such traits back to life when they have fallen dormant. Similarly, community policing's ability in the 1980s to shoulder aside competing strategic innovations to become the paradigm of law enforcement is more comprehensible when considered alongside the urban unrest and relentlessly rising crime of the preceding decades that stripped the police of a good deal of their public esteem and self-confidence. Adherents of community policing were not simply peddling another tactic; they were offering a resonant tale of a fallen golden age and the promise of redemption through community participation.

The second narrative—in which historians cast serious doubt on the existence of a golden age for "beat cops" a century ago—underscores the importance of the history of the Housing Police to understanding the benefits and pitfalls of community policing. Considered as a case study, the HAPD's successful experience from 1952 through the 1970s with strategies remarkably similar to community policing provides scholars with a uniquely relevant, sustained, and detailed precedent. A history of the Housing Police demonstrates how well community policing can work and why—but that history also reveals weaknesses inherent to the strategy. Indeed, several of the problems of the "golden age"—insufficient supervision, for example—also appear in the HAPD in the 1970s, suggesting some immutable truths about "beat cops." At the same time, the HAPD experience also points to more recent and often unexplored challenges to community policing, including the consequences for law enforcement of the informal economy, and the effects on officers of their ambitions to achieve professional status, political power, and career advancement.

Advocates of community policing rely on a periodization of law enforcement history that presents their approach as a necessary remedy to the flaws of the "reform era" of policing, which stretched from just before World War I until the 1970s. This period, in turn, is presented as a reaction to policing's "political era," which lasted from the mid-nineteenth-century birth of modern police departments until the early-twentieth-century reforms.[37]

From the mid-nineteenth century until the advent of the reform era, early police departments served as appendages to the urban political machines that provided community services, a modicum of public safety, and the security of municipal jobs for recent immigrants—all in return for votes on election day.[38] According to the textbook story of community policing, however, the "malfeasance and abuse" born of this arrangement was offset by the benefits it permitted. Those seeking to restore the lost ethos of the "beat cop" point out that the police once took on many social obligations before city halls viewed such tasks as municipal services. Even without the benefit of a guiding theory, officers often fed the hungry, housed the homeless, and collected the neighborhood's garbage. Most important, since the police recruited from and operated out of the communities they served, they enjoyed a social legitimacy that today, we are frequently told, they have lost.[39]

To students of turn-of-the-twentieth-century law enforcement, this historical account is pure fantasy. Treated as electoral spoils, police headquarters were less places of law than marketplaces of corruption. Matters were little better on the street. Supervisors found it almost impossible to control patrolmen. Snow, rain, or simply a hot day—all sufficed for officers to while away their tours of duty in barrooms and barbershops. Moreover, officers were too few in number and turned over too frequently to develop the close neighborhood relationships celebrated by advocates of community policing. Official records divulge that many officers frequently drank excessively at work and off; on their beats they employed physical abuse with little restraint.[40] Despite such evidence, the sepia-toned image of the helpful officer who knew his beat continues to exert a powerful hold on the popular imagination and still plays an important role in arguments in favor of community policing.[41]

Urban Policing in the Reform Era

Late-nineteenth-century reformers held no such romantic views of urban police departments. Drawn largely from elite Protestant circles, these reformers channeled public outrage at police lawlessness and lobbied to insulate urban constabularies from the corrosive effects of local politics. Their campaigns would, not accidentally, also weaken the electoral muscle of working-class, heavily Catholic immigrant communities. Reformers introduced civil service requirements that curbed patronage, while a new generation of police chiefs responded to emerging notions of scientific management by centralizing authority within their departments.[42] As these reforms gradually reshaped departments' ranks, the telephone and, by the 1930s, radio-equipped patrol cars transformed officers' routines. The telephone allowed citizens to summon the police directly; the radio allowed headquarters to dispatch patrolmen efficiently; the prowl car allowed them to arrive at the scene quickly.

This new state of affairs had a number of important consequences. First, chiefs came to equate managerial supervision with radio communication, while communities—increasingly socialized to "call the cops"—saw rapid response time as the best proof of police effectiveness. Second, officers now had both more and less contact with civilians. On the one hand, emergency calls ushered the police—in a way previously impossible—into the intimate sites of personal disputes and family troubles; officers now found themselves maintaining order in hallways and kitchens as well as in streets and squares. On the other hand, squad cars isolated officers from the ordinary lives of the law-abiding. In many cities, police lost contact with the workaday world of stable households and sturdy wage earners while gaining a great deal of exposure to lives gripped by crisis or criminality. Consequently, officers' and civilians' perceptions of each other deteriorated.[43]

The reform era had an additional consequence, say advocates of community policing. Police departments, eager to establish legitimacy via neutral legal procedures rather than close neighborhood ties, redefined their purpose around the skills and tools of law enforcement. The legacy of reform thus included departments that pursued a narrow crime-fighting mission and officers who assumed that making arrests under the criminal law best served that goal.[44] Historians of policing, however, offer a more complicated account, arguing that the new model changed what police *said* they were doing more than what they actually did. Although police officers and departments embraced their new self-image as "professional" crime fighters as a way to secure greater political autonomy, officers spent remarkably little time responding to crime—less than a tenth of their day, found one study—and far more on tasks unrelated to enforcing the law, as an avalanche of research in the 1970s documented.[45]

Scholarly comparisons of crime-fighting imagery and operational reality, however, can obscure an important change. Although order maintenance remained a large part of officers' daily routines, the police *had* adopted a new yardstick for understanding their role. Departments increasingly measured their performance—and that of individual officers—with statistics, tracking and reporting the rate of serious crimes as calculated by a uniform system of classification developed by early-twentieth-century reformers.[46] Likewise, the number of arrests made by an officer increasingly attracted the attention of supervisors and promised rewards, such as days off for a "good pinch" or a nod for the detective division.[47] The principles of scientific management pushed by reformers emphasized the quantifiable—crime rates and arrest totals—while making less room for the less measurable.

The damaging consequences of the reform model of policing remained largely invisible until the 1960s and 1970s, when a combination of urban unrest and empirical research shattered both its philosophical assumptions and its crime-control image. The hundreds of riots nationwide between 1964 and 1968—largely in inner cities, and almost all triggered by incidents involving the police—exposed an enmity seemingly produced by reform-style policing. Although many blamed "outside agitators," others took seriously the explanations offered by the National Advisory Commission on Civil Disorders (popularly known as the Kerner Commission), which had been tasked with identifying the causes of the unrest. The Commission found the riots had sprung from a "deep hostility between police and ghetto communities," and it held a bundle of police practices responsible for adding fuel to the resentment burning in urban America. Aggressive, "stranger" patrols "which move[d] into high-crime districts without prior notice and conduct[ed] intensive, often indiscriminate, street stops and searches" embittered the community, while the patrol car fostered alienation between officers and citizens.[48] Police departments, having achieved reformers' aspirations for politically detached law enforcement, now faced the liabilities of their estrangement from many of the communities they served. And that rift, as a presidential commission on law enforcement had noted the previous year, jeopardized police effectiveness by provoking residents into withholding the assistance essential for identifying suspects.[49]

The next decade brought a wave of academic studies that eroded the earlier confidence in the three key tactics of reform-era crime control: random patrol, rapid response, and investigative follow-up. An experiment in Kansas City seemed to demonstrate that motorized, random patrol had no real effect on crime control or citizen fears. Subsequent studies revealed that radio-driven response to emergency calls netted few wrongdoers; nearly always, crimes were reported to the police "too slowly for a response-related arrest to be made." One criminologist observed that, even if police were to travel "faster than a speeding bullet to all reports of serious crimes," the on-scene arrest rate would rise to no higher than 5 percent from 3 percent.[50] Similarly, a RAND study of detectives found that investigative expertise barely mattered in most cases. Additional research documented that when police did identify suspects, it generally occurred before a detective was assigned to the case and most often from information provided by witnesses at the crime scene rather than evidence derived through specialized technique. In short, squad cars didn't deter criminals, detectives didn't sleuth cases, and officers didn't inspire gratitude; modern policing, it seemed to many, was failing.[51]

Community Policing

The emergence of community policing in the 1980s proved to be law enforcement's most significant shift since the reform era, but the strategy borrowed from earlier police experiments (and failures) initiated in response to the profession's perceived crisis. Urban unrest had exposed, on national television, the unpopularity of the police. In response, many departments resurrected a program dating from the *last* wave of antipolice riots in the 1940s—community relations units.[52] Like their predecessors, these warmed-over efforts rarely reconnected police to communities. As one study at the time noted, such units were simply "one-way public relations" campaigns without even the pretense of "being reciprocal."[53] Still, these units created a cadre of officers exposed to community priorities, even if they were unable to respond effectively. The strategy of "team policing"—stable teams of officers accountable for geographic areas—also enjoyed a fleeting vogue in the 1970s in an effort to stem the deterioration of both neighborhood conditions and police–community relations. The effectiveness of these programs varied, and suspicious supervisors, resentful colleagues, and cost-cutting city councils generally saw to it that the initiatives did not last very long.[54] But team policing had succeeded in suggesting the value of greater attention to neighborhoods and more discretion for line officers. Collectively, then, community relations programs and team policing efforts set the stage for the development of community policing theory.

Community policing has been invoked in so many contexts by so many people—law enforcement personnel, politicians, activists, and scholars—that defining it becomes tricky. Indeed, the National Research Council has declared that the nebulousness of the term, which has been attached to innumerable and varied programs undertaken in its name, makes research on community policing almost impossible.[55] Despite the vagueness of the concept, however, it is possible to identify and describe three fairly distinct theoretical approaches to the subject that emerged in quick succession in the late 1970s and early 1980s: problem-oriented policing, community-oriented policing, and, finally, broken-windows policing.

The first significant reassessment of the reform model came in 1979 with Herman Goldstein's concept of problem-oriented policing. The police mission, this law professor contended, focused too narrowly on enforcing the criminal code in reaction to discrete events. Responding to citizens' calls for service ate up police resources, leaving officers with neither the inclination nor the time "for acting on their own initiative to prevent or reduce community problems."[56] According to Goldstein, escaping this predicament required recognizing that the unit of police work should be the problem, not the incident. Such crime-producing conditions, and the appropriate responses, could only be identified with the help of the community. In retrospect, Goldstein's insight can seem so commonsensical that it's easy to miss how dramatically it turned the prevailing wisdom on its head. For two generations, reformers had insisted that professional policing meant shielding officers from the dangers of community ties, but Goldstein argued the community was not the source of policing's problems but rather its best solution.

Goldstein's emphasis on neighborhood problems inspired other scholars, who extended his thinking by casting the community not simply as a source of tactical intelligence—the "eyes on the street" that spotted problems—but as a fresh wellspring of support for police departments' badly withered political legitimacy. If reform-era policing had justified its authority by invoking the values of an impartial enforcement of the law and a detached professionalism on the street, community-oriented policing could establish a new legitimacy rooted in community support.[57] That mattered, claimed advocates, because although criminal law could authorize an arrest, it couldn't negotiate conflicts or maintain order.[58] Those tasks require the backing of neighborhoods—precisely what police had lost during the long decades of reform.

Transforming the relationship between officers and the neighborhoods they serve, argued community-policing advocates, also required changing the relationship between officers and their superiors. Because the strategy invites residents to nominate problems for officers' attention, community policing obliges expanding the police role beyond the familiar (and failed) "three R's": rapid response, random patrol, and reactive investigation. Line officers, this thinking continues, need to be freed from the reform era's rule-bound hierarchy to respond to community concerns. Those closest to the ground should make the tactical decisions that had previously descended from the top brass. And so by the early 1990s, community policing manuals had come to resemble corporate management tracts, urging department chiefs to "decentralize" authority while "empowering" their rank and file.[59]

For the strategy to work, however, officers had to know their beats. Community policing has historically privileged those tactics, such as foot patrol and community organizing, that bring officers into both more personal relationships with neighborhood residents and more working partnerships with other city agencies. In short, community policing promises to restore the bygone era of close police-citizen bonds without the corruption that once greased such linkages.

Broken-windows policing—a more aggressive and sometimes disavowed cousin of community policing—emerged at much the same time, pushed by the 1981 Newark Foot Patrol Experiment. That study had reintroduced neighborhood beat patrols, but found that crime rates didn't budge. Citizens, however, *felt* safer because foot patrols—investigators claimed—had reduced their fears of encounters with the city's disorderly denizens: drunks, panhandlers, streetwalkers, and unruly youths.[60] Expanding these conclusions in an influential 1982 *Atlantic Monthly* article, James Q. Wilson and George L. Kelling argued that the reform-era focus on pursuing criminals—making more arrests with an eye toward a commission or gathering more evidence to insure a conviction—encouraged police to neglect their vital role in promoting a community's quality of life. The anxiety "endemic in many big-city neighborhoods" stemmed as much from a fear of disorder as from a realistic appraisal of the chances of being victimized.[61] Moreover, Wilson and Kelling maintained, disorder breeds crime. Leaving a broken window unrepaired signals that "no one cares," and soon many more will be broken; tolerating inebriates slumped on the sidewalk or teenagers loitering on the corner frightens the law-abiding off the streets, weakening "informal control" and exposing neighborhoods to criminal invasion.[62] Managing street life by policing low-level infractions, the theory holds, not only punishes petty crimes of disorder but also prevents major crimes of violence. Critics have extensively attacked this latter claim, pointing to studies documenting both that disorder doesn't cause crime and that its absence doesn't reduce it. Others decry the violation of civil liberties that they believe the strategy fosters.[63]

Community policing has come to dominate law enforcement, some scholars observed, "not because it has been proved to work," but because previous approaches have been shown to fail.[64] Indeed, evaluations of community policing's effectiveness have been, as even the strategy's adherents admit, inconclusive at best.[65] Many assessments of community policing are as notable for their cataloging of a locality's failure to execute the strategy fully as they are for their evaluation of the approach's efficacy. Such studies detail the causes and consequences of a perceived gap between community policing's tenets and its real-world manifestations in a particular context. Left unexplored is what might have occurred with a fuller realization of the strategy. For example, a late 1990s study of an experiment in community policing at several Philadelphia public housing complexes described a department whose established culture of "avoidance" policing by line officers and "continually distracted" commanders severely limited the implementation of community policing—and, by implication, the significance that could be attached to the relatively minor impact made by community policing in that setting.[66] Likewise, Wesley Skogan's twelve-year study of Chicago's Alternative Policing Strategy (CAPS) attributed community policing's "failure" to benefit the city's Latinos to that population's low "commitment" to CAPS.[67] In these evaluations, community policing's failings lie not with the strategy itself but with its intended beneficiaries—the community and the police—who are said to fall short of community policing's ideals.

In contrast to such studies of ephemeral or incomplete efforts to put community policing into action, *The Last Neighborhood Cops* chronicles a rather robust and impressively sustained embrace of the strategy by both the community and the police. Because NYCHA intentionally formed its police force as a community-oriented department just as New York's public housing started to expand, the HAPD was unburdened by the institutional legacies—such as department chiefs clinging to control or police unions resistant to change—that scholars often fault for thwarting more recent efforts to enact community policing.[68] In short, while contemporary evaluations of community policing ask "can it be made to work?" the historical perspective adopted here instead explores "what ultimately happens when it does work?" The disbanding of HAPD in 1995 made it possible to answer that question because it provided rare access to usually closed police records and wide-ranging oral histories that often revealed subtle shifts in the interactions between residents and officers over decades.

Oral Histories

Although *The Last Neighborhood Cops* is an historical study, not an ethnographic portrait, oral histories with thirty-five housing officers and fifty-seven NYCHA residents inform the arguments presented here. Researchers interested in topics related to those living at society's margins—such as public housing residents—often have no choice but to use oral histories. They do, however, have options about how they conduct such interviews and handle the stories that emerge. Accordingly, some discussion of methodology is in order. The personal accounts that undergird aspects of this book are in many ways the product of the unique institutional mission of the John Jay College of Criminal Justice at The City University of New York, where I've taught since 2000. At this urban public university, I was lucky enough to have former Housing officers as well as current and past NYCHA residents among both my colleagues and my students. Indeed, this book opens, appropriately enough, with the memories of a former NYCHA resident and grandmother of one of my students; it ends with the recollections of Arthur Brown (1933–2006), a colleague in John Jay's Interdisciplinary Studies Program, who retired from the Housing Police as a deputy inspector after three decades of service and who, for a number of years, lived in NYCHA's Lincoln Houses. Without the generosity and insights of such individuals I might have been obliged to write a very different book. And although *The Last Neighborhood Cops* follows the paper trails left behind by the Housing Police and NYCHA, the vivid personal accounts used here consistently shed light on and filled in gaps within the inert documentary record I encountered in the archives. In doing so, the oral histories helped bring to this study the voices and experiences of tenants and police officers whose perspectives might have otherwise gotten lost in a flurry of Housing Authority white papers.

John Jay's public service mission nourished my efforts to get to know those NYCHA residents whose experiences stretched back to the Authority's 1952 founding of the Housing Police. Early in my research for this book, I had the opportunity to teach in a service-learning program combining academic learning with a focused volunteer experience. Thus my class on public housing blended course readings and archival research with extensive service at the Amsterdam Houses, an NYCHA development one block from campus whose many older residents had needs that could not always be met by its own senior center. My students and I cleaned apartments, escorted seniors on visits to doctors and markets, and distributed information to homebound tenants.

The students and I, however, also wanted their academic research to make a contribution to the Amsterdam Houses. We hoped to avoid repeating the familiar pattern of outside researchers failing to give back to communities they study, so the course partnered with a local preservation group, Landmark West! (LMW!), to research the historical significance of the Amsterdam Houses in order to assist LMW! in making the case for landmark status for the development. Such a designation was an important goal for the residents, who believed that neighborhood gentrification might encourage NYCHA to exploit the financial value of the complex's location by turning the land over to private developers. The residents' fear was seemingly later confirmed when Sean Moss, then New York State regional director of HUD, suggested in a public forum that the cash-strapped Authority should consider selling its valuable properties and agreed with others who identified the Amsterdam Houses as one such property; NYCHA officials have since publicly rejected such a plan.[69]

With this mission in mind, the students pored through the extensive documentary record on the Amsterdam Houses at the La Guardia and Wagner Archives and the Citizens Housing and Planning Council. As they did so, they conducted extensive interviews with the older NYCHA residents they had been helping throughout the semester. Many of the accounts used here, accordingly, were not elicited by formal interviews with the author but rather coaxed out during more relaxed, although taped, conversations between tenants and these undergraduates—some of whom were residents of public housing themselves. The students then wove those oral histories together with their archival findings into an illustrated exhibit on the history of the community. The exhibit opened first at the Amsterdam Houses for the residents before moving on to a local museum and, eventually, the Web. At the same time, partly as a consequence of the research by the students, LMW! succeeded in its application to the New York State Historic Preservation Office to designate the Amsterdam Houses as eligible for the National Register—an important first step toward winning landmark status.

As news of LMW!'s accomplishment spread, tenant leaders at other complexes reached out to me and, in an example of what is often referred to as a snowball methodology, put me in touch with additional long-term NYCHA residents to interview. Through such contacts I found myself invited to old-timers reunions at a number of NYCHA developments. These lively summer affairs gathered around plates of home-cooked food precisely the older former residents I wanted to interview. All oral historians should be so lucky (and well fed).

A similar chain of events connected me to former Housing Police, as officers I met through Arthur Brown introduced me to their old partners and commanders. Critically, Assistant Chief of Department Joseph Keeney—who ran the Office of the Chief for many years—sat for several long interviews. And if NYCHA's former residents have their reunions, so too do the Authority's former police. The Fraternal Order of Police Lodge #997 for the Housing Authority Police Department graciously allowed me to attend their Florida reunion and conduct interviews amid their own jovial story swapping and backslapping. Officers I met there agreed to subsequent follow-up telephone interviews.

All of these interviews, whether conducted by me or by mostly undergraduate research assistants under my guidance, adopted a semistructured approach. Our oral history protocol employed scripted questions in an established sequence but also allowed discussions to range far afield as the interviewees raised unexpected topics and issues. A biographical narrative approach guided the interviews: we inquired about family, work, educational, and residential histories; we invited subjects to describe their relations with other tenants or officers and with NYCHA; and we asked what questions we had failed to ask and should have in order to understand their lives.[70] All participants in the study, of course, gave "informed consent" and maintained control over the final disposition of the digital recordings and subsequent transcripts. In addition, these oral histories with officers and residents always phrased questions about activities that violated either NYCHA policies or the law in ways that allowed interviewees to describe such events as matters they had witnessed or heard about rather than actually participated in. Although all the interviewees but one gave me permission to use their names in this publication, at the request of my editor I have changed the names of all the informants who appear here—except where distinguishing details make it impossible to disguise their identity.

FIGURE 1.1 Work Projects Administration poster, "Eliminate crime in the slums through housing," New York: Federal Art Project, 1936. Photograph courtesy of the Work Projects Administration Poster Collection, Library of Congress.

1

"Our Buildings Must Be Patrolled by Foot"

Policing Public Housing and New York City Politics, 1934–1960

On an unseasonably warm October evening in 1941 on Manhattan's West Side, the residents of New York City's second-largest black neighborhood, San Juan Hill, took to the streets for a block party. A swing band led by local son "Hubbie" James—soon to become the trumpeter for the nation's first black marine battalion—roused on the dancing until the guest of honor, Mayor Fiorello La Guardia, mounted the podium. "Farewell to the slums," La Guardia proclaimed, gesturing to the district's notorious tenements, whose slated demolition would make way for a bold housing development to be designed by three of the city's best architects and ultimately financed by $7.7 million of the public's dollars. "Let in the sky! Let in the light!" Gotham's mayor continued. "Down with rotten antiquated rat holes. Down with disease. Down with crime." La Guardia was hardly alone in his faith that public housing could banish crime by replacing the slum's squalor with the spacious designs of modern architecture and by supplanting the slumlord's rapaciousness with the benevolent competence of civil servants. As historians of the period have observed, a generation of reform-minded municipal officials and metropolitan planners conceived of air and light as immutable forces of urban progress because these factors embodied the opposite of the overcrowding and grime that had characterized—and so seemed to have caused—poverty in America's cities.[1]

By 1930, a broad coalition of the public-spirited had begun to urge a loosening of the municipal purse in order to remake New York City's blighted tenements into modernist landscapes open to "sunshine and air." Such advances, predicted housing advocates (or "housers" as they christened themselves), would uplift not just the conditions of the poor but their morals as well. The chief probation officer of New York's Court of General Sessions, Irving Halpern, was particularly enthusiastic about the crime-eradicating powers of public housing. Scrutinizing police files in 1934, Halpern and his coauthors gauged that

58 percent of Manhattan's arrested crooks and wrongdoers resided in the borough's slums. There, "narrow streets" with "seven-story walk-ups towering on each side" denied the inhabitants what "has always been free—a glance at the heavens and some air." Halpern and a fellow probation officer rendered their expert opinion: "in the face of such evidence, slum clearance means crime prevention." Only the antidote of well-regulated government housing could "unquestionably reduce delinquency" by counteracting the pernicious influences of Gotham's meaner quarters. Catalyzed by the Depression's unemployment crisis and the New Deal's collectivist ethos, City Hall in 1934 started to hire thousands to build just such housing—uneconomically, perhaps, and on a small scale, certainly. But for many reformers, as East Harlem settlement house worker Ellen Lurie recalled later, "redemption seemed upon us."[2]

By the late 1940s, however, it was clear that redemption was a more elusive goal than the optimistic housers had imagined. Even as New York's young public housing program surged rapidly after World War II, propelled by the receding of wartime scarcities and subsequent passage of the federal Housing Act of 1949, crime erupted in the newly erected projects.[3] Generous measures of sunlight and fresh air could not immunize the new housing developments against what was a citywide outbreak of youth crime. Much of New York, as chroniclers of the mid-century city have revealed, experienced an unprecedented increase in juvenile crime in the late 1940s and 1950s. The same powerful postwar economic and demographic forces that unleashed crime elsewhere in the city also threatened to undermine the tightly managed order the housers had aimed to create in New York's public housing.[4]

Unemployment was a significant part of the problem. During the war, more than half of the city's teenagers abandoned high school amid new job opportunities that allowed them to earn money and assert their independence. But when the war ended, the long-term prospects for these dropouts quickly dimmed as competition for blue-collar jobs stiffened during New York's sluggish postwar recovery. The large number of migrants to the city in these years further intensified the impact of New York's stagnating manufacturing sector on young job seekers.[5]

The southern African Americans (629,487) and island-born Puerto Ricans (approximately 572,000) coursing into the city between 1940 and 1960 were not only younger than New York's broader population but also quickly became more geographically concentrated. During the 1950s, when teenagers made up a little more than a quarter of the city's Euro-American population, an estimated 35 to 40 percent of New York's African Americans and Puerto Ricans were under the age of twenty.[6] Discrimination and poverty funneled these young newcomers and their families into the city's most crowded districts, where they competed with each other—and often with more established white working-class youths—for jobs as well as for space in which to live and socialize.

But such space was in short supply, shrinking under pressure from urban renewal schemes—encouraged by the 1949 and 1954 housing acts—that razed hundreds of blocks and, in the process, upended familiar neighborhoods and their informal boundaries. And so in postwar New York, as historian Eric Schneider has documented, economic dislocation, demographic transformation, and public policy came together to give rise to the dramatic upsurge in both youth gangs and juvenile crime that *West Side Story* made famous.[7]

Public housing did not escape these citywide patterns in the first decade after World War II; indeed, it sometimes exacerbated them. Fifty-five percent of public housing residents in 1955, for instance, were under the age of twenty—nearly twice the average for New York as whole. And the construction of vast blocks of public housing destroyed thousands of stores—two thousand by 1957 in East Harlem alone—that had often hired local teenagers.[8] Youth crime certainly dogged the city's new housing program in this decade, but it also reflected larger convulsions in New York's working-class world that delivered such troubles to many neighborhoods.

In response to the unexpected ills of delinquency, vandalism, and crime in the projects, the New York City Housing Authority (NYCHA) would spend much of the 1950s reluctantly forming (in 1952) and re-forming (in 1958) its own separate police force, eventually called the Housing Authority Police Department (HAPD). Given public housing's present realities, it is tempting to see this early period of policing in NYCHA's developments as having little relevance for today and offering few lessons for tomorrow. But the questions that faced the Housing Authority and its tenants during the HAPD's first decade—about community influence over police behavior, the dangers of police corruption, and the regulation of social infractions in addition to violations of law—continue to animate community policing debates and practices as well as broader social policy. At the heart of the HAPD's significant growing pains in its first decade was a tension between two competing visions for the new patrolmen. On the one hand, building managers wanted a security force that derived its legitimacy, goals, and methods from public housing's larger social mission: fostering decent and stable communities in NYCHA's complexes. In essence, the managers sought to realize the housers' vision through a civilian-directed police force that was of a piece with the Authority's efforts to build tightly supervised neighborhoods. On the other hand, the officers—and eventually others as well—imagined a police force whose authority, aspirations, and tools were grounded in both its distance from civilian interference and its use of specialized police knowledge. In short, they sought a professional police department that simply happened to work in public housing. The ensuing clash of visions would not be resolved until the end of the decade, when police officers, building managers, and NYCHA's tenants achieved a tacit balance of power. Although many events in HAPD's first decade were shaped—sometimes dramatically—by the political battles and social confluences peculiar to postwar New York, the style of law enforcement that developed in the projects after 1960 anticipated more recent innovations in urban policing—innovations that under the name of community policing continue to attract both broad interest and considerable controversy.

The story of these policing efforts begins before World War II, when NYCHA relied on "special patrolmen" trained, deputized, and armed by the NYPD to provide security for its ten projects: First Houses (1936), Williamsburg Houses (1938), Harlem River Houses (1937), Queensbridge Houses, Vladeck Houses, Vladeck City, South Jamaica Houses (all 1940), East River Houses, and Kingsborough Houses (both 1941). By all accounts, this arrangement worked effectively. The Williamsburg Houses (1,630 units) in Brooklyn, for example, had a total of twelve crime complaints, largely misdemeanors, from 1938 to 1941.[9] But as the conflagrations abroad pulled young patrolmen into the armed forces, NYCHA was forced to replace them with older watchmen drawn from a lower-paying civil service list. Shortly after the war's end, informal commentary from building supervisors and tenants suggested that vandalism and petty crime had taken hold in the projects. Unsettled by these accounts, early in 1948 NYCHA dispatched staff, accompanied by a New York Police Department inspector, on a program-wide survey to size up the situation in its developments. What the staffers found confirmed the reports: the watchmen "were generally incapable because of age, physical strength, and other factors from dealing with teen-age delinquents and adult trouble-makers." Moreover, replacing vandalized windows, light bulbs, and other fixtures chipped away tens of thousands of dollars a month from the Authority's coffers. And while vandals hardly confined themselves to public housing—private landlords at this time also increasingly saw their properties intentionally wrecked—NYCHA staffers recommended the creation of a special police force for the Authority's developments. Senior NYCHA management, however, quickly tabled the proposal, announcing themselves "reluctant" to approach the Authority's state and city lending agencies with such an expense until less costly means of managing crime had been undertaken.[10]

And so followed several years of strategies that aimed, as one NYCHA official wrote, to "secure the cooperation" of tenants in policing their own communities. Stair hall meetings, home visits by social workers, and more play space for children—all were tried, but accounts of hooliganism continued to spill in from project supervisors. In 1950 another round of program-wide building reviews revealed "serious vandalism at thirteen projects, plus vandalism in varying degree at practically all others." But NYCHA continued to resist approaching public officials hat-in-hand to fund a separate police force for the Authority—an expenditure that could signal its program was stumbling at a time when public housing nationwide faced steep opposition in Washington.[11] This calculus, however, would shift when New York City unexpectedly played host to a national media spectacle that made the fight against crime, particularly against juvenile delinquency, a new political priority in postwar New York.

The Kefauver Hearings and the Birth of a New Police Force

Although eclipsed in historical memory by McCarthyism's rise and fall, the high drama of Senator Estes Kefauver's (D-TN) 1950–1951 crime hearings made for a pivotal event in both television and crime fighting. The hearings not only provided the country with its first, if unlikely, political television star ("homely" was *Time* magazine's tactful term for the bespectacled, mushroom-nosed legislator) but also transformed American criminal justice by making clear the potential power of crime as an issue for electoral politics nationally. Kefauver, after securing the chair of the new Senate Crime Investigating Committee and assuring skeptical colleagues that he wasn't seeking "a lot of notoriety," promptly took his crime probe on the road. As the investigating committee made its way across the country, convening hearings in fourteen cities over fifteen months, Kefauver fastened national attention on both crime and himself. The crusading legislator rocketed up from his previous obscurity; opinion polls the next year placed the freshman senator second only to Harry Truman for the Democratic presidential nomination. Indeed, Kefauver's success with crime obliged another freshman in the Senate, Joseph McCarthy (R-WI), to settle for what had been his second choice for a big issue to drive his 1952 reelection bid: anti-Communism.[12]

But the hearings' most sensational moments came in New York. In March 1951, Kefauver brought his committee to the city for the final investigations. Few expected the New York affair to attract more than the usual attention. But Kefauver's chief counsel was Rudolph Halley, nephew of a Broadway producer; Halley possessed a theatrical flair and arranged for television coverage. As chance would have it, *Time* magazine was engaged in a subscription drive and so sponsored a national broadcast of the event—a first for television. An estimated twenty to thirty million people across the country stayed home and tuned in, leaving movie theaters deserted and obliging Consolidated Edison, newspapers reported, to fire up an additional generator in New York to meet the spiking demand for electricity. *Life* magazine concluded, "Never before had the attention of the nation been riveted so completely on a single matter."[13]

No doubt the appearance of underworld figures and accumulating evidence of former New York mayor William O'Dwyer's complicity in various rackets generated the most drama at the hearings.[14] But in addition to the familiar rogues' gallery of colorful mobsters and corrupt politicians, the investigations also raised two fresh targets for national concern: juvenile delinquency and teenage narcotics trafficking. Senator Charles Tobey (R-NH) of the investigating committee saved his longest moral outburst for revelations of drug dealing outside the schools. "The school children of Brooklyn," intoned the legislator, "are corrupted by these emissaries of evil, these ambassadors of evil." Tobey's solution tended more toward theology than criminology; he concluded by quoting the nineteenth-century Quaker poet John Whittier that "solution there is none / Save in the rule of Christ alone." This drew applause from the spectators, and the day's hearing finished on an appropriate note of moral indignation.[15]

Kefauver adroitly continued the campaign. In *Crime in America*, his *New York Times* best seller published later that year, he urged a determined response to youth crime, including a mandatory "five years' imprisonment for dope peddlers." By early summer, amid mounting press accounts of teenage drug addicts, Kefauver quadrupled his sentencing recommendation to a mandatory twenty years. Not to be outdone, Senator Herbert O'Conor (D-MD), Kefauver's eventual successor as chair of the committee, promoted the death sentence for drug racketeers as a punishment likely to inject "the fear of God in the hearts of these outlaws."[16]

In New York City, the Kefauver hearings altered the political landscape and paved the way for the establishment of the Housing Police. Making the most of the political moment the hearings had ushered in, Halley vaulted from serving as the committee's chief counsel to opening an ultimately successful bid for New York City Council president—without the support of either the Democratic or Republican parties. The recently kindled popular concern over crime had noticeably shifted the city's electoral winds. This swing had implications for NYCHA as well. In the wake of these mounting calls to arms against the newly discovered threats to public order, creating a police force for the Authority had now become much less of a political risk; in fact, it now seemed like a winning political stratagem.[17]

Two months after the Senate Crime Investigating Committee left town, NYCHA management reversed its policy and formally asked the city's police commissioner to "assign a top member of his staff to survey all the projects and recommend a system of protection that would be able to cope with the current conditions." A handwritten internal NYCHA routing slip on the subsequent report, tendered in July by Deputy Police Inspector William Reilly, revealed the influences behind the Authority's change of heart: "Perhaps we should consider this before Kefauver asks us to pay a visit."[18] This would not be the last time that sensationalist media coverage would trump sober analysis as NYCHA made decisions about security in its complexes.

Deputy Inspector Reilly, an artistic man who whose hobbies included crafting illuminated Latin scrolls that he gave as gifts to New York's famously authoritarian Francis Cardinal Spellman, offered blunt words for NYCHA in his July 1951 report.[19] "In many projects there is a general disrespect for the rights and properties of others," while gangs "roam throughout the grounds and buildings committing acts of violence and vandalism without any serious efforts being made to curb their activity." Buttressing his case, Reilly attached the summer's crime summaries from each project. Some building supervisors, such as the one at Amsterdam Houses (1,084 units) in San Juan Hill, could detail little more than "Rowdyism: May 1st, Fire Hose turned on by boys. Lights turned off in basement by boys." Other projects were manifestly troubled. The manager of the Lincoln Houses (1,286 units) in Harlem, for instance, provided a litany of felonies over a six-month period, including a rape, an attempted rape of a nine-year-old girl, an armed robbery, and a sixteen-year-old girl's fatal heroin overdose.[20] Reminding the Authority of its original mission to fight crime with wholesome housing, Reilly lectured NYCHA that continuing to ignore the conditions that prevailed in some projects would "discredit public housing and defeat its purpose by creating new crime breeding areas."[21]

Reilly concluded that only around-the-clock coverage by special patrolmen as part of a new and separate police force within NYCHA could protect the municipal investment in public housing. The price tag, however, was enormous: more than two million dollars above the six hundred thousand the Authority was already spending annually on security. NYCHA management recoiled at the expense and concluded that Reilly's plan represented "a police point of view and sets forth an optimum coverage." The officials settled on a lower-cost middle ground. The Authority would commit itself to creating a police force but would assign officers only to "problem areas" while leaving projects located "outside of slum and blighted districts" with the existing guard service—cutting down the price to merely one-sixth of Reilly's proposal.[22] In November of 1952, NYCHA publicly announced the creation of its police force, known as the Property Protection and Security Division. Invoking public concerns in the wake of Kefauver's hearings, the Authority's annual report, published the next month, stressed that the new "special officers would help develop respect for law and order in young citizens" and illustrated its point with a photograph of a housing patrolman befriending a multiracial group of docile children. The publicity photo was, unsurprisingly, staged: the first forty-seven officers wouldn't actually start their patrols of NYCHA's twelve most troubled complexes until January 10 of the following year.[23]

Running a police force was a novel undertaking for the Authority. How were New York's newest police officers to go about their work? To whom would they report? To NYCHA's managers, the answers to these questions at first seemed a simple matter of institutional mission and actuarial logic. The patrolmen should be instruments of the Authority who served the social goal of decent "project living" for the poor. Building managers who knew the needs of their tenants, accordingly, were best positioned to oversee the new police officers assigned to their respective developments. This initial priority and choice about chain of command set the early housing police on a course that emphasized the maintenance of community norms over simply targeting criminal behavior. In a more practical vein, this arrangement also meant no additional expenses were added to the balance sheets of individual projects, which were independent financial entities at the time and "obliged to operate within their own public subsidies and rental revenue."[24]

Indeed, the arrangement represented an economy for the Authority, which was eager to spend its limited financial and political capital elsewhere. As one NYCHA official wrote, the Authority's penny-pinching made it impossible to recruit a cadre of higher-paid supervising officers immediately, so they "placed the duty of the supervising the [Housing Police] employees at the project on the manager of the project."[25] While the Authority recognized that the new chief of the Housing Police, Captain John Lennox, served as commanding officer over the new recruits, it also mandated in its 1952 "Procedures For Housing Officers" that individual project managers would instruct the patrolmen "in their on-the-job tasks." Lennox codified the Authority's view of the chain-of-command in a ten-page manual he distributed to the new patrolmen: "[T]he Housing Officer will be responsible to the Housing Manager for the proper execution of his duties."[26] As Lennox explained to the force's new hires, the Housing Police's mission was to support the building supervisors in their efforts to "insure the safety, health, comfort, and convenience" of the projects through "the enforcement of numerous regulations" that NYCHA placed on its tenants. Chasing criminals, in contrast, constituted "a small part of the job." The chief housing officer, accordingly, expected his officers to make arrests only "occasionally." Instead, "enforcement," Lennox charged the new patrolmen, "should ordinarily be sought along educational and cooperative lines."[27] Relying on the building managers to supervise his patrolmen, Lennox's vision of law enforcement, not surprisingly, mirrored theirs.

Although building managers were pleased with Lennox's progressive notions of policing, the patrolmen bristled under the organization and policies set up by the Authority and its chief housing officer. Daily supervision by civilians did not sit well with the officers who were eager to establish the new force's credibility and, as former housing officer Vic Romano recalled, "feel like cops."[28] Lennox's assistant, Sergeant Anthony Baldwin, observed in 1958 that almost as soon as the officers had started patrolling five years earlier, they began objecting that "nearly everybody" in NYCHA's management gave "them orders and instructions." The patrolmen's perspective was confirmed by a 1957 report, which concluded that although Lennox had "nominal supervision" of the force, in truth the civilian housing managers enjoyed "primary control" over the officers.[29] The New York City Police Department it wasn't.

The Housing officers were frustrated not only by what they saw as meddlesome civilian supervision but also by the philosophy of criminal justice that shaped their command and training. The rank and file had little patience for the psychogenic view of crime to which their civilian managers and chief housing officer subscribed. As sociologist David Garland has noted, criminal justice professionals at this time borrowed liberally from Freudian depth psychology. Schooled in the era's popularized theories of psychoanalysis, they directed their efforts to the "delinquent personality"—assumed to spring from distant childhood traumas—and the expert cures it seemingly required.[30] Chief Housing

Officer Lennox was not shy about using psychoanalysis for criminological insight, and he eagerly tutored his new patrolmen in this weapon against crime. "Every day the housing officer is confronted with the problem juvenile delinquency," Lennox began in one general order, and so "should be familiar with the cause." It was all rather simple: when "the basic need for love and attention is not satisfied in a child . . . they develop an inferiority complex which asserts itself in aggressive, anti-social behavior." Fortunately, experts were developing "crime preventive techniques comparable to preventive medicine" and so surely would be able to "scientifically handle this problem" in "the next few years." But until then, Lennox urged his officers, a "sympathetic understanding and an intelligent approach will accomplish more than an arrest."[31]

To many officers, the Authority's vision of policing "was just a bunch of socialism," recalled Sal Brazini, a former officer and eventual union leader who joined the force in 1954. The blunt judgment of the patrolmen in these years, recounted Vic Romano, was that the building managers and even some of the police supervisors who eventually joined the force simply "lacked balls."[32] Certainly, Lennox's understanding of the professional role of police officers differed dramatically from that of New York's police commissioner at the time, Francis Adams. Adams, for example, had explained in 1955 to an audience gathered in the oak-paneled hall of the Williams Club, his alma mater's business club in the city, that the police officer was not a "social worker, a psychiatrist . . . or a rabbi" and patrolmen should, accordingly, be expected to limit themselves to the "business of enforcing the law."[33]

It is not surprising, then, that the Housing Police officers were particularly unhappy with the small phalanx of social workers and organizations that, as Lennox described them, were "interested in promoting racial, cultural or civil welfare" in the projects and so often attempted to shape the new force's practices. Lennox had to issue repeated written commands reminding the patrolmen that these "specialists in their field . . . rendered an invaluable assistance to the Property Protection and Security Division." He eventually had to order that the social workers "receive the cooperative interest of all housing officers."[34]

The clash between the officers' professional self-assertions and the Authority's managerial penchants likely fed the patrolmen's grumblings noted by Lennox's assistant, but the consequences seem to have been minimal.[35] In fact, despite the widespread discontent, policing in the projects was a success. Crime in NYCHA's projects, according to the period's best surviving study, was significantly lower than in comparable neighborhoods. An independent NYPD crime survey late in 1954 paired two NYCHA complexes—Harlem's Abraham Lincoln Houses (1,286 units) and James Weldon Johnson Houses (1,310 units)—with two adjacent control areas of similar population size and poverty rates. Collectively, the housing projects had felony complaint rates less than one-third that of the control areas. Moreover, of the 228 total crimes reported in both the projects and control areas, only 38 occurred in NYCHA developments and in "only a small percent" were public housing "tenants involved as perpetrators." The favorably impressed NYPD concluded in its report that the "task of the policeman [had] become less difficult " because of public housing and its new patrolmen.[36]

Nor did the divisions within the Housing Police impede the force's evolution or growth. The first members of NYCHA's Property Protection and Security Division had been "special patrolmen," a civil service title that the city's police commissioner coined to empower them to carry a firearm on patrol but with an arrest authority limited to duty hours. By 1956, however, state legislation conferred upon the force "peace officer" status, enabling the men to be armed and make arrests at any time within city limits. The Security Division's ranks grew with its powers: the original force of 47 officers had become 165 within a year and 232 by 1956. And that fall, Chief Housing Officer Lennox could proudly, if somewhat cryptically, congratulate his men for being "ten percent ahead in all phases of operation" compared to the previous year.[37]

Scandal and Politics Transform the Housing Police

In 1957 and 1958, however, the tensions between Housing officers and their supervisors became—at the hands of ambitious politicians—ingredients in a dramatic City Hall power struggle. As a result, a volatile cocktail of McCarthyism and graft shook the force, leading to its reorganization, a sharp reduction in building managers' influence, and the death of Chief Housing Officer Lennox by his own hand. John Lennox's suicide is broadly remembered in Housing Police lore as a private tragedy, unrelated to larger events. But while his death was certainly tragic, private it was not. Rather, his suicide originated in and helps reveal the political context of the department's formative phase, which was marked by municipal corruption, opportunistic red-baiting, and the power of race in a metropolis where, historian Martha Biondi reminds us, housing and employment discrimination were not only pervasive but legal and flights from Idlewild Airport enforced Jim Crow seating.[38]

A full accounting of the Lennox tragedy begins in City Hall with Tom Shanahan. Formally a bank president, Shanahan was more widely known for a decade as the Tammany Hall political organization's lead money man—the influence peddler who demanded and collected the payoffs that greased the wheels of the local Democratic Party machine. Mayor O'Dwyer appointed Shanahan, his former campaign manager, to NYCHA's five-member board in 1948. Shanahan found the position a convenient perch from which to accumulate the spoils that accompanied public housing's explosive growth during the 1950s.[39] Historian Nicholas Bloom has argued recently and convincingly that NYCHA suffered from corruption less than did housing authorities elsewhere in the country, but many of the underhanded dealings that did occur bore the prints of Shanahan's well-placed fingers. Anyone wanting to do business with the Authority, recalled one architect, "had to do business with Tom Shanahan."[40] Successful recipients of lucrative NYCHA contracts did their banking at Shanahan's Federation Bank and Trust and made their contributions to Tammany through him. But such arrangements, as biographer Robert Caro has chronicled, seemed insignificant next to the decision by Robert Moses, the city's redevelopment maestro, to deposit the Triborough Bridge and Tunnel Authority receipts (ultimately totaling fifteen million dollars) into interest-free accounts with Shanahan's Federation Bank and Trust. The deal profitably expanded both the bank's lending capital and Moses's political influence at NYCHA.[41]

Shanahan continued to prosper from such shady connections until 1955, when Mayor Robert Wagner, hoping to avert a scandal, sought to curb the banker by appointing his trusted special assistant, the corncob pipe–smoking, former *New York Times* political columnist Warren Moscow, as executive director of the Housing Authority.[42] The inevitable showdown occurred the following year, when Shanahan requested a paid, full-time aide in his position on NYCHA's board. Suspecting that Shanahan's real ambition was for a "bag man" to serve as an intermediary in bribes, Moscow, joined by Authority Chairman Phillip Cruise and two additional board members, blocked the move. Shanahan fired back by announcing a boycott of further meetings unless the board relented.[43] The other members held the line until early 1957, when Moses apparently intervened through his man on the board, architect William Wilson. As Moscow later recounted to Caro, Wilson informed the board, "I have a message for you from Mr. Moses. You give Tom what he wants or we'll turn the *Daily News* loose on you." The bullying was well aimed. Ever since anti-Communist hysteria had started escalating in the city during the late 1940s, Caro argues, NYCHA's board had dreaded a tabloid exposé of the Authority's staff, several of whom, during the heady 1930s, had passed through organizations later tagged as "Communist fronts."[44] In what was likely no coincidence, the board's fears were realized shortly after Wilson's threat.

The *Daily News* launched its red-hunting series about the Authority on February 18. The first of ten articles prominently featured Shanahan's photograph and praised both his stand against the "Communist clique that had all but taken over [NYCHA's] vast billion-dollar empire" and his boycott of meetings given the "futility of his battle against the Red Menace."[45] By the time of the fourth article ("Housing Execs Admit Red Role"), the Authority's board caved, voting to allow Shanahan his man.[46]

That man was William F. Hartnett, a thirty-two-year former FBI agent and, more recently, a "loyalty investigator" for the city's Board of Higher Education, who was to conduct "special and confidential studies" under Shanahan's direction.[47] His hiring was just the start of events precipitated by the *Daily News* coverage, however. The paper's sensationalistic treatment of public housing obliged both NYCHA and City Hall to respond to the attacks on the Authority's loyalty and competence.

Four days after the final *Daily News* article, Mayor Wagner set the city investigator, Charles Tenney, to ferret out the supposed Communists; then, at the Authority's behest, he appointed his own team under City Comptroller Charles Preusse to look into the charges of mismanagement and incompetence. After the *Daily News*'s accounts of teen lawbreakers running amok in the "criminal paradise" of NYCHA projects barely policed by a security force that hamstrung its patrolmen, the Authority hired Arthur Wallander, O'Dwyer's square-jawed police commissioner, to study the force and recommend reforms.[48] This cavalcade of investigations had significant consequences for NYCHA and would eventually dramatically reshape both the Authority and its new police department.

Tenney came up mostly empty-handed in his red hunt, snaring only seven low-level employees out of a staff of 5,800; this largely spared NYCHA from future anti-Communist attacks, even as they became a feature of housing politics elsewhere.[49] Preusse, however, turned up significant management failures at the Authority that ultimately produced what historian Nicholas Bloom has described as timely and effective reform and handed Mayor Wagner sufficient ammunition to edge out Wilson, Shanahan, and Cruise the following year.[50] Wallander's investigations coupled with Hartnett's ambitions set in motion a more calamitous series of events, however.

Although in his report Preusse had applauded Lennox for making the best of limited resources, when Wallander was preparing his second round of proposed reforms for the Housing Police, word circulated according to Lennox's assistant, Anthony Baldwin, that the former police commissioner might not recommend Lennox's reappointment as chief housing officer. This uncertainty created an opportunity for the ambitious Hartnett. As reported by Baldwin, Hartnett suggested to Lennox that "the Security Division was growing and it really needed a person with greater experience"—such as himself.[51] Threatened, Lennox hatched what can only be described as a profoundly misguided scheme to save his job by exploiting not only old animosities between civil rights organizations and Wallander but also the new mood in the city's fast-growing black neighborhoods.

Taking out his 1927 Underwood, Lennox typed and mailed a series of anonymous hate letters that attacked the appointment of African Americans to the Housing Police on his own watch. Lennox addressed these letters not only to city officials but also to himself and Baldwin, signing each letter: "The White Council of Housing Officers."[52] "Nigger," began Lennox in a letter to George Gregory, the city's first black municipal civil service commissioner and a notable figure in local Democratic politics who championed increased job opportunities for African Americans.[53] "For a long time housing officers and other responsible people have been wondering why there were so many niggers on the housing police force," continued Lennox. "You certify them and nigger lovin [sic] lennox puts them to work." Lennox's intent in crafting these fabrications becomes even clearer in his description of himself in these letters: "Thanks to a lot of decent people in public office this bastard lennox is going to be fired or demoted because of his love for niggers." Revealingly, Lennox added: "Mr. Hartnett will see to it that this lousy bastard is fired next week. After lennox we will whiten up our little force."[54]

Lennox then arranged a series of secret meetings with the *New York Amsterdam News* and the Mayor's Commission on Intergroup Relations (COIR)—meetings to which he brought the letters he had sent himself and others. Baldwin, who also attended the meetings but did not yet know the origin of the letters, reported that Lennox hoped to "gain aid in retaining his position of Chief Housing Officer." Lennox, Baldwin recalled, told his contacts at COIR he thought the civil rights organization "might be able to help him in his personal case." Lennox likely appealed to *Amsterdam News* editor James Hicks hoping to leverage the newsman's recent role as go-between in the edgy relationship between the city's black population and its nearly all-white police force. In April, Hicks had helped avert a riot by persuading a hesitant Malcolm X to engineer a peaceful end to looming racial violence in the wake of the NYPD's brutalizing of Nation of Islam member Johnson X. Hicks, who had also covered the infamous Emmett Till lynching for Baltimore's *Afro-American*, wrote shortly after Lennox's visit that the chief housing officer had asked him to use his influence "to get a high city official to see that he did not lose his job solely because he was fair to Negroes."[55] Hicks recalled that as Lennox prepared to leave the paper's Harlem offices, he looked the journalist "squarely in the eye" and pleaded, "I'm only asking for a fair break."[56]

Lennox's accusation of racism at the Housing Police, particularly when the force was in the process of being reformed by Wallander, would have received a sympathetic hearing with black activists at the time. As police commissioner in the late 1940s, Wallander had notoriously resisted organized efforts by civil rights advocates to control police brutality in Harlem, publicly denouncing what he saw as "a concerted campaign of calumny against members of this department, without investigation, facts or justification." As historians Martha Biondi and Marilynn Johnson have documented, Wallander also defended officers who had severely beaten a Harlem candy-store owner arrested after a warrantless search (the precinct commander in the case asserted confidently that "we have our own law in New York"). Lennox very likely would have been familiar with all of these events, as he had been assigned to uniformed duty in upper Manhattan during those years.[57]

Civil rights activists had other reasons to be alarmed by Lennox's story of racism in NYCHA's police force. In the 1950s, public housing, which until 1963 was the only housing in all of New York State both subject to and complying with antidiscrimination laws, had increasingly become home to racial minorities. As historians have extensively documented, this trend was intensified by racially motivated federal and state policies designed both to help underwrite the mushrooming expanses of suburban housing and block African Americans from purchasing those same homes. For blacks eager to escape the deteriorating housing stock of the city's "Negro areas"—with streets that were overcrowded and landlords who overcharged—NYCHA's doors were often the only ones not jammed shut by the contrivances of realtors, banks, and government officials. In these years, then, African American leaders generally lent their voices to the call for public housing, echoing their constituents' embrace of the rare chance to live in recently constructed, modern apartments. NYCHA's rent rolls register the intertwined consequences of government-sponsored residential segregation: between 1950 and 1960, NYCHA experienced a net loss of more than 14,000 whites—with roughly half, the Authority estimated early in the decade, leaving to buy their own homes in the suburbs. At the same time, NYCHA's total population of African Americans and Puerto Ricans increased by 11,497 and 6,486 respectively. Lennox's accounts of racism, accordingly, would have seemed both credible and threatening to the civil rights leaders with whom he met.[58]

But just before dawn on January 10, 1958, the day after the meeting with COIR, John Lennox stirred his wife from her sleep to tell her he intended to take his own life. Then, with a single shot from his service revolver, he did so.[59] Why Lennox chose suicide before giving his plan time to work is not clear. Perhaps he discovered he was about to be exposed; perhaps he had begun to doubt the plan's chances; or perhaps he simply—as his widow told reporters—had grown despondent over the potential loss of his command. But Lennox *had* accurately predicted how readily New York's civil rights organizations would take his bait. After meeting with Lennox, COIR held an emergency conference and then informed the mayor of its intent to investigate the chief housing officer's charges. Meanwhile, the *Amsterdam News* published one of Lennox's letters, offering it as evidence that there were "forces at work in New York which are determined to ruin and destroy all independent-minded Negroes who occupy positions of honor." The Urban League joined COIR in urging the mayor to make a "full and public investigation" of racism at the Housing Police. While no records of that inquiry survive, by late May the police had traced the letters to Lennox's own typewriter and COIR quietly dropped the case.[60]

Once Lennox's machinations to rally civil rights groups behind him became known, Arthur Wallander—the former NYPD commissioner busily reforming the Housing Police—recast the tragedy as a parable of corruption. Lennox's attempt at fraud, Wallander argued, made plain the dangers posed by civilian oversight of police forces. This notion, in fact, had been the animating theme of the reforms Wallander had been proposing since arriving at the Authority as a consultant. In a memo to NYCHA's board, Wallander echoed a generation of police thinking about professionalism as a shield against the corrosive effects of the public on police operations. "The sad Lennox affair," Wallander wrote, "reminds us the men of the Police Division must be placed beyond the temptation of corruption by outside groups." Too much familiarity with the community, Wallander explained to NYCHA's top bureaucrats, exposed officers to "undue influences."[61] This sentiment mirrored his first white paper of October 1957, in which he had stressed "the police force must be autonomous," while the superintendent of police (his proposed change in nomenclature from "chief housing officer") should be free from "outside pressures . . . in accordance with the best concepts of policing." Applying those modernizing precepts to the housing police, Wallander detailed for NYCHA's board, required an end to the Authority's practice of "service ratings of patrolmen made by managers"; instead, supervision would be placed where it belonged—with uniformed sergeants.[62] Wresting away "the authority now exercised by project managers" would require transforming the force's chain of command—or so Wallander assured NYCHA's board. Rather than assigning patrolmen to particular projects, which were the fiefdoms of building managers, Wallander urged that the officers be organized into police precincts, each composed of several projects collectively under the command of a lieutenant. Such a precinct model, akin to the NYPD's, would provide a layer of police supervision that would, Wallander hoped, displace the influence of individual building managers.[63]

But Wallander's efforts to isolate building managers from the policing of their projects had already triggered a backlash against his law enforcement approach by NYCHA staffers who doubted the wisdom of police professionalism for the low-income communities they oversaw. Shortly after Wallander's second round of recommendations in December of 1957, the newly formed Public Housing Managers Association, claiming to represent nearly all of NYCHA's building managers, assembled its own thirteen-page rejoinder to the former police commissioner. Citing their ten to eighteen years of experience each, the managers mapped a conception of law enforcement that was very nearly the polar opposite of Wallander's—and that anticipated to a remarkable degree the law enforcement practices that would later become known as community policing.

Wallander's modernizing visions of a police force supervised from centralized precincts, focused efficiently on crime-fighting, and insulated from external pressures left the managers unmoved. The "more we 'professionalize' the organization of the Housing force," they countered, "the more officers would seek to justify their existence by the apprehension of criminals" and "the less will be their inclination to devote their attention to" the real "needs of the project population." And the managers believed that those needs properly embraced duties that neither the patrolmen nor Wallander saw as police work: "providing escort services for deposits, assisting tenants in emergencies," and "mediating disputes." Indeed, while the managers conceded Housing officers "occasionally" arrested criminals, they concluded that the quality of life in their projects more realistically depended on policing "violations of Authority regulations rather than of law."[64]

Anticipating by several decades the criminological theory of "informal control," the managers' experience told them that it wasn't the police at all who prevented most crime; it was the tenants themselves.[65] As one NYCHA consultant observed in 1957, managers believed that their first and most important line of defense against disorder was not the housing patrolmen, but "what women say to one another as they sit on the benches with their babies." Similarly, managers thought that they, not the courts, could best correct the behavior of wrongdoers through a "warning, service charge," or "referral to a social agency or other community group."[66] These are assumptions that would sit comfortably with nearly all community police advocates today.

Moreover, unlike the narrowly defined crime-fighting mission Wallander saw for the Housing Police, NYCHA's managers presented security and maintenance issues as two sides of the same coin. In doing so, they foresaw a core assumption of community policing as it later emerged. Today, champions of community policing contend that because many neighborhood crime concerns stem from problematic conditions—abandoned buildings that shelter drug dealers, for example—fighting crime requires partnering with other municipal agencies, such as the sanitation or health departments, rather than relying solely on traditional police methods. And so, argues this line of thinking, the definition and practice of police work should expand accordingly. However innovative this insight might appear in contemporary discussions of community policing, NYCHA's managers had already hit upon it by 1958.[67] As the Public Housing Managers Association pointed out in response to Wallander's reforms, a range of tenant complaints—everything from "roaches, vandalism, heating [to] crime"—landed on managers' desks, because the tenants themselves did "not differentiate between maintenance problems and other problems." The managers believed that, with their broad understanding of building problems and tenant concerns, they occupied the best vantage point from which to deploy patrolmen along with other building staff for "programs to reduce useless expenses of vandalism and increase the overall physical and social attractiveness of a project." The managers concluded that "control of the housing officer force can therefore not be left solely in the hands of professional police officers."[68] Where Wallander envisioned an autonomous police force under uniformed commanders guided by the "best concepts of policing," the managers saw the patrolmen as instruments of decent project living, properly directed by specialists trained in the goals and tools of social uplift.

Battling over Fort Greene

The Authority, after the pummeling over crime it had taken in the press, was in no position to challenge the expert opinion of the former police commissioner. By early 1958, NYCHA had largely agreed to Wallander's package of proposals—ignoring the counsel of its increasingly discontented building managers. The managers were left believing that there was now, as one complained to the *New York Times*, "an anti-social worker concept on the part of certain people in the Authority."[69] In particular, the Authority saw the creation of precincts as the best way to reestablish the badly bruised crime-fighting credentials of the city's public housing program. But the precinct model required the construction of precinct headquarters, and New York State was slow in approving the necessary funds. When it finally did, the state forced NYCHA to scale back the concept to a single precinct.[70] In the summer of 1958 NYCHA announced the completion of the headquarters for the first of what it—inaccurately—predicted would be twenty such precincts throughout its system.[71] The new Fort Greene Police Precinct covered three Brooklyn projects: the Farragut Houses (1,390 units), the Marcy Houses (1,717 units), and NYCHA's single largest project at the time, the Fort Greene Houses (3,503 units, subsequently divided by the Authority into the Walt Whitman and Raymond V. Ingersoll houses). The precinct quickly became contested terrain as NYCHA's building managers and police force battled over the proper law enforcement approach for New York's public housing. In the end, both sides would acquiesce to a compromise that curtailed the power of building managers even as it halted the remaking of the Housing Police along the lines of the era's "reform model" police department, marked by centralized authority and a strictly supervised paramilitary hierarchy. The Housing Police would remain a distinct—and distinctive—department whose presence and practices demarcated New York's public housing from surrounding neighborhoods.

Signs of the conflict between building managers and housing officers first materialized that fall, when the manager of the Marcy Houses protested to NYCHA's director of management that although the inclusion of her project in the "Ft. Greene Plan" had produced better police coverage, the "manner" of the patrolmen had changed with the change in their supervision. She complained that the Housing Police's new "get tough" policy was "being over done" and that the officers, emboldened by reorganization of the force, had started to "harass" tenants. She reported that her tenants had witnessed officers "approaching teen-agers with profanity and . . . indiscriminate actions." Indeed, the manager passed on, the problem had become so severe that parents threatened to "go higher" if the patrolmen did not show more respect. Likewise, she reported that as the officers increasingly focused on fighting crime, their reports "contained nothing of value to her" about particular tenants "which she could include in her records."[72] It was a persistent complaint from managers, recalled Officer

Vic Romano, who started working the Fort Greene precinct in 1959. Managers encouraged officers to enforce NYCHA's regulations so that management could "know who the troublemakers were." In this way, Romano recalled, managers hoped to "get something on tenants," as a NYCHA file thick with such violations could strengthen management's hand in eviction proceedings against a resident. Although such cooperation was common at projects where building managers supervised housing officers, the experimental precinct was, Romano recalled, "a completely different job." At Fort Greene, "managers had less influence," so officers "answered to the sergeant, lieutenant, the captain"—all of whom had less incentive to instruct those under their command to write up tenants for violations of the Authority's regulations.[73]

Others noted similar changes afoot in the housing police. In July, Brooklyn's *Williamsburg News* reported that it had received complaints from residents of the borough's Williamsburg Houses (1,630 units) about the Housing Police's new strategies. The article looked back to public housing's "early days," when NYCHA had employed watchmen whose "chief task was not so much to guard against major crimes as it was to prevent vandalism." The paper noted that although it "commended" the steady "increase in stature of the Housing Police" from "mere watchmen to a present status just about on par with the regular New York City Police," the editors and the tenants objected to the recent "attitude and technique" of the force. "Apparently enraptured with their new status," the *Williamsburg News* wrote of the Housing Police, "the constables are concentrating solely on the chore of policing major crimes in the project." But in the process the officers had "seemingly forgotten about the very important job of curbing vandalism," a task the paper concluded the patrolmen now deemed "below their dignity."[74]

NYCHA could no longer rebuff the growing discontent over the Housing Police. Indeed, the Authority felt compelled to remind the patrolmen, "all members of this division will keep in mind that the foremost duty . . . is to curb vandalism at all housing projects."[75] And despite assurances from the new superintendent of police that the precinct model, particularly the use of the headquarters's air-raid siren to break up teen rumbles, "has had a good effect on the tenants," NYCHA soon shelved its once-elaborate plans to put the Fort Greene plan into action throughout its now sizable (seventy-nine) collection of projects.[76] As NYCHA explained to its funding agencies in May 1959, "information gained from such experimentation" at the Fort Greene precinct "had led the Authority to conclude that it was not necessary at present to extend the precinct model." Nor did NYCHA "intend to provide the type of police station as constructed at Fort Greene Houses in any other project."[77] By 1960, NYCHA had disbanded the precinct. But the observant urban archeologist can still find two green lamps with the barely discernable markings "Precinct 13" hanging from what had been the Fort Greene Precinct headquarters on 4 Auburn Place in

Brooklyn—silent testaments to Arthur Wallander's aborted vision for the Housing Police.

The end of the Fort Greene experiment brought about a peace of sorts between NYCHA's police officers and building managers. The force would be autonomous and managers would no longer write up patrolmen's service ratings; however, the Housing Police would also preserve its chain-of-command structure organized around individual projects—an arrangement that encouraged daily contact between managers and officers. This decision, as I will detail in chapter 2, allowed a form of community policing to flourish in New York's public housing for more than two decades. But it also set the stage for a labor showdown in the 1970s between police commanders and their own rank and file, assisted by NYCHA's residents, who in that decade would pressure the department to adopt precincts throughout the city—an issue explored in chapter 3. Thus, the conflicts of the 1950s were replayed twenty years later, as the founding vision of the "housers" faced criticism from politicians, the HAPD's rank-and-file, and the tenants themselves.

Surveying the first decade of the Housing Police from the vantage point of the present, however, it is clear that it was in these early years that the Authority and its security force initially encountered four crucial tensions that would persistently influence and sometimes alter the Housing Police for the next half-century. The first such tension was the struggle by NYCHA to determine its own policing policies despite the power of the media to shape the political landscape in which the Authority operated. The second was the opposing visions held by managers and their tenants on the one hand and the Housing Police on the other hand as to the proper extent of the force's autonomy within NYCHA. The third tension was the conflict over the primary mission of the Housing Police: should officers be curbing disorder or pursuing criminals? The fourth and final dynamic was the Housing officers' occasionally anxious efforts to bolster their own professional identity as police officers. Collectively, these tensions would structure the sometimes competing efforts by NYCHA's management, police, and tenants to fashion a distinctive style of crime control tailored to the Authority's high-rise architecture and low-income communities.

FIGURE 2.1 Swearing in first class of Housing Police, December 15, 1952. Photograph courtesy of the New York Housing Authority and La Guardia Community College, CUNY Photograph © New York Housing Authority.

2

"A Paradox in Urban Law Enforcement"

Residents, Officers, and the Making of Community Policing in NYCHA, 1960–1980

On January 10, 1953, forty-seven "special Housing officers" began patrolling twelve New York City Housing Authority (NYCHA) complexes for the first time. They were dressed not in the gray attire of watchmen but in new blue uniforms indistinguishable, except for an identifying arm patch, from those worn by the regular New York Police Department (NYPD). From a distance, one might easily have mistaken a Housing Officer for a New York City cop; up close, however, there were important differences—differences that tenants and officers both knew went far beyond the uniform.[1] The Authority, aiming to build a police force suited not only to its sprawling developments but also to its tight budgets, created a department that was unique in the postwar United States—and uniquely revealing of the possibilities and limitations of community policing.

The tenants' sense that the Housing Police were the "last neighborhood cops" developed from the conditions under which the force unavoidably operated: the need for foot patrol; the distinctive demographics of its personnel; a decentralized organization; and structural ties to NYCHA management. These unusual characteristics created opportunities for tenants to influence both community order and law enforcement practices in ways that surprised the few outsiders who paid any attention to the new force, which operated largely out of sight of the vast majority of New Yorkers. Because of the reciprocal nature of their interactions with the officers who served them, NYCHA tenants only partially shared in the contempt for the police that many city dwellers began to express in the 1960s. Thus, at a time when minorities in northern cities identified police brutality as a graver threat to their communities than unemployment, inadequate housing, or unequal education, NYCHA's growing population of black and Latino tenants repeatedly declared their approval for the officers patrolling the city's low-income developments. The relationship between

NYCHA residents and their police was indeed exceptional. As residents frequently described it, "Housing" was "our police force."[2]

NYCHA and Vertical Patrols

As NYCHA's glass-and-brick empire expanded after World War II and its complexes progressively broke with the street grid, public housing became isolated from the services provided by the NYPD—particularly as that department increasingly shifted to what it termed a "radio motor patrol" style of policing.[3] As one NYCHA official wrote, "we have created superblocks" where most of the crime "occurs within the stairwells and on the roofs"—crimes that "would not be corrected by the ordinary type of police patrol."[4] And although since 1947 the Authority had repeatedly asked NYPD for special officers to be assigned to the interior of NYCHA developments, just as repeatedly the police commissioner had refused, agreeing only to patrol the perimeters of complexes.

Recognizing that the protection provided by the NYPD was "not particularly suited to project needs," in 1952 the Authority—as chapter 1 details—reluctantly formed its own Property Protection and Security Division. This new police force, however, would increasingly differ not only from the NYPD but also from other departments nationwide as a consequence of both NYCHA's policy decisions and project designs. Elsewhere in the country, excessive reliance upon squad cars meant, as historian Lawrence Friedman notes, that "a ton or more of steel separated the motorized officer from the community." By creating its own police force, NYCHA avoided this "ton of steel" divide as well as a grab bag of urban law enforcement problems that had accompanied the drive to "professionalize" policing. The NYPD and other big-city police departments at this time, for instance, were pursuing more exacting hiring standards that soon filled precincts with officers who had little in common with the people in the neighborhoods they patrolled. Similarly, urban police commissioners, enamored with popular notions of administrative efficiency, had increasingly sought to concentrate into their hands a more centralized command and control structure—eroding local influence on law enforcement in the process. In contrast, Housing's path was dictated not by national trends in police practice but by the unique law enforcement requirements of NYCHA's distinctive complexes. The Housing Police were free to evolve in their own direction.[5]

As police departments increasingly pulled officers out of neighborhoods in order to fill squad cars, many urban communities in mid-century America experienced the loss of patrolmen walking stable beats. But NYCHA's architecture spared its residents that fate. An officer behind the wheel of a cruiser could neither see the goings-on within public housing's superblocks nor enter its corridors, roofs, and stairwells. To prevent crime—rather than merely arriving "after a crime has been committed"—NYCHA concluded, "our buildings must be patrolled by foot."[6] Called "vertical patrols," Housing officers' regular beats included walking down busy stairwells and through long hallways, in the thick of the daily domestic worlds of NYCHA's residents. As Morton Bard, a prominent City College of New York psychologist, concluded in a 1970 study of NYCHA residents' interactions with the Housing Authority Police Department (HAPD), the department was a "paradox in urban law enforcement." Although NYCHA's buildings had some of the highest population densities in the nation, they also represented the last place in America where "the citizen is still in direct and regular association with the police officer."[7]

While on vertical patrol, the HAPD helped to regulate many aspects of the everyday lives of residents; housing officers not only enforced the law but also monitored adherence to NYCHA rules. Ball playing, rowdiness, and even walking on the grass provided grounds for the Authority to fine a tenant. Enforcing NYCHA regulations meant that Housing officers worked more closely with the civilian managers of their particular projects than the police supervisors of their "borough command," whose offices were generally in another neighborhood. Within the majority of projects, Housing Police "record rooms" served as diminutive precinct houses, tethering the work routines of the officers to the geographical space of the communities they served.

Race and Residency in the HAPD

The HAPD was also, to a degree unprecedented nationally, a black and Latino police force. In 1965, when the Housing Police was the fourth largest force in New York State and the twenty-fourth largest in the country, 45 percent of Housing officers were minorities. Merely ten years later, that figure surged past 60 percent—all at a time when roughly nine out of ten New York Police Department officers were white.[8] Even had the Housing Police merely drawn its recruits from the city's various ethnic groups in proportion to their numbers, minorities would have represented a larger slice of the HAPD than the NYPD simply because of timing. The HAPD formed, expanded, and hired in growing numbers just as the city's African American and Puerto Rican populations soared—swelling 45 and 230 percent respectively between 1950 and 1960 in a city whose total population actually diminished by more than 100,000 in those same years. In contrast to the Housing Police, the ranks of the older and slower-growing NYPD continued to reflect the hiring patterns—and the prejudices—of an earlier and whiter period in New York's history. Indeed, as late as 1969 the NYPD remained 40 percent Irish. As New York City journalist Jimmy Breslin quipped at the time: "If you want a rug seller, get an Arab. If you want a cop, get an Irishman."[9]

Two additional factors intensified the effects of demographic trends on the hiring patterns in the NYPD and Housing Police. First, the two forces had different employment qualifications. Ever attentive to costs, Housing would hire applicants with a misdemeanor record, while the NYPD refused such candidates until 1965. Disproportionately arrested and convicted, minorities were much less likely than were whites to be eligible to join the NYPD. In addition, Puerto Rican migrants—historically smaller than better-fed, mainland-born Americans—often met Housing's 5'70" height cutoff but fell short of the NYPD's, which demanded an additional inch (5'8") until 1973. Second, white New Yorkers, enjoying greater options in a racially segregated job market, less frequently had to settle for the lower salaries offered by HAPD from 1952 until 1965, when Housing's pay finally caught up to NYPD levels.[10]

Chronology and policy, then, converged in the HAPD to produce a police force with the nation's highest percentage of black and Latino officers during these years—a fact surprisingly unheralded by the many historians of minorities in law enforcement.[11] Indeed, in 1975, when the share of black and Latino HAPD officers in the 1,786-person force peaked at 60 percent, that figure was twice as large as the equivalent number in Housing's closest competitor for minority representation, the Atlanta Police Department. In short, when New York's roughly 600,000 public housing residents, over half of them minority by 1960, interacted with the Housing Police, they had a good chance of doing so with a black or Latino officer.[12]

Tenants' perception that the Housing police force was uniquely theirs stemmed from more than racial affinity, however.[13] Many Housing officers both served and lived in public housing. Although NYCHA did not keep records documenting this phenomenon, Assistant Chief of Department Joseph Keeney—who ran the Office of the Chief in the 1970s—estimates that until at least 1980 one in five HAPD officers was also a NYCHA resident, with the number growing through the 1960s and peaking sometime in the 1970s.[14]

Tenants' sense that Housing patrolmen, unlike NYPD officers, were "our cops," received further confirmation in 1960 when New York's state legislature carved out exceptions to the civil service residency requirements for police officers in the name of "professionalization" (as would numerous other state legislatures at roughly the same time). The rule change encouraged many, mostly white, NYPD officers, unsettled by New York's rising costs and declining services, to decamp for surrounding suburbs even as Housing officers, more likely to be minorities, increasingly lived in NYCHA's developments. This growing residential disparity emerged, in part, as a consequence of suburbia's federally subsidized racial barriers, which were maintained through the 1970s in New York's suburbs by a powerful alliance of builders, realtors, and banks. These barriers were so effective that even black police officers had trouble penetrating them.[15] Moreover, once the NYPD became free to hire nonresidents after the 1962 removal of the Lyons Law, the department began reaching beyond the city's borders to small, outlying towns for new recruits, stalling what otherwise would have been a significant ethnic turnover in Gotham's largest police force as whites left New York and blacks and Puerto Ricans poured in.[16] As the ranks of the NYPD and other police forces in the urban North remained overwhelming white by becoming increasingly suburban—joining, in essence, the tidal flows of commuters in and out of the cities that employed them—the Housing Police developed in the opposite direction. The HAPD grew both more urban and less white until the 1980s, when, as we will see in chapter 4, institutional changes transformed hiring patterns and practices in both the NYPD and Housing.

The Structure of the HAPD and Community Policing in NYCHA

Oral histories with NYCHA residents and archival HAPD documents testify to the extent to which, before the mid-1970s, project tenants and housing officers relied on each other to enforce community norms. Residents in particular describe a braiding together of informal social controls and formal police presence in terms that might have been lifted from a current community policing manifesto were they not expressed in the cadences of the residents themselves. Listen to Mary Alfson and her daughter Tricia Alfson recalling the Housing Police in the McKinley Houses (619 units) in the Bronx during the late 1960s and early 1970s:

MARY: The housing officers took interest in the people in the community.

TRICIA: Yah, they knew your name, if they were walking they'd say "Okay now, so and so, don't ride that bike too fast or I'll take you to your parents."

Similarly, Maria Vasquez recalls of the HAPD in Manhattan's Amsterdam Houses (1,084 units) at the same time:

> They did their jobs, but they knew the kids . . . they knew what apartments they came from. So if they did something wrong, they take you by your coat, take you to your parents.

Another former resident, Rachael Ryans, captured the dynamic among officers, children, and parents with impeccable concision when she described her memories of "Larry," the Housing patrolman who guarded the Amsterdam Houses in the 1960s when she was growing up. "If you did something wrong," she recalled, "Larry would tell your momma and you know you would get a whopping."[17]

Such recollections of officers who knew where to track down an errant teen's mother are common among older NYCHA residents in part because of a unique feature of the Housing Police in these years: record rooms. These miniature police stations were the legacy of both the piecemeal expansion of HAPD's operations and the failure of the Fort Greene pilot precinct described in chapter 1. Unable to predict where mercurial municipal politics might locate the next NYCHA development and discouraged by the Fort Greene experiment, the

HAPD decided not to organize its patrol force into fixed precincts with centralized and expensive command posts as the NYPD had done. Rather, when the supervisors of the growing Housing Police detailed officers to a new development, they simply commandeered an apartment or basement space as an additional small office for the use of patrolmen (and they *were* all men until 1973). So it was in the record rooms of their assigned project, and not at a distant police station, that patrolmen filed their incident reports, collected their paychecks (until 1965), interviewed their suspects, kept their firearms, and reported to and from their daily tours.[18] In short, record rooms ensured that nearly every manifestation of police presence or exercise of police authority, other than formal booking and incarceration, occurred locally. The proximity of record rooms could imbue NYCHA's lively hallways and airy courtyards with a remarkable sense of security. Allen Jones, recalling his youth in the South Bronx's Lester Patterson Houses (1,788 units) during the 1950s and 1960s, observed that unlike many black New Yorkers at the time, his family "felt safe in our neighborhood" because "the Projects had its [*sic*] own police force, which operated out of the management office where we went to pay our rent."[19]

That the policing of the city's public housing occurred within the compass of each NYCHA complex was a distinction with important consequences. As Raymond Henson—a building manager at the James Weldon Johnson Houses (1,310 units) in East Harlem in the late 1950s and early 1960s—remembers, managers conferred daily with the officers who "turned out" from the record rooms, exchanging details about tenant concerns and neighborhood conditions. Such discussions, Henson recalled, were as likely to be about "broken light bulbs" in a hallway as an "apartment that had been broken into."[20] This daily contact allowed managers, Henson argues, to hold "officers accountable" for problems in the complex. Former Housing officers concur. "The managers knew the families and they knew the cops," explained one retired HAPD lieutenant, who joined the force in 1965. "So if there were complaints, you heard about them right away even if you didn't want to."[21]

Project record rooms kept the enforcement of law close enough to tenants that they could on occasion shape its practice, ensuring that the institutional force of the police didn't entirely eclipse the informal control of family and community. Terri Sheeps, who moved into the Bronx's Castle Hill Houses (2,025 units) in 1967, recalled how one officer, whose name had not escaped her even three decades later, often turned detained teenagers over to neighbors as he walked his unhappy charges to the record room. Sheeps recounts:

> If Miss Betty saw Officer Marson dragging you off to the record room, Miss Betty would interfere, and ask Officer Marson what did you do, he'd explain, and she'll say, "No give him to me, he'll stay at my house until his mother comes," and then she'll go BAAAP and swipe you on the head.

But even for those fortunate enough to escape a neighbor's scolding slap and make it to the record room, Sheeps explains, "their family knew where they were and where to look for 'em." The room's small holding cell, she argued, was:

> sort of an early scared straight program . . . you would walk in and those kids would be sitting shaking and they would be scared to death, it was just the sound of that closing that metal gate that scared them straight.

And, Sheeps observes, if the offense wasn't severe and the officer knew the family's reputation in the project, "You could take care of it in the record room" and "the kid wouldn't get a sheet."[22] Call it record room adjudication.

It was a practice that Barry Gottehrer, Mayor John Lindsay's assistant tasked with monitoring neighborhood unrest, credited with cooling police–community tensions. In late September 1968, in the wake of nationwide rioting following Martin Luther King's assassination in April of that year and just weeks after Chicago's "police riot," Gottehrer was hunting for ways to keep the lid on New York's own witches' brew of racial animosities, heated to the boiling point by the city's continuing teachers' strike. The prolonged teachers' strike had been sparked by white resistance to school integration and black demands to manage neighborhood schools. An experiment in such "community control" in Brooklyn's Ocean Hill–Brownsville neighborhood had gone badly, culminating in black militants purging much of Junior High School (JHS) 271's white staff. That act triggered a union walkout that shut down the city's schools and seemingly pitted the United Federation of Teachers, which at the time was 85 percent Jewish, against New York's largely black and Puerto Rican students.[23] And just five minutes from JHS 271, the school at the center of the storm, lay NYCHA's Cypress Hills Houses (1,444 units). There, Gottehrer noted in a memo, a Housing patrolman, Ivan Kelly, had arrested a "14 year old disorderly male, over 6 feet tall" who was "bent on resisting the police." But as Kelly restrained the boy, a restless crowd of hundreds of idled and embittered teens encircled the pair in the project's courtyard. Alone, as HAPD officers usually were on their beats, Kelly rushed the boy into the nearby record room. Relying on his familiarity with the Cypress Hills families, Kelly was able to summon the teen's mother from her apartment in the complex. She marched her son out of the record room and back home, defusing the situation and allowing Kelly to disperse the crowd. Gottehrer concluded that because the record room (unlike a precinct station) was close at hand and the patrolmen had relied on parental authority (rather than police power), "a serious incident" in an explosive neighborhood had been averted.[24]

Although few incidents were as dramatic as this one, reports that underscored the value of local police stations appear repeatedly in HAPD's daily memos and departmental records. By their very nature, the HAPD documents most often register those occasions when the relationship between police and tenants failed seriously enough to warrant the attention of report-writing supervisors. In documenting the most difficult interactions, however, these reports often reveal residents' expectations of how that relationship *should* have worked by describing tenants' reactions to the exercise of HAPD power. The reports show, for example, that parents assumed that if their children were arrested, they would be "dealt with," as one NYCHA mother asserted, "in the housing police office of their own building" rather than "downtown" by the NYPD. And the proximity of record rooms meant that it was not unusual for the family of residents taken into police custody, as one NYCHA official wrote, to be "informed by neighborhood children," often arriving, as another official noted, "within minutes." The tenant association of Brooklyn's Albany Houses (1,229 units), the *Amsterdam News* reported in 1971, so appreciated the presence of a record room in their development that they collected money from fellow residents in order to donate curtains and other fixtures to the HAPD for the spartan police quarters. As one tenant recalled of her Harlem complex's record room of in the 1960s, "that place made the officers like neighbors seeing as how you saw them everyday, not just when something went wrong."[25] And so, tucked away within the modernist landscapes of NYCHA's projects—so often decried as oppressively monotonous symbols of institutional indifference—there was, in fact, a chain of neighborhood HAPD stations that encouraged a remarkably local form of policing within reach of the people it served.[26]

The daily interaction that evolved among Housing officers, building managers, and project residents often enabled the HAPD, as one retired officer put it in the colorful parlance of the city's police, to "nip shit in the bud before it got the fuck out of hand." As the officer (and eventual detective) described of his eight years as a patrolmen in the Sound View Houses (1,259 units) in the Bronx during the late 1960s and early 1970s:

> If I saw someone from the roof selling fireworks, well you just knew that was gonna be a problem on the Fourth of July so you went and talked to their parents. . . . Or you see a husband and wife disputing on the street, so you stopped by their place later. . . . No one told you to do it, you just did it.[27]

Nearly all of the officers interviewed recalled such preventive policing—a key aspect of contemporary community policing.

Judging from the HAPD records, until the late 1970s it was not unusual for tenants, officers, and management to collaborate to avert potential problems An episode from Brooklyn's Cooper Park Houses (699 units) usefully distills the ways in which these groups regularly worked together to maintain peace in the city's public housing in the 1960s and so merits a close look.

In October 1966, Cooper Park's manager called a meeting of tenants and leaders from local churches and community groups to explore how "to obtain better tenant cooperation to improve the appearance of the houses and diminish vandalism." The community, however, had more than scuffed grass on its mind; the residents' anxieties this evening, instead, fixed on a riot they feared the weekend would bring. The daughters of one of the development's larger families, it was said, had taken to throwing "rent parties" and had recently started to ask boys from the nearby Williamsburg Houses (1,630 units) to join. But to some of Cooper Park's young males, this gesture had sounded less like a social invitation than sexual competition in what they took to be their exclusive space. Tenants reported that at the last party resentful threats had followed angrily after the Williamsburg boys' appraising glances of several Cooper Park girls until someone had fired four shots—harmlessly—into the night air. The pistol had been seized by, as the manager described it, "our police," and Housing officers had already started "meeting with both groups of boys" to "prevent a future clash." But the gathered tenants and community leaders still feared that juvenile swagger and teenage jealousy might combust again at the next event. Learning that the girls planned another party for Saturday, the manager left the meeting to speak directly with the family. He returned with a promise from the parents that there would be no further parties and announced to the vocally grateful tenants that he had "already started termination action" against the family for their repeated violations of Housing rules.[28] The HAPD, likewise, pledged additional officers over the weekend.

The full articulation of community policing's basic tenets was still decades away, but the residents, police, and management of Cooper Park were already engaged in what could be seen as a textbook example of how that strategy, as envisioned by its adherents, should work. The neighborhood identified a problem; the police worked to negotiate the root conflict and adjust resources accordingly; and management used its own power to help arrive at a solution the neighborhood could live with. And in this case at least, the community policing blueprint that was being worked out by tenants, patrolmen, and building supervisors throughout NYCHA in the 1960s and 1970s succeeded: that October weekend passed uneventfully in the Cooper Park and Williamsburg Houses.

This is one example among many preserved in the HAPD archives of a phenomenon that is called, in the jargon of today's community policing advocates, NYCHA's residents and police regularly "coproduced order."[29] Coproduced order was also achieved, to cite another example, when the HAPD, responding in 1969 to demands from a tenants' association that believed most of its complex's crime was committed by outsiders, agreed to "change the method of patrol of our housing police" by shifting the officers' beats to the open grounds of the housing unit rather than its interior spaces. Only a 33 percent spike in crime complaints from inside the buildings within two weeks of the policy change "compelled [HAPD] to terminate the experimental exterior patrol," with apparent approval from the tenants' association.[30]

The steps taken by NYCHA in the 1960s and early 1970s closely resembled what two decades later became a central, if generally unrealized goal, of community policing: allowing neighborhoods a voice in identifying, prioritizing, and solving problems. As one housing official wrote in 1964, "we need more security officers," but the knowledge necessary to achieve "project stability" could only come "from the tenants themselves."[31] This attitude was in marked contrast to the culture and practice of the NYPD, where, as one academic study noted at the time, "the rules of the game have prescribed that any alteration in enforcement policy must be a product of decision-making wholly within the Department." The HAPD, on the other hand, went so far as to sit down in 1968 with residents who aimed to expand job opportunities by forming a "Special Police Force" composed of armed tenants and funded by the Authority itself. Obvious legal constraints kept such notions from being put into practice, but the negotiations did later lead NYCHA leaders to push the HAPD to be "more active in the organization of tenants patrols," so as to bolster their standing in residents' eyes by "lend[ing] an air of official police" affiliation to the volunteers.[32]

Fines and Community Order

As both NYCHA tenants and HAPD officers tell it, however, linchpin in the maintenance of the daily order they constructed together during these years was the Housing Authority's system of fines for violations of NYCHA regulations. The Authority first turned to fines in the 1940s, hoping to restrain "vandalistic activities" without resorting to the more drastic—and in NYCHA's eyes, embarrassing—step of creating its own security force, as the New York Police Department had urged. Initially, the Authority planned that its civilian employees would issue summonses for minor breaches of tenancy regulations and then NYCHA courts—composed equally of residents and employees—would review the evidence and impose fines when appropriate.[33] Advised by lawyers that such courts could not be "proper agents" of the Authority; NYCHA dropped this idea in favor of what it believed to be a more legally sound—if also more paternalistic—approach.[34] The plan eventually adopted by NYCHA allowed building supervisors to tack on small "service charges" to the next rent statement of a tenant who had breached a regulation. Managers, however, were required to enter the tenants' side of the story into the case file, and residents had the right to appeal the decision in city court. The Authority rewrote its leases to hold tenants responsible for "reasonable charges" for "extra services as required by reason of the infraction by the Tenant or any member or his family of requirements or rules established for the proper administration of the project."[35]

With the creation of the Housing Police in 1952, the power of such fines to shape daily life in NYCHA increased, as officers walking their beats wrote up tenants for violations of Authority rules—from shaking mops out of windows to shattering lightbulbs in hallways—and conveyed that information to building managers. By 1959, HAPD officers were reporting an average of two hundred breaches of Authority rules a month in the seventy projects they covered.[36]

As East Harlem social worker Ellen Lurie described the system of fines in 1955, managers saw the charges not so much as a source of revenue—they rarely even covered the cost of processing—but as a means to "pinpoint" for residents the social conventions contributing to "decent project living." Moreover, the fines served "to bring the family into the manager's office for a conference." The Authority left managers free to calibrate the "service charge" to the seriousness of the infraction and the circumstances of the family. Such broad discretion no doubt shaded into bureaucratic capriciousness on occasion. Former police commissioner Arthur Wallander, hired by NYCHA to study its housing force, faulted the Authority in a 1957 report for a "lack of uniformity in imposing fines," noting that charges for the same offense ran "from 50¢ to $15.00."[37] Some residents clearly would have agreed with Wallander. As Lurie observed, tenants in the East Harlem developments where she worked "resented the arbitrariness" with which managers enforced fines. But Lurie also concluded that the majority of residents, as one mother reported to her, thought the fines "forced people to raise themselves up and better themselves."[38]

Lurie might well have been thinking of residents such as Sarah Martin, a young parent who in 1956 left a decrepit Harlem tenement to move into the recently completed General Grant Houses (1,940 units) nearby. Martin, a South Carolina native, vividly recalled her first service charge:

> My son had wet his bed and I hung the sheets out to dry out the window. Right away I received a letter notifying me NYCHA was fining me. From then on I wouldn't hang nothing ever again. But I commend the Authority, I thought it was just. Where I moved from those things were kinda allowed. But public housing meant new behavior, new respect, new everything. And I treated it accordingly . . . and it felt good.[39]

Martin's faith in NYCHA's system of fines to prod tenants into what she saw as better behavior was not unusual and echoes throughout the recollections of the Authority's older residents and former officers. Less punitive than the criminal code but possessing more bite than a neighbor's reproach, fines helped define and enforce community standards in the city's public housing until the early 1980s. Consider the memories of Peter Grymes, the son of southern migrants to New York City; he grew up largely in the Bronx's Castle Hill Houses in the late 1950s and early 1960s and became a Housing officer in 1968. Written up and summoned with his parents to the manager's office several times for "loitering," Grymes nonetheless credits fines with nudging residents to make "an effort to be responsible" and allowing Housing officers to signal "we mean business here" without having to make arrests.[40] Terri Sheeps, a Castle Hill resident since 1967 and a tenant leader for more than two decades, also believes the fines sustained neighborhood standards of behavior because they made clear to residents that "we had a responsibility not only to our families but to our community." Victor Gonzalez, currently a tenant leader in Manhattan's Stephen Wise Towers (399 units), recalls the impact of fines in much the same fashion. The child of wartime Puerto Rican migrants who grew up in Harlem's Manhattanville Houses (1,271 units) in the early 1960s, Gonzalez remembered that although some "on the wrong end" of the rules opposed fines, most residents praised the system for "keeping NYCHA for what it was supposed to be: a nice, decent place to live." Residents' belief in the power of fines to reinforce order was so great that when budget cutbacks, policy changes, and court challenges of the 1970s made the NYCHA reluctant to impose "service charges," tenants' organizations citywide demanded that NYCHA enforce the rules as vigorously as it had in the past (a topic explored in detail in chapter 3).[41]

Although all of the resident interviewees whose tenancy stretched back to at least the 1970s remembered tenants supporting NYCHA's use of fines—and nearly all those interviewed paid at least one "service charge"—the accuracy of such recollections, taken on their own, invites speculation: how much of what these tenants remember has been rose-tinted by nostalgia? And how representative are their stories? Interviewing older residents, for example, will hardly capture the perspectives of tenants who chafed under the Authority's fines and so moved out of NYCHA—or were forced to do so. Other accounts of public housing in New York and elsewhere, however, lend credence to long-term residents' convictions about both the popularity of fines in NYCHA and their role in preserving "decent project living." Tenants' recollections of Chicago's public housing in the 1940s and 1950 and studies of resident-managed public housing conducted during the 1970s in a variety of cities, as well as ethnographic fieldwork from NYCHA complexes in the 1980s, all testify to residents' support for Housing rules backed by fines.

When a past Chicago Housing Authority official and a team of oral historians conducted extensive interviews with current and former residents of Chicago's public housing, they documented a firm and broad belief by tenants that fines—even without a separate housing police force—helped to protect a cherished civility in their communities until the late 1950s. As the African American historian John Hope Franklin observed, the study's largely black tenants succeeded in creating "healthy and attractive communities" in public housing during these years partly because the Authority had fines and other tools at its disposal to "adequately serve the social and economic needs" of their tenants.[42]

Whether in Chicago or New York, however, elderly tenants' memories are easily burnished by time in ways that contemporaneous records are not. Although no opinion pollsters ventured into NYCHA complexes to measure residents' attitudes about the Authority's management of project life through fines, between 1978 and 1980 academic researchers did survey public housing residents in six other cities, including neighboring Jersey City, New Jersey, and found deep support for firmly enforced rules of tenancy. The Manpower Demonstration Research Corporation—a Ford Foundation spin-off—dispatched shoe-leather social scientists to study what was then a new and promising factor in the urban equation: tenant-managed public housing. To the Manpower researchers' surprise, not only were the tenant managers proudly and emphatically stricter than the previous city-appointed managers, but extensive surveys revealed residents' satisfaction with their housing actually grew the more firmly the tenant-managers enforced the rules—a finding confirmed by subsequent studies.[43] The tight management of daily behavior seemed to enjoy broad backing in public housing.

To outsiders, tenant support for fines could be baffling at times—particularly to a new breed of poverty experts for whom resistance against oppressive institutions and systems seemed to hold the key to empowering the poor.[44] When sociologist Lawrence Grossman, assisted by a team of graduate students, attempted in the late 1960s to mobilize tenants in a Brooklyn development, he found to his surprise that residents refused his suggestion that they oppose certain housekeeping fines levied by the complex's manager. Faced by resistance not from the Housing Authority but rather the very tenants whom he had hoped to rally, Grossman resorted to psychological explanations. Such residents suffered, he concluded, from undue "identification with authority" because they sought "contact" with and "entry points to an upper-class world." "What kinds of people," he asked rhetorically, "are usually attracted to 'keeping things clean'" besides such "identifiers"?[45] From the perspective of many residents, however, such daily order *was* the goal of neighborhood striving. As tenant leader Gonzalez recalled, NYCHA's willingness to maintain standards by imposing fines had demonstrated to residents that management took seriously their desires for "dignity in our homes."[46]

NYCHA's system of fines was pervasive in the residents' daily world chiefly because of the Housing Police, whose "vertical patrols" extended the reach of management's supervision. But the HAPD was nearly unique: not only was NYCHA the nation's largest public housing authority, the HAPD was, by an order of magnitude, the largest of the handful of public housing police forces.[47] Only in New York, then, did Housing officers regularly intercede in project life, writing up the roughhousing teens loitering in the building lobby or the neglectful parent too overwhelmed to take out the garbage from a filthy apartment. As former NYCHA resident Peter Grymes quipped of his years on the HAPD, "I wrote up people on a daily basis, hell, I wrote up some of 'em three times a day."[48]

Grymes's recollections are echoed in ethnographic data collected a little over a quarter-century ago that provide insight into the Authority's practice of using HAPD officers to fine residents for housing violations—as well as evidence of that the system continued to be supported by tenants even as late as the 1980s. Between 1980 and 1982, noted criminal ethnographer Mercer Sullivan closely observed the lives and life choices of a small number of New York youths as they edged in and out of crime. Sullivan's informants came from three different lower-middle or low-income Brooklyn neighborhoods, including a cluster of public housing complexes he dubbed "Projectville" to preserve the anonymity of his sources. Apparently unknown to Sullivan, however, by the time of his research the Projectville complexes were a bit of a rarity within NYCHA. Institutional changes in the late 1970s had left Projectville one of the few sites where managers still levied fines—a task that had already been complicated by legal challenges a decade earlier. Nonetheless, Sullivan encountered a stubborn if besieged oasis of social control in Projectville, where fines were still used to maintain order. The system depended on the cooperation of tenant groups willing to alert officers to persistent violations, patrolmen authorized to investigate and write up tenants for such infractions, and an overseeing officialdom ready to wield "service charges" when it could. Sullivan found that this alliance of bureaucracy and community was "partially successful" in reducing crime in Projectville—or at least displacing it.[49]

Rather than risk being detained and fined by the local HAPD for loitering or other infractions, the Projectville youth studied by Sullivan at times took their preferred criminal pursuits—drug dealing and chain snatching—elsewhere. In contrast, their counterparts in the study's other low-income neighborhood stuck closer to home when preying on victims or peddling marijuana in this pre–crack cocaine era.[50] Indeed, Sullivan observed that much of Projectville life was a "struggle between the youths on the one hand and on the other the tenants who feared them and allied with the police and Housing officials." Whatever the precise relationship between fines and crime, the process of levying "service charges" transformed housing officers, building managers, and older residents into allies, knit together around the promise of local sanctions for neighborhood menaces.[51]

This system of clear rules and swift (if occasionally arbitrary) fines that NYCHA residents spoke of repeatedly and approvingly in their oral histories characterized New York's public housing for more than a quarter-century after the HAPD's founding. By the mid-1960s, that system had come increasingly to distinguish NYCHA's complexes from surrounding neighborhoods and, indeed, most of the nation. While the HAPD would continue to try to manage project orderliness by enforcing NYCHA's regulations until the 1980s, outside of public housing a sweeping legal transformation between 1965 and 1972 made the task of regulating street life more difficult for ordinary police by invalidating the statutes they had previously depended on.

Until the mid-1960s, courts allowed the police wide discretion in their pursuit of public order.[52] Officers faced few checks on their abuse of vaguely defined statutes against vagrancy, breaches of the peace, and loitering. One observer at the time noted with only mild exaggeration that such laws were "so broad that they 'legally' authorize the police to arrest virtually anyone."[53] This legal regime, however, escaped public outcry because the police didn't arrest just "anyone" under such statutes. Instead, officers aimed these intentionally broad ordinances chiefly at the politically downtrodden who lacked the power to fight back: inebriates, to be sure, but also African Americans, Latinos, and impoverished whites. But when all-white police departments started to use such laws to arrest civil rights activists amid what seemed a larger police campaign to defend segregation in the South, federal courts took notice. After 1965, these statutes increasingly faced a scrutiny as intense at it was overdue.[54] With surprising swiftness, lower courts struck down most such order-maintenance laws, a process that culminated in the 1972 Supreme Court decision *Papachristou v. City of Jacksonville*. That ruling ultimately invalidated a medley of public order laws nationwide that the justices concluded had been designed only "to increase the arsenal of the police."

In limiting the discretion of officers in their pursuit of order, *Papachristou* and similar earlier rulings were at least as important to policing as the more well-known (and more debated) procedural revolution of the Warren Court.[55] If *Papachristou* spelled the end for a particular class of statutes as a law enforcement tool, it also symbolized, as a number of scholars have remarked, a broader shift away from order maintenance itself as a public goal.[56] Thus, in drafting his decision, Justice William Douglas attacked not simply the vagueness of order-maintenance statutes that "encourage[d] arbitrary and discriminatory enforcement of the law," but also the conformity of an American culture that fostered a "hushed, suffocating silence." Using the occasion to squeeze in references to poets Vachel Lindsay and Walt Whitman, Douglas insisted that a generous society should tolerate vagrancy as a wellspring for individual "creativity" instead of suppressing it as a peril to community stability.[57]

At much the same time that courts began challenging order-maintenance laws, police critics began to question the wisdom of controlling panhandling, loitering, and other behaviors when rising crime rates suggested the real threats to public safety lay elsewhere. According to this argument, officers busily rounding up youthful vandals and disheveled vagabonds weren't available to pursue the violent criminals who increasingly stalked both the city's streets and—polls revealed—the public's fears.[58] These shifts in popular attitudes, along with the new legal rulings, propelled police administrators themselves to question their customary practices, and departments started to slacken their enforcement of what they had now learned to see as "victimless crimes." If criminal justice in the United States changed in these years, it was in great part because increasing numbers of police, from top brass down to the rank and file, came to accept and implement the thinking of courtroom judges.

The transformation of antiprostitution law enforcement in New York provides a good example of these post-1960 developments in law enforcement. In Gotham's parched-paint courtrooms, prosecutors and judges had, by the late 1960s, started to throw out solicitation cases based on loitering or other newly suspect charges—halving the conviction rate to 40 percent, according to the *New York Times*.[59] Out on patrol, meanwhile, NYPD officers increasingly tolerated streetwalking on a modest scale in several of the city's quarters, while making arrests for prostitution everywhere else a low priority.[60] And so it was with numerous other low-level crimes. The city's overall arrest statistics tell the story: in 1964, more than four out of ten "collars" made by NYPD officers fell into the lowest grade of severity, but by 1970 such arrests had fallen to less than one-fifth of the total as patrolmen increasingly turned a blind eye to minor crimes on the city's streets.[61] The same, however, was not true for NYCHA's complexes.

Because the Authority had become a distinct region within the city's legal terrain, New York's public housing developments followed a different course. Rules for daily conduct and a system of fines, established in a more paternalistic era, remained both on the books and enforced (albeit with wide variation and declining vigor). Even after organizations primed with Great Society dollars and inspired by a suspicion of government bureaucracies brought suit against the Authority in 1968, raising issues similar to those posed by *Papachristou*, NYCHA's system weathered on. The activists based their legal challenge on the argument that the "coerced tranquility" of the city's public housing robbed residents of their "dignity and self-respect," and, in *Lockman v. NYCHA*, contested NYCHA's fines on due process grounds.[62] But the unique nature of the Authority's rules blunted the legal force of the assault. Grounded in tenant leases rather than municipal law, NYCHA's ability to impose fines for violations was limited but not eliminated by an appellate decision into which *Lockman* had been consolidated.

The court ruling did prevent managers from levying fines justified solely by grievances lodged by fellow tenants, unless the complaining residents were willing to brave direct confrontation with the accused in an evidentiary hearing.[63] Unsurprisingly, residents nearly always proved too fearful of retaliation to do so. But violations witnessed by the Authority's own police officers, who were available for cross-examined, continued to be a viable basis for fines.[64] As a consequence of the new restrictions, HAPD officers—who had previously often conveyed to management infractions based only on neighbors' descriptions—started to report solely those breaches of the rules of which they had direct knowledge, roughly halving the number of such cases that landed on managers' desks. In 1968, the year of *Lockman*, HAPD officers reported 18,406 residents to managers; in 1971, after the appellate court decision, that number slipped to 9,102 and then barely fluctuated until 1978 when it plunged amid a reorganization of the HAPD's chain of command that hobbled the Authority's ability to impose fines.[65] Through the 1970s and in some places into the 1980s, Housing officers continued to write up and apprehend tenants for comparatively minor infractions of NYCHA's regulations. In 1976, for example, HAPD officers made 1,157 apprehensions for "bike riding," 1,998 for "playing in prohibited area," and another 6,386 for loitering, noise, and even housekeeping violations. Indeed, that year HAPD officers made 13 percent more apprehensions for violations of NYCHA's rules (9,991) compared to arrests under penal law (8,129).[66] In ways that had become rare elsewhere in the city and the nation, public housing's officers policed not just major crimes but minor disorder as well.

Community Influence on Policing

It would not have been surprising if HAPD officers, authorized to enforce Housing rules for remarkably small incivilities, had abused their broad discretion—as police elsewhere had long done, turning many African American and Latino neighborhoods in northern cities into tinderboxes of resentment by the late 1950s.[67] Instead, the HAPD's policy choices and daily practices largely spared New York's public housing the bitter alienation between residents and the police that increasingly characterized city life beyond NYCHA's complexes. Indeed, in ways large and small, minority communities signaled their preference for the brand of law enforcement they witnessed in NYCHA's projects.

At a citywide conference in 1973 that was intended to quiet seething enmities between New York's police and its African American and Latino communities, a reporter was startled to find that residents "constantly juxtaposed" the practices of the NYPD with those of the HAPD. While the Housing officers on foot patrols were "available" and "visible" in the projects, NYPD's squad cars left "indifference" in their wake as they swept through neighborhoods resentful of a police force no longer close at hand.[68] Likewise, when in the "long, hot summer" of 1967 anger at police brutality finally and riotously exploded in American cities—prompting officers of any race to think twice before entering minority neighborhoods—Harlem's United Block Association had already welcomed the Housing Police by sponsoring a well-attended parade for both the black and white members of the force. HAPD officers marched down 125th Street, the neighborhood's symbolic heart, under a banner that proclaimed, tellingly, "Active in Community Affairs." The procession represented an unusual and public gesture for a neighborhood that had witnessed three antipolice riots in four years, and at a time when for many African Americans, as writer James Baldwin observed, respecting law enforcement usually meant surrendering "self-respect."[69]

Of course, NYCHA in these years was no Shangri La of tranquil police–community relations. Nation of Islam members, for example, led a mob that briefly stormed a Brooklyn HAPD record room in 1962, insisting only their presence could insure justice for a fifteen-year-old detained inside. A decade later in East Harlem, two white Housing patrolmen were pelted by bottles hurled by an unruly crowd angered by a fatal shooting the night before by an HAPD officer.[70] Nor did all Housing officers embody racial progressivism. In 1976, Robert Barbieri, an HAPD sergeant, served prison time along with three neighbors—another sergeant from the NYPD, a corrections officer, and a vice president of a prominent Wall Street brokerage firm—for repeatedly vandalizing a house in their all-white Staten Island neighborhood in an effort to prevent a black family from moving in. Over the course of three weeks, the four shattered the house's windows, flooded its basement, and eventually set fire to the structure—all to dissuade a black Venezuelan-born psychologist and his Princeton-educated wife from settling into the home that they had rented with an option to buy.[71]

As NYCHA documents, press coverage, and tenant recollections testify, such incidents were few and far between. New York's African American and Latino communities generally drew a sharp distinction between the city and NYCHA police forces. As one African American recruit explained in 1973, "I wouldn't want to work for the City Police Department . . . only [Housing] deals with the community."[72] That sentiment echoes in the recollection of Haile Selassie, a Ghanaian-born former HAPD officer named by his Ethiopian father after his country's celebrated emperor, who had been forced into exile by the Italian invasion the year of the patrolman's birth. Selassie refused to work for the NYPD out of a dislike for the "abusiveness of the police" he had witnessed in Harlem, where he moved to in 1959. But when the possibility of joining the Housing Police emerged in 1969, Selassie signed up, eager to serve the growing black and Latino communities in public housing, whom he came to view as his "real employer" and so intended to "treat with respect."[73]

The differences between police–community relations inside and outside of public housing complexes would likely have been obvious to the close observer of one particularly ill-fated NYPD program. To much fanfare, the NYPD announced early in 1972 that with the stroke of Police Commissioner Patrick Murphy's pen it was reversing a musty reform era policy prohibiting officers from working their home precincts, allowing the NYPD to start the experiment of posting "resident patrolmen" to walk beats in their own neighborhoods. The pilot project's new patrolmen, explained the commissioner, would police "their own community" and so have a special stake in "working directly" for "neighbors, home, family, and self." But the press coverage had included the names and photographs of the officers, and within weeks residents of the "model precincts" had taken to harassing the new—and apparently unwelcome—patrolmen. The NYPD, in turn, took the hint and quietly transferred the officers to new details for their own safety. Meanwhile, despite tenant newsletters that often lavished attention on them, hundreds of HAPD officers continued to live in NYCHA housing without incident, as they had since 1952.[74]

In contrast to New York City at large, where the sources of power could seem remote and inscrutable, the very structure of NYCHA reduced municipal bureaucracy to an approachable size, allowing some residents individually and collectively to enforce responsible policing. NYCHA's grounds may have sometimes been patchy and the tenants nearly always poor, but its building managers and Housing patrolmen, working out of local offices, were known by name to the residents who, as the Authority's rich records chronicle, felt free to express grievances. In 1969 Mrs. Larleen Moses, for example, complained to the HAPD that an officer had improperly written up her son for "simply being in the hall" near their apartment in Staten Island's Mariners Harbor complex (607 units). Such overbearing use of power would, Mrs. Moses worried, "decrease [her son's] respect for the police." But she refused NYCHA's offer to take her grievances to a formal hearing, explaining that her sole "concern in making this complaint was to establish a better understanding between her son and the police." The next year another mother, Ruby Hogans of the Pink Houses (1,500 units) in Brooklyn, reported an officer for handling her son a mite too roughly, but similarly declined to file a charge because the officer in question was a "new member of the force" who had now "been made aware that people [in Pink Houses] are interested in the welfare of their children."[75] Hogans withdrew her complaint, content that through her actions the novice officer had learned the unspoken conventions—developed through countless daily interactions between officers and tenants—that governed policing in her complex.

In demanding changes in police behavior, NYCHA's tenants not only raised their individual voices but also exerted the collective power that had developed in their communities during the era of expanded rights and neighborhood activism ushered in by the War on Poverty. As historian Rhonda Williams has demonstrated in her study of Baltimore's public housing, "In providing living space and setting forth rules governing working-people's tenancy," the government "set a standard for decent housing and government responsiveness for tenants as renters [and] citizens." Structures built into public housing intended by NYCHA and other housing authorities to build community—such as tenants' associations and patrols—quickly became vehicles for more politicized forms of engagement with the state.[76] In New York, public housing tenants could mobilize relatively quickly on behalf of their communities in ways that the citizens of the city's other poor neighborhoods could not. During the 1960s and 1970s, through lobbying of elected officials, demonstrations, and rent strikes (both threatened and actual), NYCHA residents demanded, and frequently secured, what they saw as their fair share of protection from the city's law enforcement agencies. They achieved not only expansions in the Housing Police ranks but also alterations in HAPD practices. Even today, when community policing has become the byword for more than three-quarters of the nation's departments, the strategy's supporters have had to acknowledge that few poor communities enjoy a comparable place at the policy table.[77]

This record of collective action by NYCHA residents rarely figures in popular accounts of New York's public housing complexes, which are more often portrayed by present-day observers as little more than depressing warehouses for their "demoralized" and "disorganized" tenants.[78] Historians have done little to modify this image of hapless passivity.[79] Historical discussion of tenant mobilization in New York City's public housing began, and largely ended, with Joel Schwartz's pathbreaking early research in the 1980s. Schwartz detailed what he saw as NYCHA's golden moment of resident organizing: the campaigns of the largely Jewish activists of the 1930s and '40s who had been "touched by radicalism and the union movement" even before moving into public housing. But collective action by tenants "foundered" and then vanished entirely, Schwartz concluded, with the exodus of these leaders in the 1950s as both the city and its low-income housing changed. Postwar affluence coupled with NYCHA's maximum-income restrictions pushed the Authority's early residents, activists included, out of public housing and into the outer boroughs, making "room for non-whites in numbers and in projects unthinkable before the war." But these "newcomers," Schwartz argued, were "largely unexposed to the radical traditions that had animated" the previous tenant activists.[80] And so the "new black residents never did share the sense of project citizenship" that the first generation of tenants had. While Schwartz may have gotten the story right for NYCHA's early white residents, he overstated the contrast between these "hardy pioneers" (as he called them) and the largely African American and Latino tenants who followed.[81]

In struggling to preserve the safety of their communities, in fact, these "newcomers" often enlarged their engagement with the state and deepened their expectations of citizenship. And while certainly "unexposed" to the specific leftist traditions of the largely Jewish activists celebrated by Schwartz, the Puerto Ricans and African Americans filtering into postwar public housing had collectivist traditions of their own upon which to draw, in particular a heritage of community mothering well suited to the new public housing developments of East Harlem that were thick with children by the late 1950s.[82]

Even Ellen Lurie, a committed settlement worker at the time, found these networks of women in the city's public housing hard to identify at first, although their effects were plainly visible.[83] In 1957, as a representative of the East Harlem Project, Lurie went in search of neighborhood groups and leaders that her organization could help mobilize, with the assistance of private foundation funds, into a "voice for decisions which involved their own futures." Only after two years of meetings with NYCHA residents in East Harlem did Lurie encounter the most "formidable" association in the neighborhood: Las Vigilantes, an anticrime organization of mothers "well known" to their fellow tenants in the Lexington Houses (448 units). "In reflecting as to why this group had not been discovered earlier," Lurie pointed to a male building representative ("domineering and easily threatened," she observed) who had insisted that no other associations existed in the complex and blocked her inquiries. Only by outflanking him and making her own connections had Lurie discovered the "real" source of energy that had begun organizing the building's tenants.[84]

As Lurie discovered, this group of six Puerto Rican women enjoyed prominent status in the building because of their roles as neighborhood caretakers, reflecting a seasoned tradition of "othermothers" and "activist mothering" that scholars have traced in African American and Latino communities.[85] First, the women's "high incidence of children" (twenty-seven) brought Las Vigilantes credibility in the building. Second, the hours they logged in their particularly visible meeting place—the benches outside the building's laundry room—made staying involved with Las Vigilantes as inevitable for the building's women as doing the week's wash. Finally, the group had an "interest in promoting social change" among the broader "bench society" of mothers in the building. However modest their organization's "office," their accomplishments were significant: stimulating a mass protest of residents that persuaded the Authority to install window bars on the first floor after a ground-floor tenant was brutally attacked; organizing the building's "different fathers so that they would take turns at various times day or night, depending on their shifts, to help patrol the building" for several months after a rape of a child; working with the HAPD to "discourage the illegal use of [their complex's] street by vehicles"; and winning from management the right to plant flowers around the complex—a practice NYCHA would later adopt systemwide.[86]

Tenant organizations would mushroom throughout the city's low-income housing in the 1960s, fostered by NYCHA's efforts and dollars. As historian Nicholas Bloom details in his study of the Authority, after 1958 NYCHA increasingly worked to build community in the projects, hoping to stave off vandalism and disorder through tenant commitment. Official residents' organizations, the Authority calculated, could help it meet its management challenge. By 1965, all but 28 of NYCHA's 134 developments had tenant associations. The results, however, didn't always match the Authority's expectations.[87]

To begin with, NYCHA discovered that funding tenant groups didn't necessarily result in improved order. Tenant organizations, it turned out, were as likely to divide the Authority's residents as they were to bring them together. NYCHA—having created an official base for tenant power, however narrow, and having offered money, however little—now regularly found itself obliged to serve as a neutral arbitrator in what proved to be frequent clashes between black and Latino tenant factions over the new benefits. NYCHA, indeed, resorted on several occasions to hiring outside firms to oversee disputed tenant elections in an effort to bolster the integrity of the voting process and the credibility of the leadership that emerged.[88]

In addition, the Authority wasn't the only government agency in town hoping to enlist disadvantaged people in plans for their own uplift. President Lyndon Johnson's War on Poverty sought to persuade the poor of the virtues of bettering themselves through their own political muscle—if only within the existing system—rather than relying on the allegedly enfeebling charity of the federal government or philanthropic institutions.[89] By 1968, over one thousand "community action" groups opened offices in predominantly black and Latino neighborhoods across the country, four-fifths of them funded by the Office of Economic Opportunity (OEO), the agency administrating the bulk of the new Great Society programs.[90] From 1964 to 1975, the Authority's complexes buzzed with the activities not only of NYCHA-backed groups but also a throng of community action organizations brought into existence by the OEO. To such organizations, NCYHA's readily rented community facilities and clearly defined neighborhoods made the developments particularly attractive places to set up shop. Indeed, NYCHA officials publicly offered up the Authority's complexes as "social laboratories" for "involving the poor in planning and administrating the programs they require," noting that "with the community facilities and the tenant body at hand, it is comparatively easy to test emerging hypotheses in community living." By 1965, forty-nine of the Authority's one hundred community centers were operated by OEO or other volunteer associations. As historians have noted, over time "community action" organizations nationwide—brought to heel by existing city and federal agencies and moderated by their own creeping professionalization—lost much of their early radical edge. But the groups could, at times, expand residents' influence on NYCHA decisions.[91]

Whatever notions NYCHA and the OEO had regarding improving the lives of residents, tenants associations and community action groups tended to have ideas of their own, and these strong opinions often put them at odds with their government sponsors. Despite the variety of tenant organizations and their rapid growth through the 1960s and 1970s, they generally shared three goals that frequently conflicted with those of the Authority's personnel: expanded and more responsive HAPD service, enforcement of Housing rules, and the eviction of troublemakers. The new spirit of collective action in NYCHA complexes, in other words, meant the Authority often found itself being held accountable by its own tenants for failing to use its institutional power to curb disorder in New York's low-income housing.

This pattern was at work, for example, at the October 1966 Cooper Park Houses meeting on the subject of "rent parties," described earlier in this chapter. Even though the building manager, responding to tenant demands, had already promised to evict the disruptive family hosting the "rent parties," and despite the fact that the HAPD brass had agreed to step up that weekend's patrols, the gathered residents and community leaders were looking for more durable changes. Linsy Hart, the tenant association president, and Mrs. Mildred Tudy, the former president who had recently been hired as an organizer for a local OEO community action group, took the assembled NYCHA officials to task. These two women—mothers and veteran civil rights activists—complained that the building manager was rarely forceful enough with the many Cooper Park families who violated Housing rules.[92] Tudy and Hart insisted that NYCHA officials should be "more severe in these cases." They put the Authority "on notice" that Hart's tenant association and Tudy's Community Progress Center would be watching to see that tenancy regulations were "firmly enforced" at Cooper Park. To these activists, preventive policing and community security required both fines and evictions—and they used their leadership positions to prod the Authority to action.[93]

Such popular pressure, focused on neighborhood safety rather than individual rights or other causes historically championed by the political left, often remained invisible even to sympathetic outsiders. The radical social theorists and activists Richard Cloward and Frances Fox Piven, for example, concluded at the time that NYCHA had successfully deployed tenants' 'organizations to channel residents' discontent "away from actions troublesome to the Authority" and into "middle-class" endeavors such as "project beautification." Moreover, the maintenance of public order in NYCHA, the two academics argued, reflected the efforts and interests not of the tenants themselves but rather of the Authority, which wielded "policing practices" to "contain the poor" and "reinforce their powerlessness."[94]

Cloward and Piven's analysis would have surprised Mildred Tudy, whose insistence that NYCHA enforce its rules against her unruly neighbors fit squarely with her concept of political action on behalf of her community. Indeed, Tudy, looking back decades later, described her central goal in a lifetime of activism in African American struggles as fighting for " 'basic needs': the opportunity to be healthy and independent in one's environment." Demanding that the Authority impose standards of behavior in Cooper Park was no exception to her politics. Rather, Tudy's sense of her community's positive right to the "basic need" of neighborhood safety meant individuals' claims to their NYCHA lease should be conditional on responsible behavior. This fusing of group rights, conventional volunteerism, and more radical demands shaped Tudy's participation in neighborhood campaigns that, over the course of forty years, included efforts to expand black employment and education opportunities, fighting lead poisoning in poor communities, resisting racist violence, and protecting what Tudy saw as poor people's rights to government assistance.[95]

And Tudy was hardly alone. NYCHA's new tenant associations often pressured managers for evictions. Although until 1971 management could evict families for the criminal offenses of any of their members, removing tenants was a last resort for public housing managers who generally, as one noted, preferred stability and low turnover to evictions, as long as families paid their rent.[96] Evictions for "non-desirability," accordingly, occurred infrequently—even in the late 1950s when NYCHA's institutional power over tenants was at its peak. Although it is impossible to be certain of the reasons for tenant move-outs from the surviving records for NYCHA's city- and state-funded programs, the paperwork for the Authority's federal program—which included four out of ten tenants at the time—is more revealing. In 1958, the Authority either evicted or asked to move out a total of 110 families from federally funded complexes: 7 for "noncooperation," 15 for "breach of regulations, " and 88 for "objectionable conduct." The 487 individuals involved represented merely 1.2 percent of all residents in the federal program. But the rarity of evictions does not seem to have lessened residents' confidence in their power as a deterrent against misbehavior. As tenant leader Terri Sheeps reported, "eviction was absolutely key" to the fragile order the police, tenants, and management had forged in the Castle Hill Houses where she lived in the 1960s. This conviction was shared by other tenant association leaders, who often demanded that NYCHA evict particular families for serious violations. Tenant leader Sarah Martin, for example, remembered residents throughout the city in the 1960s organizing to send petitions to building managers requesting action against unruly residents. NYCHA's files from these years even contain numerous telegrams from tenant groups sent to the Authority's chairman identifying families they no longer wished to have as neighbors.[97]

One clear measure of NYCHA residents' investment in policing their complexes is the frequency with which they interrupted their days—already crowded by the demands of fussy children and difficult bosses—to deliberate about community order with each other, the HAPD, and the Authority. In contrast to the often sparsely attended neighborhood "beat" meetings that have disappointed advocates of community policing in New York and elsewhere since the 1990s, NYCHA residents participated in both police meetings and community organizations in impressive numbers during the 1960s and 1970s.[98] One study of three representative Authority complexes from 1970 found that tenant association meetings—which regularly included an HAPD or NYCHA representative—enjoyed turnout rates of close to 40 percent of the adult residents. In comparison, even in the most intensive and sustained recent community policing effort—the Chicago Alternative Policing Strategy (CAPS)—participation at "beat" meetings in largely African American neighborhoods in the 1990s averaged merely 25 attendees per 10,000 residents (a figure that, however low it might seem, actually exceeded the rates for predominantly white and Latino neighborhoods).[99] But in NYCHA in the 1960s, even meetings focused exclusively on policing consistently drew significant, though much smaller, numbers of residents.

The fortuitously preserved records for 1963–1965 from the community center at Harlem's George Washington Houses (1,515 units) provide rare quantitative evidence of residents' anticrime activism. In addition to the tenant association gatherings, the development—88 percent black or Puerto Rican—held meetings nearly monthly with HAPD police officers, to which an average of 37 of the 5,940 total residents turned out.[100] In other words, despite the meager budget of their community center, NYCHA's Washington Houses residents in the 1960s were close to two and a half times more likely to participate in meeting with their police than were residents from racially comparable neighborhoods in Chicago thirty years later—even with CAPS' sizable resources for outreach and training. As these numbers suggest, NYCHA's investment in both community and security was more than matched by residents' activism in these years.

The synergy of government funding for community groups and neighborhood mobilization also proved powerful in fostering responsible policing in the city's public housing. An incident in Brooklyn during the summer of 1968 reveals just how effective the dynamic could be. The killing of NYCHA tenant Edward Troutman at the hands of a Housing officer was one of the most significant ruptures in community relations during the half-century of the HAPD's existence, but in the end it was not catastrophic. This case provides a insight into the ability of tenants and the HAPD to repair such cracks in their relationship by drawing upon both the neighborhood organizations and personal trust that were fostered by Housing's distinctive style of policing and NYCHA's management policies.

On a June evening in 1968, several hundred teens gathered around the courtyard benches of Brooklyn's Marcy Houses (1,717 units), enjoying the freedom afforded by summer to flirt and drink, away from watchful parents in cramped apartments. As Thomas Johnson, an HAPD officer, walked past the high-spirited group, someone tossed a stick at the patrolman who—unlike others working the development—had never been popular with the residents. Johnson, the New York–born son of West Indian parents, spun around and, unable to extract an admission of guilt from any of the teens, ordered the crowd to disperse.[101] One youth moved too slowly for Johnson's liking and received a jab from the officer's nightstick. Provoked, the group started to hurl bottles at Johnson; one teen, Zachary Merritt, went further—no one ever figured out why—and struck the patrolman with a hammer. Confused and under assault, Johnson used his service revolver to fire back at Merritt. The shot, however, merely nicked its intended target and continued into the crowd, striking a seventeen-year-old in the throat. The youth, Edward Troutman, died en route to the hospital.[102]

By the next morning, when news of the killing spread through the Marcy Houses, the complex crackled with anger. And as evening fell, the hastily called tenants' meeting seemed to promise violence. As chance would have it, however, Mayor Lindsay was also in the neighborhood on one of his famous night walks. Learning of the tensions, the mayor, according to the *New York Times*, quickly "changed the itinerary of his stroll and headed for the low-income development."[103]

Lindsay's arrival at the Marcy Houses met with chants of "Black Power, Black Power." Undeterred, the mayor shouldered his six-foot-three-inch frame through the crowd of jeering residents in the basement community center, ducking the exposed pipes along the way. Surrounded on all sides by restive tenants, the Lindsay challenged his audience: "One of the marks of greatness is to allow the other fellow due process when it has not been allowed to you." Lindsay, however, also promised to "do everything in my power to see that justice is done—and that word justice means a lot." To the astonishment of the journalists accompanying him, the words of the patrician mayor won over the public housing tenants, who drowned out Lindsay with their approving shouts. As the *Amsterdam News* described it, Lindsay magically "changed the crowd from anger to loud cheers." The night was, in fact, a small reprise of Lindsay's celebrated walk through Harlem following Martin Luther King's assassination only ten weeks earlier: a demonstration of the mayor's personal charisma triumphing over the weight of accumulated grievances.[104]

The temporary calm achieved by Lindsay's magnetic presence failed to hold. The Marcy teens who had witnessed the killing remained unconvinced by the mayor's promises, and the next day found them milling about angrily in the complex's grounds. The threat of violence again hung heavy over the Marcy Houses. Lindsay's visit had been dramatic, but in the end it would fall to tenant leaders and a local antipoverty group to restore the peace.

Edward Troutman, the teenager Patrolman Johnson had shot to death, had been a member of the Pioneer Civic Action Organization, a short-lived outpost in the War on Poverty that operated out of rented space in the Marcy Houses. Eleanor Ford, the wife of Pioneer's director, was a Marcy tenant, and she quickly grasped that the shoestring organization might succeed where the mayor and his sleeves-rolled-up aides-de-camp had failed. Making the most of the trust she had built with Housing officers during the many tenant–police meetings Pioneer had held at Marcy, Ford convened a gathering of both Housing and NYPD brass, City Hall officials, and the teens of Marcy Houses. As Mrs. Ford explained to the assembled young people, she had called the police so that they could hear the youths' side of the incident.[105]

It is not hard to imagine that the high-ranking NYPD officials whom Ford had persuaded to appear at the meeting feared it would feature more of the antipolice diatribes that had become commonplace in the city by the late 1960s. Indeed, one of Mrs. Ford's invitees, Lloyd Sealy, then an assistant chief inspector and the highest-ranking African American in the NYPD, had recently been lured by a similar invitation into a publicity trap set by Sonny Carson, head of the Brooklyn chapter of the Congress of Racial Equality (CORE) at the time. Carson had requested the presence of Sealy and City Hall officials at what he promised would be a private meeting to discuss police–community tensions. Sealy and the mayor's staff tramped up to the second-floor meeting hall of Brooklyn's Moorish Science Temple only to discover that they had been set up to play unwitting roles in a media circus devised by Carson. Flanked by disciples, Carson seized upon the arrival of Sealy and the mayor's representatives to launch a tirade against the police and City Hall in front of the television crews he had surreptitiously invited. Matters then quickly spiraled out of control. One CORE member assaulted a *Daily News* photographer without provocation while others outside the Temple busied themselves by vandalizing a car belonging to a mayoral aide at the meeting.[106] More of the same seemed in store for any police official committed, bold, or foolish enough to appear before a community meeting, particularly one in the wake of a teenager's killing by a patrolman and growing calls for Black Power—calls that were often misinterpreted by outsiders.

Historians a generation removed from the era have begun to rescue Black Power from its media caricature as the civil right movement's "evil twin." A growing scholarship has documented Black Power's nuanced analysis of urban problems as well as its role in strengthening the resiliency of African American protest in the face of deepening white intransigence. But what was profound or pragmatic about Black Power was often eclipsed when its leadership exploited a cooperative press in order to cultivate its own provocative brand of celebrity. In response, law enforcement often took the movement's militant posturing at face value—or saw images of decapitated pigs in the *Black Panther* as programmatic threats and not as ideological metaphors. Only three months before Mrs. Ford invited police officials to Brooklyn's Marcy Houses, a leader from the nearby Ocean Hill–Brownsville local control movement had indeed created a menacing spectacle by urging his heavily school-aged black audience to "obtain weapons and practice using them" in order to defend themselves against the New York Police Department's "occupying army." Lloyd Sealy and the other NYPD officials who agreed to Ford's request had good reason to expect yet more overheated rhetoric at the community meeting.[107]

But at the Marcy Houses' gathering, the harangues never came. Unlike Carson and other emerging male black militants, Mrs. Ford had no use for revolutionary theater. Indeed, she reckoned her role was to safeguard her community, not achieve iconic status. "Not much sense," she told a Housing official, in "turning things upside down when it won't get either of us what we want."[108] The meeting with the Pioneer Civic Action teens at Marcy, accordingly, must have surprised Sealy and the assembled NYPD officials.

Crowded into the same community center the mayor had visited earlier in the week, the teens insisted it wasn't the policing of the projects or even most of the officers assigned to their complex that gave rise to their rage. No, as the young residents angrily explained it, Patrolmen Johnson was the problem. Indeed, the youth compared Johnson, who was black, with a white officer—"Larry"—who also worked the Marcy Houses. Although Larry had made "numerous arrests in the project," the teens considered him a "good cop" because he reasoned "with the kids like a parent." In contrast, the teens described Johnson as "walking around in a belligerent manner" on his patrols and then "going beserk [*sic*]" when he encountered trouble. And Johnson's unrestrained use of his firearm, the teens recounted, was not unusual. The day before killing Troutman, Johnson had "pulled his gun on a group of nine-year-old children."[109] After verifying the Marcy teens' accounts, the HAPD decided it had heard enough. Under pressure from Housing's brass, Johnson quietly resigned from the force (but escaped any criminal charges stemming from Troutman's death). As Assistant Chief of Department Keeney recalled of Johnson's departure from the HAPD, "a guy like that wasn't going to last long in a department that listened to the community."[110]

Being heard by the police, however, wasn't as simple a thing as Chief Keeney's comment might suggest. In truth, as the Johnson affair underscored, tenants' ability to shape policing hinged on two aspects of life in New York's public housing that during the 1960s and '70s often distinguished the Authority's developments from other low-income neighborhoods. First, NYCHA residents could generally turn to tenant associations or community groups like Pioneer to advocate their interests before both the HAPD and the Authority. Second, the Housing Police could draw on their sustained interaction with residents to know whom to trust when complaints did arise. Both conditions took hold readily in NYCHA complexes, where the Authority and its tenants made good use of clear community borders to build resident organizations and where the HAPD, organized around local record rooms and not precincts, walked regular beats in ways the city police increasingly did not.

At the NYPD, putting such police decisions—even to a small degree—into neighborhood hands amounted to professional heresy, particularly when the neighborhood was poor and the hands weren't white. This attitude was most unequivocally expressed in 1966 by John Cassese, then president of the NYPD's Patrolmen's Benevolent Association, who exclaimed during the fight over Mayor Lindsay's effort to contain police brutality with a Civilian Complaint Review Board: "I'm sick and tired of giving in to minority groups with their whims and their gripes and shouting."[111]

Subsequent events seem to have ratified the assessment of Marcy House tenants about the danger Johnson posed to their community. After leaving

Housing for the Transit Police, Johnson continued to behave erratically, racking up two serious weapons violations within a decade. Then, in April 1982, he shot at two NYPD detectives who had angered him—and was killed when they returned fire in a case the city police deemed self-defense after a brief investigation.[112]

Rent Strikes and Political Leverage

From the late 1950s until the end of the 1970s, tenants' most urgent and insistent political goal was always the hiring of more housing police. At nearly every meeting with Authority staff, in a flurry of letters to elected officials, and—starting in 1966—with increasingly strident demonstrations, residents demanded that NYCHA increase police coverage in their complexes. Indeed, between 1963 and 1980, New York's public housing residents engaged in at least thirty-nine significant protests of varying kinds—demonstrations, rent strikes, sit-ins, and vigils—calling on NYCHA to provide more officers.[113] Such activism by NYCHA residents neatly inverts Cloward and Piven's notion that the Housing Authority aimed to disrupt tenants' political aspirations by enforcing orderliness in its complexes. Instead, the records show that neighborhood order was frequently the purpose of NYCHA residents' political struggles and that tenants believed they could achieve greater order by increasing the presence of Housing Authority patrolmen.

The tenants' most dramatic strategy in this campaign was the rent strike, a tactic borrowed from civil rights agitation elsewhere in New York and the country. By the late 1950s, housing activists in Harlem had demonstrated the advantages of aiming for exploitive landlords' pocketbooks rather than their consciences, inspiring a community organizing effort that spread throughout the urban North in the mid-1960s. The movement's glowing press coverage and increasing political clout left established civil rights groups scrambling to preserve their relevance by launching housing campaigns of their own, suited to the newly combative temper in black neighborhoods.[114] Historians of "black freedom struggles," looking beyond the South and beyond the activities of major civil rights organizations, have documented the role of rent strikes in cities such as Philadelphia, Baltimore, Los Angeles and New York during this period of widespread and accelerating protest. Surprisingly, however, the important chronicles of black and Latino grassroots activism have not only overlooked public housing residents' rent strikes in New York but also failed to acknowledge their goal: an increased police presence in their neighborhoods.[115] The larger rent strike movement may never have sparked the mass mobilization of the ghetto dreamed of by its leaders, but NYCHA tenants used rent strikes (or the threat of them) to help secure what they defined as real benefits for themselves.

The link between the rent strike movements in private and public housing was Jesse Gray, the famed and fiery organizer of the Harlem campaigns. After his successes uptown, Gray allied with the organization Mobilization for Youth (MFY) on Manhattan's Lower East Side. Originally formed to quell gang delinquency, MFY quickly reinvented itself into an antipoverty group and self-proclaimed vanguard of radical change. Gray brought to the organization, as one member recalled, "a kind of gutsiness " that MFY "wouldn't have otherwise had." Early in 1964, aiming to "disrupt the slum system," MFY and a cluster of Lower East Side organizations inaugurated a rent strike against private landlords with a three-hundred-person torchlight march through the districts' streets. Within weeks, however, the Lower East Side Rent Strike Committee had disintegrated. According to Piven and Cloward, who served at the time as MFY's in-house intellectuals, the strike was undone by legalistic requirements such as documenting building violations and depositing monies in escrow. Before granting approval for a rent strike, the courts demanded compliance with these "bureaucratic rites," which, Piven and Cloward argue, ultimately "exhausted organizers and bewildered tenants."[116] Others in the coalition blamed the alienating style of Gray himself, whom many civil rights workers viewed, as one recalled, as "a real opportunist and a hustler."[117] Whether the 1964 rent insurgency dissolved because of calcified municipal bureaucracy or unseemly leadership personality, the failure of New York's first wave of rent strikes was not the end of the story. MFY's supporters and detractors alike have tended to omit from their rent-strike tales the occurrence of a second wave of strikes in 1968—this time undertaken by public housing residents on the Lower East Side and in Harlem and the Bronx, and all focused on getting more Housing officers into NYCHA's complexes.[118]

This second, largely forgotten mobilization lasted far longer, gathered more support, and in many ways required greater courage of the tenants than had the first strike in 1964. State law provided seventy-six violations for which tenants could legally withhold rent from a landlord—from rodent infestation to plumbing defects—but insufficient security was not on the list.[119] So while Gray's strategy of "No Repairs, No Rent" had actually shielded strikers from legal eviction (and, in fact, gave them priority for admission to NYCHA), those already in public housing who withheld rent in a bid for more patrolmen enjoyed no such legal protections. Even so, a mother protesting with her children for more police for their Harlem housing development boasted to the *Amsterdam News*'s famed reporter Simon Obi Anekwe, the rent strike was, "one of the most beautiful things that ever happened here."[120]

This "beautiful thing" also reflected a compromise of sorts between the radical ambitions of MFY's staff and the practical needs of the poor whom they hoped to organize. Although MFY activists had assumed they could ignite the city's oppressed in an uprising against callous municipal bureaucracies, the masses had instead inundated them with routine service requests—usually for access to those very agencies. One historian found, for example, that close to half of MFY's casework in the summer of 1966 involved applications for public housing. Eager to push beyond the seemingly limited impact of social work in the mold of old-line settlement houses, MFY had to adapt its favored strategy of "direct action" to the residents' expressed hopes of greater order through more police.[121] It was an unlikely tactical compromise. MFY had, in fact, long cultivated a reputation for being antipolice, publicizing its practice of stationing lawyers at precinct houses to curb police excesses. Gray himself had electrified crowds during the 1964 Harlem riots (triggered by the NYPD killing of a teenager) with his call for "100 skilled black revolutionaries ready to die" to wage "guerilla warfare" against the city's police.[122] But MFY soon learned that "maximum feasible participation" of NYCHA tenants, who generally supported the Housing officers patrolling their complexes, required a different strategy: not a war against cops, but a strike for more of them.

Launched in February of 1968, MFY's rent strike for more Housing police was a multi-neighborhood affair. MFY-led strikers in the Jacob Riis and Lillian Wald houses (1,190 and 1,86 units respectively) on the Lower East Side and the Paterson Houses (1,791 units) in the Bronx coordinated their effort with tenants in five additional complexes in Gray's original base of Harlem: Manhattanville, Grant, Douglas, St. Nicholas, and Drew houses. Lawyers from or affiliated with MFY defended all the tenants—except at Manhattanville, where traditional electoral politics trumped public housing's new pro-police insurgency. Running for reelection and eager for visibility on a popular issue, Charles Rangel—then a New York State assemblyman—saw to it that he represented that complex's tenants.[123]

MFY helped the residents deposit payments into escrow and then filed a lawsuit on behalf of tenants in the Lillian Wald Houses against the Authority on the grounds that the complex lacked adequate police. The court ruled against MFY in that case (*NYCHA v. Medlin*) in June, but the strike continued for eight more months, punctuated by attention-getting vigils and demonstrations to keep the pressure on the Authority. Only in January of the following year—when NYCHA commenced eviction proceedings—did the rent defiance end, having held together roughly four times as long as MFY's much-discussed 1964 rent strike. The Authority, however, quickly accepted back rent and restored the strikers' tenancy.[124] But both the strategy itself and the demand for more officers spread as other groups eager to lay claim to the popular movement for greater law enforcement in public housing took up the residents' cause.

Consider, for example, the Young Lords Organization (YLO), a former Chicago Puerto Rican street gang eagerly reinventing itself in the late 1960s as a political movement in the style of the Black Panthers. YLO's bold rhetoric and combative stance had caught the attention of Puerto Rican activists in New York. As Pablo "Yorúba" Guzman explained later of Chicago YLO chairman Cha

Cha Jimenez's speeches: "Revolution, and socialism and the liberation of Puerto Rico . . . I hadn't never heard no Puerto Rican talk like this—just Black people."[125] Inspired, Guzman and others established a YLO chapter in the city the summer after *NYCHA v. Medlin* and promptly canvassed the needs of Spanish Harlem. The chief complaint of YLO's *barrio* neighbors, to the evident astonishment of the organization's leadership, was the filthy state of the quarter's streets. And so was born the YLO's famed 1969 "Garbage Offensive"—a riff on the Viet Cong's Tet offensive unleashed the previous year. Using uncollected rubbish to barricade the barrio's main avenues, the YLO briefly shamed Mayor Lindsay into delivering a fairer share of sanitation services. For a while at least, the "mean streets" immortalized by Piri Thomas's 1967 autobiography were as clean as those in any middle-class neighborhood.[126] Hoping to leverage their heightened community profile garnered by the garbage offensive, Young Lords leaders announced—in further emulation of the Black Panthers—a Thirteen Point Program of political objectives in October of 1969. But the Young Lords would soon be making exceptions to their newly crafted party line.

The manifesto's twelfth item had called for "revolutionary war" against the "the businessman, the politician, and the police," warning "ALL PIGS" that "BORICUA IS AWAKE!"[127] Young Lord organizers working NYCHA complexes, however, discovered they had to break with ideological purity; *Nuyoricans* in East Harlem's public housing wanted more Housing Police officers, not a racialized war against them. And so 1970 found the Young Lords organizing NYCHA residents in a rent strike for an increased police presence in their communities. The Young Lords settled on the George Washington Carver Houses (1,246 units) for their campaign. Fifty-three percent of Carver's residents were Puerto Rican, making it the most Latino of the many NYCHA developments that blanketed much of East Harlem with a nearly unbroken landscape of modernist high-rise towers. In December, the Young Lords announced their threatened strike at Carver with a disciplined sit-in at the manager's office by 150 tenants, who chanted in unison their willingness to withhold rent until the Authority provided them with more police officers.[128]

Other groups organizing rent strikes were not as famous as the Young Lords, but they gathered impressive support nonetheless. In the same month that the Young Lords held their sit-in, 600 tenants in Brooklyn's Red Hook Houses (2,545 units) stormed a management office and threatened a rent strike unless their call for more housing patrolmen was met. That spring, the Harlem Youth Federation, an African American tenant group at the Lincoln Houses (1,286 units) led by Hannibal Ahmed, blocked arterial traffic on Fifth Avenue near their complex to draw attention to a rent strike they had declared in the hopes of getting both more officers and "police booths" installed at the entrances to their development. And 1971 would see more of the same: tenants at Brooklyn's Ingersoll Houses (1,802 units) withheld their rent and demanded both better maintenance and more officers. At NYCHA's largest complex—the Queensbridge Houses (3,142 units)—tenant association president Ralph Dominguez organized residents in a rent strike to get more police with the help of an OEO-funded organization, the Queensbridge-Astoria-Long Island City Community Action Group. Capturing the collective mood of the Authority's tenants, the systemwide Residents Advisory Council ended the year by threatening a larger strike in all of NYCHA's complexes until more officers were hired; Council spokesperson and NYCHA resident Ralph Rangel (brother of by-then Congressman Rangel) bolstered the warning by claiming that "90 percent" of tenants backed the proposed action.[129]

The willingness of NYCHA residents to risk their tenancy by withholding rent is certainly a tribute to the HAPD as well as clear evidence of community support for "our cops." Measuring the effectiveness of particular strikes, threatened and actual, is trickier. The promised rent strikes, for example, often failed to materialize because the Authority frequently—if temporarily—reassigned police officers from elsewhere to pacify the protesting residents. After a single day of protest and a threatened rent strike at the Whitman Houses, for example, NYCHA committed additional officers immediately, prompting the tenant leaders to declare they were "holding off on the rent strike for now."[130]

But more broadly, on a systemwide level, the Authority did, in fact, significantly expand the Housing Police in these years. NYCHA boosted the HAPD's ranks by more than 17 percent in 1968, again in 1969, and by more than 7 percent in 1970—despite no more than minor increases in the tenant population. While City Hall had agreed in 1969 to base its subsidies of newly hired Housing officers on the number of new NYCHA units, the growth in the HAPD far outpaced that calculus. The 60 percent expansion that the Housing Police enjoyed during the most active years of tenant militancy (1968–1970) was roughly double the increase the force experienced during the previous six years of tenant quiescence—suggesting that the residents' political pressure had real impact. In a telling contrast, the NYPD, which inspired no similar populist protests demanding its expansion, grew by merely 13 percent from 1964 until 1970, the year Lindsay's cash-strapped administration froze municipal hiring and ended growth in both the Housing and city police departments for several years.[131]

Beyond the numbers, internal NYCHA documents reveal the extent to which the new tenant insurgency shaped the Authority's thinking. By the late 1960s, NYCHA officials recognized the need to contend with residents' political leverage not just at individual projects but throughout the Authority. When NYCHA's top officials, for example, convened for a closed meeting about "Project Security Problems" in 1968, they acknowledged that citywide, the now "well organized tenants . . . are able to make their complaints known more readily than the general public."[132] Moreover, the Authority administrators took advantage of tenant militancy in their efforts to draw more money from the city's coffers. NYCHA's chairman, for example, concluded his 1968 plea to Mayor Lindsay for an increased Housing subsidy by invoking the tenants as a political force to be reckoned with. "Unless . . . we voluntarily meet the demand . . . for enlarging our police force," he wrote, "pressure from our tenants and their representatives will become so great that compulsory legislation may well be adopted."[133]

By the mid-1970s, however, the possibility of rent strikes increasingly troubled the Authority—in part because housing authorities elsewhere had been crippled by such tenant mobilizations. The well-reported scenes of strikes in other cities, generally for basic services in poorly run and often corrupt public housing systems, clearly haunted NYCHA officials. "With rent-striking the familiar tumble begins," wrote the Authority's general manager, Simeon Golar. "Service cuts, layoff, physical deterioration; more rent striking. . . . It's not a nice picture. Consult the recent memory of St. Louis, Newark, Boston." Begging for additional money from City Hall for the HAPD in a confidential 1974 memo, another NYCHA official invoked the power of dissatisfied tenants to wreak havoc, arguing that further cuts to the force's ranks would mean, "rent strikes and project deterioration similar to the disastrous results in Newark and St. Louis."[134]

NYCHA's simultaneous roles as proprietor, caretaker, and constable created unusual fiscal incentives for the Authority to be responsive to its residents' security demands—demands that New York's private landlords to the poor were of course able to ignore. Rent strikes by public housing residents, and even the mere threat of them, proved potent as both a protest symbol and a bargaining tool in their campaigns to increase the police presence in their communities.

Against the backdrop of the dramatic civil rights battles that unfolded nationwide in the 1950s and 1960, the tenant activism that emerged out of the Authority's complexes, whether holding NYCHA accountable for enforcing community order or demanding that the city provide what residents saw as their fair share of policing services, can seem trivial. It was not. Public Housing in New York survived America's "urban crisis"—even as cities elsewhere saw their public housing implode into national symbols of failure—in large measure because of the NYCHA tenants who drew upon their collective strengths to help preserve the security of their communities. In demanding that the Housing Police and the Authority work on their behalf, NYCHA residents made their homes, and their daily lives, political—even if the goals of their activism deviated from the era's more visible channels of protest and prominent ideologies of resistance.

The success of this tenant activism was built in part on years of relationships fostered by the unique structure of policing in NYCHA. These relationships did not happen by chance. With vertical patrols rather than squad cars, on-site record rooms rather than distant precinct houses, and officers who might be neighbors rather than suburbanites, tenants had every reason to consider Housing officers "our cops" rather than a hostile presence. The mutual understanding and structures for communication generated by years of such interactions, while not perfect, helped carry NYCHA, its residents, and its police through two decades of urban change and turbulence. Together, in the daily world of the sprawling complexes, the Authority's officers and tenants forged and practiced a distinctive form of community policing long before think tanks and foundations had even worked out a theory.

FIGURE 3.1 Family outside Brooklyn's Red Hook Development, 1980. Photograph © Jamel Shabazz.

3

A Confluence of Crises

The 1970s and the Undermining of Community Policing

Despite its popularity, community policing in New York's public housing stumbled badly in the 1970s. The political and economic turmoil of that decade not only destabilized the individual lives of New York City Housing Authority (NYCHA) residents and police officers but also disrupted the delicate relationship between them. Attempting to weather the hard times, each group adopted strategies at odds with the other's interests. For residents, making ends meet now often meant "hustling"—turning to an underground economy that deepened as formal jobs disappeared. But hustling tenants also had reason to conceal much about their daily lives from the Authority and its officers. For Housing Authority Police Department (HAPD) officers, refashioning their force along the lines of the New York City Police Department seemed the surest way to realize their middle-class aspirations. These changes also undermined Housing's steady presence as "neighborhood cops" in NYCHA complexes. Inevitably, the tacit alliances and informal rules that had undergirded community policing in the projects gave way, under economic pressure, to more adversarial perceptions and practices. By the decade's close, little remained of either the institutional structure or human sentiment necessary for the community order the two groups had previously cooperated in maintaining.

Compounding the cracks in the once-shared interests between tenants and officers was a legal assault from an unexpected quarter: rights activists eager to curtail the power of the state to enforce conformity and impose morality. In the 1930s, as one radical "houser" reflected, public housing thrillingly "smacked of socialist Vienna, Red Moscow," but three decades later a new generation of activists saw the New York City Housing Authority as simply another government bureaucracy.[1] Amid what historians have called the "rights revolution" of the 1960s that sought to expand individual social freedoms, NYCHA's screening, fining, and eviction of tenants seemed more redolent of oppressive paternalism than liberating socialism. Not surprisingly, such policies came under attack by what amounted to a new professional group: poverty lawyers. Thanks to federal grants, this reforming cadre multiplied sixfold between 1963 and 1971. And the lion's share of the ultimately more than 2,500 poverty lawyers settled on New York City as the laboratory for testing litigation's potential not just to serve individual poor people but also to right social wrongs on a sweeping scale.[2]

To the Housing Authority, however, rights advocates' successful court challenges to their social-engineering practices stripped NYCHA's policy cupboard bare. No longer able to exercise a firm hand in the choosing of tenants or the enforcing of rules, the Authority came to believe it had little to offer residents struggling to preserve order in their communities. Little, that is, except a greater reliance upon police services. But as federal support for both cities and public housing dried up, meeting tenants' demands for more officers who could respond more quickly to their emergency calls meant weakening the very community policing strategies that had distinguished NYCHA's complexes from other low-income neighborhoods.

Police Union Politics and the Model Precinct Experiment

New York City's tumultuous labor disputes during the 1960s provided the political context for decisions made by the Housing Police that would eventually magnify the gulf between officers and tenants. Driving the public sector labor unrest were new threats to the interunion peace that had long prevailed among the city's uniformed services. New York's Depression-era politics had bequeathed a tradition of guaranteeing cops and firemen equal base pay—salary "parity"—at a level that would, in turn, always hover a status-conferring 10 percent above sanitation workers' earnings. Likewise, within each department, supervisors would take home more than the rank and file by a formula-determined percentage consistent across the uniformed services.[3] The potentially divisive question of the Housing Police's place in this finely filigreed equation remained largely moot—even as Housing's ranks and salaries grew—so long as NYCHA's officers lacked formal New York State recognition as a distinct police department in the city.[4] Without that title, at least according to the New York Police Department (NYPD) way of looking at things, Housing officers continued to be no different from any of the poorly paid "special patrolmen" employed by various city agencies, such as the Welfare Department, which maintained a police force into the 1970s.[5]

NYPD officers, ever attentive to their enviable place in the pecking order of city employees, opposed an "amalgamation" with the Housing Police. City police, explained one journalist in 1962, "felt [their] standards of enforcement were higher" than those of the heavily black and Latino Housing force.[6] NYPD officers did their best to define and emphasize their identity as the city's only real police. Studs Terkel, the famed collector of working people's stories, encountered this rivalry in blue while interviewing a former Housing officer in the late 1960s. "City cops," explained Tom Patrick, "think they're the elite. Housing is H.A.—They call us ha-ha cops." The attitude of the NYPD officers was sufficiently obvious that even the *New York Times* noticed it, observing wryly that NYPD officers viewed Housing officers as "Keystone cops," unworthy of the status of real police.[7] Many of the Authority's officers, pointing to the fact that as early as 1965 nearly half of their force was black or Latino, believed the tensions reflected the racism of the then nearly all-white NYPD. As Haile Selassie, the Ghana-born Housing officer first introduced in chapter 2 explained, "Even if it wasn't admitted, the problems were racial. The animosity was mostly on their side—we wanted to be like them." Officer Peter Grymes, also introduced in chapter 2, agreed. "Back then," Grymes noted, "NYPD thought you could be black or you could be a cop, but you couldn't be both."[8]

Blocked from merging with the NYPD, the Housing Patrolmen's Benevolent Association (HPBA), Housing's bargaining unit, pushed for the state legislature to designate their force as a separate, but equal, police department—as it had done with the Transit Police in 1964. Acknowledging that Housing was New York's fourth largest police force, serving a population the size of Cincinnati's, the legislature approved the Housing officers' request in 1966.[9] This change in nomenclature for NYCHA's police force gave it the same stature, at least on paper, as the New York City Police Department. Just as the Housing Police acquired their new status, however, the labor law governing the compensation of the city's three formally recognized police departments (NYPD, Transit, and now, Housing) altered dramatically.[10]

Responding to a series of disruptive strikes by municipal workers, city and state officials enacted reforms they hoped would avert future walkouts. In April of 1967, the state legislature passed the first comprehensive labor relations law for public employees—the Taylor Law—which authorized Mayor John Lindsay to establish the Office of Collective Bargaining (OCB) to oversee collective bargaining procedures for New York City. These seemingly straightforward legal and administrative changes emanating from Albany and City Hall unintentionally fostered competition among the city's three departments that ultimately helped erode community policing throughout New York's public housing complexes.

The backers of the Taylor Law and OCB had, of course, aimed for something quite different. Their goal had been to defuse growing militancy in public sector unions by substituting what they saw as the dispassionate expertise of technocrats for the municipal *realpolitik* of labor chieftains. The principal instruments for this rationalist transformation were to be independent fact-finding panels that would examine workplace conditions and recommend appropriate policies free of political pressures. But the HAPD quickly grasped the implications of these changes: if a panel found that the jobs of the Housing and NYPD officers differed, the HAPD's salaries, which had only recently caught up to the

NYPD's, might suffer in either absolute or relative terms. And so the Taylor Law and the OCB generated powerful incentives for NYCHA's officers to make the Housing Police resemble the NYPD in both form and function. As the *New York Times* noted of the ensuing interunion jockeying in the city, the "hazards" faced by both firemen and NYPD officers argued for parity in their compensation, but "the justification for giving as much to . . . Housing police" was "less clear-cut" and required "an exhaustive job analysis."[11]

Sensing the new political reckonings augured by the Taylor Law, the HPBA immediately pushed for two novel but revealing conditions in its upcoming contract negotiations with NYCHA. First, the HPBA demanded that the name of the force be changed formally to the New York City Housing Authority Police Department from its official, if seldom used, designation of Security Division (and before that, Property Protection and Security Division). This shift would confer upon Housing patrolmen a departmental identity semantically equivalent to that of the NYPD. Second, the HPBA proposed the institution of a "precinct plan" to replace Housing's decentralized, project-based organization. Each precinct would be overseen by a centrally located headquarters from which the officers would "turn out" for their tours. Such an arrangement mimicked the command structure of the NYPD.[12] Future fact finders, the HPBA hoped, would discover more similarities than differences between the two departments and dig into the city's coffers accordingly.

NYCHA readily agreed to the first of these proposals, which proved to have little impact on relations between tenants and officers. The Authority, however, rejected the HPBA's second proposal after what appears to have been no more than minor consideration. As the Housing Police's Chief Weldon wrote to NYCHA'S vice-chairman, past circumstances had occasionally obliged the force to cobble together the policing of multiple housing projects into a temporary precinct command, and the department had always found that tenants "complained that their protection has been lessened by having the men turn out and return to the central location." NYCHA saw little reason to ignore the chief's experience and turned down the HPBA's request.[13] But pressure from the tenants themselves for faster officer response times and more extensive patrol coverage would ultimately force the Authority to adopt the HPBA plan—in stages at first, but throughout the city by 1978. The consequences of this decision proved to be as dramatic as they were unforeseen and significantly reduced the daily interaction between the Housing police and the public housing community.

Within three years of its initial 1967 precinct proposal, the HPBA began calculating that restructuring the department could offer more benefits than simply matching the NYPD's chain of command. The Housing Police's decentralized organization afforded few possibilities for career advancement: a department of patrolmen on foot had little need for additional supervisors in offices. As one academic study noted in 1967, the HAPD's command structure, "in comparison with the City police force, hampers advancement," fencing in the "great majority . . . to the bottom grade."[14] Eyeing the numerous paths toward promotion in the NYPD's precinct system, the HPBA's rank and file began calling upon NYCHA yet again to do away with its distinctive local policing structure. In its stead, the HPBA insisted, the Authority should establish police precincts akin to those of the NYPD. It was an arrangement that would, the officers knew, compel their department to elevate many on the force to the new supervisory positions a precinct configuration would require. Appealing to the famously technocratic temperament of the Lindsay administration, the HPBA authored a white paper that warned darkly of the consequences for public housing if more of its membership was not promoted to correct the imbalance of too many patrolmen supervised by too few commanders. NYCHA dismissed the HPBA's arguments as merely "an appeal for an increase in manpower," particularly at the higher grades, and claimed that fiscal constraints prevented additional appointments.[15]

Stymied in their efforts to increase their pay and swell their ranks, the Housing patrolmen launched a wildcat sick-out in early January 1971. HAPD officers, in fact, caught the "blue flu" at the same time as did NYPD officers, who had become embroiled with the city in a different parity fight—this time over matching pay for police sergeants and Fire Department lieutenants. In its first written communication to the Authority after the job action, HPBA demanded that NYCHA "change the out moted [*sic*] patrol system that is currently a hindrance to our duty," and specified that the first item for negotiation would be a "precinct type operation" to be "acted on without delay." Pressured by Lindsay and unsettled by the prospect of projects without police, NYCHA reluctantly complied.[16]

By April 1971, a chastened NYCHA implemented a "pilot precinct" in the Bronx that would "require considerable expansion of the . . . command ranks."[17] That autumn found the Authority and the HPBA sufficiently reconciled to collaborate on a grant to fund the pilot program from the Law Enforcement Assistance Administration (LEAA), which under the Nixon administration had tilted from researching crime's root causes to devising more effective curbs on criminal behavior. The pitch by the HPBA and NYCHA, unsurprisingly, called for an "innovative approach to the policing of housing projects" by creating "a model police precinct, analogous in many ways to [a] NYCPD precinct." Washington's dollars flowed to Albany and on down to NYCHA. Dozens of housing officers left foot beats to patrol the pilot precinct from eleven freshly purchased squad cars, scores more commenced "turning out" from a newly created central headquarters, and the remaining officers enjoyed promotions to positions the HAPD established to meet the "acute paucity of supervision."[18] So in this small patch of the Bronx, the HAPD took its first step, with federal money, toward becoming the NYPD in slightly different garb.

For a while, however, it seemed that the Bronx experimental precinct might remain exactly that. NYCHA subjected the pilot project to numerous evaluations that raised doubts about its value: the precinct model might benefit some of the Authority's officers, but it did not serve the interests of residents or advance the mission of the Housing Police. Although some positive interim assessments indicated that patrolling by squad car and using the "advanced communications equipment" purchased by the grant encouraged "a high degree of espirit [*sic*] among the patrolmen," later reviews came to a different, and more dispiriting, set of findings. Addressing the experiment's impact on project life rather than officers' morale, these evaluations established that whatever satisfactions the new cars and radios provided the men (no women served in the precinct), such gains were "offset to a considerable degree" by a shift in the officers' orientation and behavior.[19]

The pilot project assigned patrolmen not to particular housing developments but to the new precinct made up of fifteen complexes in the Bronx. This innovation deepened officers' interaction with their new police supervisors while diluting both their contact with civilian project managers and their familiarity with the residents' worlds. The officers now patrolled many more complexes and encountered many more tenants than when they had predictable beats in a single project. With this change, "a large majority of the officers," Housing Police Chief Daley concluded in his report to NYCHA's chairman, "tended to lose perspective as to their mission and the overall goals of the Authority's Police Department as evidenced by a massive decrease in the performance of Housing Authority related duties"—that is, duties not directly related to crime fighting. NYCHA found it particularly unsettling that the changes to foot patrol "resulted in a reduction in the enforcement of the Housing Authority rules and regulations."[20] More troubling still, the numbers of burglaries in the complexes contained within the precinct rose dramatically. Indeed, NYCHA's experience with the pilot precinct in the mid-1970s closely resembled its assessment of the ultimately abandoned Fort Greene Precinct model in the late 1950s (discussed in chapter 2).

Surveying the damage, Housing Police Chief Daley recommended against any further application of a model that had failed. Indeed, so serious were the Department's reservations that when politicians from the city's Lower East Side proposed replicating the pilot project for that neighborhood's public housing, the HAPD successfully squashed the concept on the grounds that the experiment had proven to be "not satisfactory" for "crime prevention and protection of the tenants."[21]

And there the precinct model might have died. It was ultimately, and somewhat ironically, not pressure from the union but the ability of NYCHA residents to influence the policing of their complexes that breathed new life into the reorganization of the HAPD into precincts. Adopting a precinct model that freed officers from fixed foot patrols, as precincts would, eventually seemed to NYCHA's management the only way to satisfy tenant demands for expanded police coverage without hiring more officers—a move that became more difficult as city and federal dollars grew scarce.

Since 1965, as noted in chapter 2, NYCHA had been able to meet tenants' increasingly public demands for the Authority to "do something about crime" simply by hiring more Housing Police, passing the costs on to either City Hall or the newly created Department of Housing and Urban Development (HUD). But as early as the end of 1968, HUD had started warning NYCHA that despite the fact that the new federal agency had "approved ever increasing amounts of funds for housing security," Washington doubted that additional patrolmen would have "any impact on project conditions" and threatened to reject all further requests.[22] Nor was City Hall, with the first dark clouds of the decade's fiscal storm gathering, willing any longer to pick up the costs for additional officers: Mayor Lindsay froze hiring in all of the city's uniformed services early in 1970.[23]

With the presidency of Richard Nixon, HUD deepened its resistance to helping NYCHA meet tenants' demands for more officers. Although the new administration actually expanded funding for low-income housing, it did so in ways that both reflected its conservative ideology and deflected dollars away from its Democratic opponents. The White House recognized that over the years a coalition of interests had formed around public housing and the lucrative contracts and stable salaries the program supplied: property developers, unionized hard hats, housing bureaucrats, social workers, and—in some places like New York and San Francisco—even housing police. Strange bedfellows, no doubt, but on Election Day they all faithfully rewarded the politicians, usually Democrats, who backed public housing. But starting with the Nixon administration, a growing share of federal funds flowed to private landlords in the form of rent subsidies handed out directly to the poor—circumventing, and so increasingly starving, the liberal network that built and maintained public housing. HUD's new approach was evident as early as 1972, when the Authority's requests for monies to pay for additional Housing Police met with a curt federal response that NYCHA experiment with less expensive, nonunionized guards instead.[24]

With neither city nor federal dollars on offer, the Authority would somehow have to squeeze more productivity from its Housing officers without increasing their number if it hoped to answer the tenants' calls for action. The HAPD's brass found a solution, they thought, in their decision to redeploy the entirety of the Detective Bureau away from confidential investigations and toward twenty-four-hour "supervisory patrol" that would verify that officers walked their appointed beats. As Housing Police Chief Weldon had publicly lamented in 1966, in contrast to "most municipal police departments" where "the patrolman . . . is visible to the supervisor on motor patrol," Housing supervisors generally could not "determine the whereabouts of the officer" on vertical patrol within NYCHA's developments.[25] But "public relations," as the head of the Detective Bureau wrote, required that the department respond to "allegations" by tenant groups that residents "never see the police" because they spend "too much time in their office!" Oral histories confirm that tenants were dissatisfied with the police presence. Gladys Sturns, a resident of the Amsterdam Houses (1,084 units) on Manhattan's West Side, for example, remembered well tenants' unhappiness over some officers' haphazard approach to their duties during the 1970s. As she recalled, the HAPD

> would have been very good if it not had been that they had other things in mind, such as going to peoples' apartments and relaxing. You know they would meet people, the woman coming in and so forth.[26]

Sending detectives out on supervisory patrol, the HAPD brass hoped, would resolve tenant complaints by deterring officer negligence and increasing the "visibility of the uniformed Patrolmen." The infractions that Bureau turned up within just the first year of the new tactic seemed to confirm the residents' accusations and sent a ripple of unease to the highest echelons of the HAPD: the detectives had reported 304 counts of "dereliction" of patrol duties in the 1,435-man department.[27]

It is impossible to know from surviving records whether the Detective Bureau's discoveries revealed a new pattern of negligence among some Housing officers or simply drew new attention, amid growing crime, to older habits that in earlier and safer years residents had tolerated (or at least did not publicly report). Certainly, the department's leadership took the information seriously. Faced with evidence of broken links in their chain of command, in 1972 the Housing Police brass took the additional step of also assigning the newly created Internal Affairs Unit to supervisory patrol. Again, tenant demands propelled the department's decision. The "express purpose," as NYCHA's General Manager wrote of the strategy, was to "respond to . . . allegations made on a city-wide basis by tenant groups" about "the lack of patrol." In a dizzying five-month whirl of activity, Internal Affairs officers made 1,880 surprise visits to public housing developments throughout the city. Again, their findings worried NYCHA's top staff: close to 10 percent of these inspections led to either a written reprimand or a formal charge of "improper patrol" against an officer.[28]

The infractions uncovered in NYCHA's investigations and the tenants' recollections might be construed as evidence that the Housing Police were a particularly unmotivated and undisciplined band. Certainly, that was the rankling charge frequently lobbed at Housing officers by their NYPD counterparts in these years. But there is reason to believe that Housing police were not unusual in finding it both tempting and easy to shirk the often-mundane duties of a "neighborhood cop," especially under unsupervised conditions. A few years after the NYCHA Internal Affairs investigations, an external study of a six-month pilot project in Jersey City's public housing that deployed Jersey City's regular police in community foot patrols concluded that when officers were not closely managed, a sizable minority also started "holing up" rather than walking their beats. Regardless of the department, tedious community policing chores frequently could—it would seem—demoralize cops.[29]

The shared concerns of NYCHA's police commanders and its housing residents placed the Authority in a quandary. On the one hand, as the Housing police chief had warned, the Bronx experiment suggested that a precinct system diminished enforcement of the tenant regulations NYCHA thought essential to livable projects. On the other hand, that same precinct command structure could also narrow the "span of control" between the rank and file and supervisors, potentially ensuring the officers' presence would be more noticeable in the developments. That greater visibility, in turn, might answer residents' demands for better security. Perhaps, NYCHA speculated, less control over its tenants was a reasonable price to pay for increased supervision of its officers? If so, reorganizing the Housing Police Department into precincts could spare the Authority the growing embarrassment of the tenants' public accusations that NYCHA ignored crime in its projects. The decision to centralize HAPD's command structure ultimately came about, however, not through deliberations within the Authority but because of the actions of the tenants and Housing Officers themselves. Through their daily practices and the political pressure they brought to bear, residents and officers soon pushed the Authority to reorganize the HAPD into NYPD-like precincts throughout the city, transforming the institutional structure upon which the distinctive style of the Housing Police had relied.

The Informal Economy and Community Policing

The HAPD, like community policing programs today, worked from the assumption that a department integrated into and accepted by a neighborhood would be more likely to receive the informal tips and witness cooperation necessary for preventing crimes and arresting suspects. According to this argument, a community-based police force is most likely to enjoy the benefit of the community's eyes and ears. Through the end of the 1960s, tenants and officers both believed that the arrangement worked within NYCHA. But New York's economic crisis during the 1970s forced many residents to reconsider their relations with the police. As the market's invisible hand swiped at Gotham's working poor in the 1970s—shuttered factories one day, failed bodegas the next—they fought back by wrangling badly needed extra cash from underground enterprises that thrived in the cavities left behind by the disintegrating formal economy.[30]

New York's deindustrialization had begun long before the 1970s, but the accumulated consequences of that wrenching economic shift—exacerbated by a global recession and fiscal mismanagement—pressed upon the city's poor most keenly in those years. The decade's bleak litany of statistics trace the relentless hemorrhaging of jobs in precisely those sectors where low-income New Yorkers had tended to find employment: manufacturing (down 22 percent), construction (down 31 percent), and personal services (down 30 percent). Unemployment, less than 5 percent in 1970, doubled within five years. Even city jobs, whose growth in the first half of the 1970s had sheltered many African Americans from the economic storm, contracted 17 percent in the decade's second half.[31] Welfare, too, proved a shrinking refuge even as caseloads increased. Escalating prices eroded benefits that Congress refused to peg to inflation. From 1972 to 1984, for example, Aid to Families with Dependent Children (AFDC) and food stamps lost roughly one-third of their real purchasing power.[32] Overall, the proportion of New Yorkers living in poverty nearly doubled—from roughly one in ten in 1969 to more than one in five a decade later—while the median income for a family of four plunged (in constant 2009 dollars) from $46,544 to $38,055.[33]

In response to such grim economics, poor and near-poor New Yorkers took to "hustling." This much-borrowed term, coined in the 1970s, succinctly captures the determined and creative responses by those at the nation's fraying margins to generate income through informal and sometimes illicit means.[34] The off-the-books entrepreneurship that scholars have documented in New York's neighborhoods at the time was also common, as residents recall, in NYCHA's projects. Carlos Rhonda of the Amsterdam Houses, for example, remembers the sudden appearance of car repair services offered by his fellow tenants; the women of the complex, in contrast, recall a proliferation in food and child-care providers. Sarah Martin recollects that "wheelin' and dealin' to survive was an everyday thing" in Harlem's General Grant Houses.[35] Diana Perez, an immigrant from the Dominican Republic who moved into the Alfred Smith Houses (1,935 units) on Manhattan's Lower East Side in 1974, remembers clearly various tenants in her building making do in the hard times by selling goods and services in the neighborhood's informal economy: *pasteles* (a traditional Caribbean dish) to families during the Christmas holidays, flavored ices to children during the hot days of summer, and in the case of a few residents, sexual favors to Authority employees year-round.[36]

The Authority's janitors and maintenance crews, who knew the buildings in both their minutia and their totality, observed the change first. It was no mystery why. Evidence of the tenants' burgeoning new underground enterprises surfaced, inescapably, in NYCHA's trash. As one project manager interviewed in 1990 recalled, building custodians began to find enormous quantities of fish heads in the garbage in the mid-1970s. "Not a fish head here, a fish head there," the manager remembered, but hundreds of heads a day, "concentrated" from certain apartments as tenants "prepared dishes and sold them to restaurants." Likewise, "pieces of building material" began showing up in the refuse, the consequence of residents doing construction "piecework" in their units. At other times, signs of the informal economy showed up in unexpected places. In 1977–78, a Columbia University anthropology student who had arranged to install video cameras in several NYCHA apartments as part of her dissertation fieldwork inadvertently documented off-the-books enterprises among her informants, including babysitting, vegetable gardening, and—when a chicken strutted into her camera's field of vision—poultry rearing. Such entrepreneurship belied public housing residents' growing reputation as idlers indifferent to the nation's proclaimed values of self-reliance and ingenuity. But pursuing the American dream in this fashion when one's landlord was the New York City Housing Authority did have its consequences.[37]

Even though not all, or even most, of this informal economy ran afoul of the law, NYCHA's tenancy rules explicitly barred operating a commercial enterprise out of an Authority apartment. Prohibited behavior could lead to eviction almost as surely as illegal acts. Moreover, additional income, whatever the source, potentially meant an increase in rent should the Authority learn of it. Public housing residents, then, had good reason to shield their participation in the underground economy from NYCHA's sight. But such secrecy meant that when tenants did need police assistance in their domestic worlds and workaday struggles, they increasingly turned to the NYPD (who wouldn't report them to NYCHA), rather than the HAPD (who could).

Former Housing employees and archival NYCHA papers confirm a sudden recognition of this changed dynamic in the mid-1970s. As one 1974 NYCHA report observed, "many tenants did not want the Housing Authority to know they had trouble since they thought that they might be evicted as 'troublemakers.' . . . Therefore, when they needed the police, they tended to call the NYPD and not the Housing Authority Police."[38] HAPD officers, too, knew tenants had started to reckon their relationship with law enforcement differently. Testifying before the City Council in 1978, HPBA head Jack Jordan acknowledged residents' new reluctance at times to rely upon the HAPD. As Jordan explained, tenants' fears of evictions now meant that whenever an NYCHA "family does not want [something] on their record . . . they avoid on that occasion calling the Housing Police." Instead, "they feel it is better to call the New York City Police Department."[39]

On those occasions when tenants did telephone the Housing Authority for emergency police services, their calls were often handled by Sheila Renaghan, who worked NYCHA's police dispatch center in the 1970s. Renaghan's position offered her a unique perspective on residents' use of police services. Her memories confirm Jordan's 1978 observations. As Renaghan recalls, she and the other dispatchers in these years understood that tenants preferred to call the NYPD in situations involving their own families or apartments so as to avoid baring the details of their lives to the Authority. Likewise, former Housing Police officer Arthur Brown (who himself lived in NYCHA's Lincoln Houses) recounted his realization in the 1970s that tenants in trouble had begun to prefer the NYPD over the HAPD when they "had their own thing going on." Similarly, Jesus Morales, a New York–born son of Puerto Rican migrants who joined the HAPD in 1968, recalled that as the recession deepened in the 1970s, "tenants didn't want you to report them to management. So they called City and there'd be no report."[40] As such "hustling" worked its way into the social fabric of the city's public housing, fewer and fewer residents welcomed a police force that knew the community too well.

NYCHA tenants' calls to the NYPD did not, however, always meet with an eager response. Through their new citywide Residents' Advisory Council, residents complained that the NYPD operators answering their emergency calls often told them to dial the Housing Police instead. By 1974, residents' insistence on choosing which department would respond to their calls created such administrative headaches for the brass of both police departments that they began exploring ways to subvert tenants' efforts to telephone the NYPD rather than the HAPD. The two departments hoped to institute a "mechanical procedure . . . whereby calls requesting police assistance made to 911 and affecting Housing Authority tenants" would instead "be referred" to the HAPD. An experimental version in the South Bronx using police radios redirected 3,800 such calls within ten months. By 1978, NYCHA addresses had been computerized in the city's 911 system (established a decade earlier), and it automatically routed calls to Housing.[41]

NYCHA's residents were unusual neither in compensating for the financial vulnerability of their households by turning to the informal economy nor in their willingness to conceal such enterprises from the Authority. Scholars attempting to understand the social and economic worlds of the poor have noted similar patterns in other contexts. Sociologist Sudhir Venkatesh, whose work addresses contemporary low-income communities both within and adjacent to Chicago's Robert Taylor public housing development (since razed), has also documented the phenomenon. Venkatesh discovered that in the early seventies, unlike the preceding decades, households in Robert Taylor called upon both "legal dollars" and "unreported income to make ends meet." Homemade food and clothes, auto repair services, even a celebrated brothel and gambling parlor brought in much-needed income to the complexes.[42] This economy of "shady dealings," as Venkatesh dubs it, has endured in the area and today his informants—embedded in a network of gray-market exchange—consistently hesitate or refuse to call the police whenever "there are underground economic issues at play."[43] In New York's public housing, as residents recollect, the small wads of unreported cash stemming from such transactions helped pay the phone bill, feed the laundry machine, and take the kids to the movies. Less visibly, however, these off-the-books dealings also distanced NYCHA tenants from both the broader society and the unique protections afforded by a local police force.

Model Cities Meets Police Union Politics

New York's deepening economic crisis also pitted the Authority's tenants and officers against each other in unexpected ways that further undermined their mutual trust. Ironically, one NYCHA program designed to improve security while creating jobs for the poor set in motion events that widened the gulf not only between residents and police in public housing but also between the uniformed services and the unemployed throughout the city. The episode revealed just how willing HAPD officers had become—as their careers sputtered amid new municipal austerity—to side with the politically potent city police rather than with public housing's struggling communities.

These new rifts between tenants and officers had their origins in HUD's first great undertaking: the 1966 Demonstration Cities and Metropolitan Development Act—renamed "Model Cities" after a southern congressman objected that "demonstration" smacked of racial strife. For its efforts to empower poor communities, Model Cities drew conservative scorn for nearly a decade (and scholarly attention ever since), but the program's nine hundred million dollar budget also funded modest job-training programs that frequently paid small salaries.[44] In employment-starved New York during the 1970s, however, no expansion of the government payroll, whatever the size, was a simple matter.

Aiming to atone for two decades' worth of urban renewal sins that had razed neighborhoods and displaced residents, Model Cities planned to spend hundreds of millions of dollars rehabilitating the ghetto's physical condition and social workings. Turning the tide of the urban crisis, the program's architects insisted, would require including neighborhoods in city planning decisions through "citizen participation." So, in 1969, New York's freshly hired Model Cities staff went door-to-door, clipboards in hand, earnestly surveying residents of three target neighborhoods: Harlem, Central Brooklyn, and East New York. The results depressingly echoed the findings of studies dating to the 1930s that already lined library shelves.[45] Residents ranked "law enforcement" near the top of their litany of grievances (just behind "sanitation" and "education").[46] As a strategic paper by New York's Model Cities Administration (MCA) concluded, "police-community relations . . . are at low point." The cause, moreover, was not hard to divine: residents "believed that too many rookie cops are put in deprived areas, that many police display contempt for the community, and that some police use their guns needlessly." Meanwhile, close to half of the working-age population in the Model Cities neighborhoods was underemployed or jobless.[47] Daunting conditions, no doubt. But New York's MCA, swept up in the exuberant optimism of 1960s urban reform, believed it could solve the twin crises of police legitimacy and neighborhood employment with a single, bold policy punch. "Distrust for police officers" and "inadequate police protection" in the target neighborhoods would vanish as problems if only the MCA could create "job opportunities for community residents in the police department."[48] In the wake of hundreds of urban riots nationwide set off by incidents involving the police, federal money was available for precisely such a daring experiment.

The 1968 Kerner Commission had urged the creation of a Community Service Officer (CSO) program that would create exclusive "career ladders" for poor African Americans and Latinos, lifting them into the nation's overwhelmingly white police departments and transforming American law enforcement in the process. It was a tall order: as late as 1968 Alabama and Mississippi still barred nonwhites from their state police and even famously liberal Massachusetts had only 2 African Americans on its 870-man force. The Kerner Commission envisioned that ghetto recruits to the new program would receive both classroom instruction and on-the-job training by providing limited patrol service to their own communities. After such preparation, these "apprentice policemen" would take competitive examinations for a new rank of departmental personnel—community service officer—that would be set aside for residents of impoverished neighborhoods.[49] The concept quickly attracted public dollars to match its reforming ambitions. The 1968 Safe Streets Act opened the spigot of federal funds, which Congress eventually redirected to Model Cities for use by local MCAs. Had the program succeeded, it might very well have changed the face, and faces, of policing in the country's poorest urban areas. But New York's uniformed services unions, including the Housing Patrolmen's Benevolent Association, fought the program to a standstill—with important ramifications for policing nationwide.[50]

In 1968, New York's MCA approached the top brass of both the NYPD and the Housing Police with a proposal to establish CSO programs in the ranks of their respective departments. Philosophical differences nearly scuttled the negotiations with the NYPD from the start. The department questioned whether it was "appropriate" for the MCA to use federal funds to "increase the number of patrolmen on foot" in the city's police force—a key goal of the CSO program, but also one that conflicted with NYPD priorities and culture, which increasingly favored "radio motor patrol." Eugenia Flatow, the executive secretary for New York's MCA, later recalled of the department's resistance, "I've had better luck talking to pigeons."[51]

The police were not the only impediment. Once the Brooklyn MCA staff—or, in the era's distinctive phrase, "indigenous leadership"—had established a CSO program, their counterparts in the other Model Cities zones of East Harlem and South Bronx quickly lost interest. As the police department coordinator observed at the time, the local leaders of the other neighborhood MCAs, each seeking their share of the political pie, "wanted no part of a program that would be similar to that of a supposed 'competitor.'" And the small CSO experiment the NYPD eventually did manage to launch in Brooklyn in 1970 hardly suggested the dawning of a new age in police–community relations. The twenty-five Model

Cities recruits sworn in that January barely remained on speaking terms with the police officers assigned to the project in its first year. Indeed, the pilot seemed only to replicate within the halls of the Police Academy the racial tensions swirling on the streets of the city. The CSOs were, one study noted, "anything but cordial" to their police instructors, who, in turn, made clear their disdain for what they saw as "both the attitude and the atmosphere generated by the candidates."[52]

The NYPD's CSO program may have been beset by problems, but in the very different setting of New York's public housing, the concept thrived. Recruiting CSOs, after all, was not that much different than NYCHA's long-standing tradition of hiring staff, including police, from among its own residents. In the pilot project crafted by the MCA and the Authority, recruits received on-the-job training assisting patrolmen and attended high school equivalency classes, taught at first by Housing officers, to ready them for eventual hiring with the HAPD. More importantly, unlike the NYPD experiment, the NYCHA program envisioned exclusive civil-service lines, to be known as "police aides," that held the promise of a secure city job for the recruits. By the summer of 1970, forty youths between the ages of seventeen and twenty-one from Brooklyn's Brownsville neighborhood were sworn in as Housing Authority Community Service Officers (HACSO). Each received a hundred dollars a week. As a program evaluation observed, the recruits quickly accepted the Housing officers as "brothers" because "they had come from a similar background and were willing to take their own time to work with the youths." Encouraged by the success of the pilot, NYCHA and the MCA expanded the program that year to all three Model Cities areas in New York, eventually hiring 240 HACSOs—even as the NYPD program failed to grow beyond Brooklyn. The Authority, its police officers, and the officers' union, all fully backed the HACSO experiment. But such enthusiasm could not last long in the cauldron of New York's labor politics. Within a year, the HPBA would join an alliance of line organizations from the city's fire and police departments that sought to kill the Model Cities recruitment program.[53]

Ironically, the HPBA's new opposition to the CSO project had its roots in an effort by President Lyndon Johnson to contain the political backlash provoked by earlier Great Society programs. Community action agencies had incited big-city mayors into open revolt against the White House because these federally funded groups amounted to "competing political organizations in the [mayors'] own back yards," as one presidential staffer later noted ruefully. Angering southern politicians seemed unavoidable, but LBJ's administration had assumed the War on Poverty would enlist the support of Democratic political machines in the urban North. In the hope of placating these restive political allies, the Model Cities legislation backtracked by placing control of new initiatives safely in the hands of local city halls.[54] Granting mayors power over this ambitious federal aid program had the unforeseen consequence of alienating a different, if equally entrenched, set of interests, however—as John Lindsay was about to discover when his presidential ambitions collided with the city's uniformed service unions.

The summer of 1971 saw New York's Republican mayor readying for his White House bid as a Democrat, a process *Time* magazine described as possessing all the "tedium of a protracted striptease." At a Gracie Mansion press conference, Lindsay—standing before seventeen movie and television cameras and dozens of reporters—shed his GOP affiliation with a call to arms against the woes of the nation's cities: "men without jobs, families without hope, indecent housing, blighted neighborhoods, crowded hospitals, crime, poverty, polarization." Days later, the candidate-to-be strategically dispatched mimeographed position papers to the national press detailing his ambitious solutions for the problems of the country's largest city. Prominent among Lindsay's proposed reforms were plans to broaden NYCHA's successful Model Cities HACSO recruitment program to New York's fire and police departments.[55]

By establishing separate exams and job classifications, the newly expanded project, like the Housing Authority's, would create exclusive career ladders for residents of Model Cities neighborhoods. But Lindsay, whose eyes were now fixed on national politics, failed to appreciate the local firestorms that would be sparked when he tried to take the HACSO pilot project citywide. Not only did the new program's scale dwarf the Authority's experiment, it also extended the minority set-asides beyond the public housing police to the more politically sensitive old-line uniformed services. Lindsay planned to use federal money to establish in the fire and police departments—long the preserve of white ethnics working their way up—825 spots that would be reserved for residents of largely black and Latino neighborhoods. Moreover, several of the city's districts that Lindsay's staff handpicked as worthy of such largesse had been the site of recent riots, creating the impression that the mayor was about to reward urban lawlessness with city jobs. Even in better times, all of this might have been a tough pill to swallow in the Irish and Italian quarters of Queens, Brooklyn, Staten Island, and elsewhere that had come to see positions with the fire and police departments as a something between an ethnic right and a family obligation. But these were days of instability in many such blue-collar neighborhoods, as growing inflation and changing demographics challenged old certainties.[56] That September, when New York witnessed the unprecedented sight of four thousand African Americans and Latinos registering for a test that would qualify them for positions in the uniformed services, the overwhelmingly white police and fire unions attacked the project's legality.

In court, the unions argued that by restricting the opportunities for the new jobs to particular neighborhoods, the Model Cities CSO program gave preferential treatment and competitive advantage to African Americans and Latinos. Such programs, the unions claimed, would violate requirements in the state's constitution—implemented decades earlier by progressive reformers to limit patronage—that civil service appointments be made solely on the basis of "fitness and merit." The unions, however, had more than abstract legal principles in mind. In the wake of Lindsay's hiring freeze, it looked to many that employment in New York's police and fire departments might depend on Washington's dollars (which is close to what happened later in the decade when federal job-training grants hired back laid-off city employees). The Model Cities recruitment plan appeared to signal that federal munificence would benefit minorities at the expense of whites.[57] Moreover, because the CSO positions required both continued residency and deployment in the target neighborhoods, the program raised a troubling prospect for many white cops: all-black or Latino precincts in the city that would box in their chances for promotion. Indeed, the director of Model Cities' CSO program reluctantly admitted such precincts "might exist at first," but insisted "it was only a matter of time until the people in the [target] communities are educated and the present need for the programs will end."[58]

The Housing Police Benevolent Association, however, was unwilling to wait for such promised progress to come to the inner city and quickly joined NYPD officers' efforts to squash CSO program. The HPBA's political calculations were straightforward. Although the Housing Police did not initially oppose the Model Cities recruiting experiment, the union had benefited from its alliance with the New York Police Department's PBA in the sick-out earlier that year. For once, it seemed, the two departments had acted as brothers-in-blue, wringing concessions together from City Hall. The strike, in fact, had been a reassuring sign of "parity" to the status-anxious Housing Police. As one former HAPD officer recalled, "we never wanted to be seen as some kind of poverty program. We wanted everyone to know we were real cops, on par with the NYPD."[59] Such respect, however, would prove elusive in the summer of 1971, when a series of attacks on police officers by black militants strained the relationship between the overwhelmingly white NYPD and the heavily black and Latino HAPD. In particular, the murders of two NYPD officers on the grounds of a public housing development left the HPBA more determined than ever to display, and gain from, solidarity with the larger and more powerful New York City police.

On the evening of May 21, 1971, Waverly Jones, an African American NYPD patrolman, and his white partner, Joseph Piagentini, responded to a medical call from the Colonial Park Houses (984 units) in upper Harlem. The caller, though bleeding from a knife wound, refused their aid, so after a few minutes the pair strolled back to their radio car. In the project's parking lot, the patrolmen had to pass two young men slouched against a white Ford Mustang. As the officers did so, the youths—members of the Black Liberation Army, a shadowy group that had splintered from the Panthers amid government repression—gunned down the patrolmen from behind before slipping away into the night.

Jones, thirty-four, was dead even before his body hit the sidewalk. Piagentini, twenty-eight, bled to death in the backseat of a squad car as it sped to Harlem Hospital.[60]

The attacks particularly rattled the city's officers, already alarmed by a spate of bombings aimed at police the previous year. Not only were the murders exceptionally brutal—Piagentini took thirteen shots at point-blank range while begging for his life—but they came just forty-eight hours after machine-gun fire had maimed two officers guarding the home of Manhattan's district attorney after a Black Panther terrorism trial. Arriving at Harlem Hospital where the victims' bodies lay, Edward J. Kiernan, the combative PBA president, spoke for many officers when he announced, "It's open season on cops in this city"—an accusation that conveniently ignored the role of police brutality in fostering the rise of the Panthers and other black militants. But the ambush, despite appearing to present Housing and city police with a common adversary, failed to bring the two departments together. Instead, the incident exacerbated their earlier tensions. Many NYPD officers, in fact, blamed Housing for the murders, seemingly ignoring press reports that HAPD officers' "knowledge of the people in the area" had allowed investigators to identify key eyewitnesses.[61]

Whether out of fear, racism, or simply a desire to assert departmental status, the NYPD's rank and file had long made known their displeasure at having to handle domestic dispute and medical emergency calls from NYCHA complexes. They contended that Housing, not city police, should respond to routine calls of the sort that had brought Jones and Piagentini to the projects on the night of their deaths, and it wasn't long before some NYPD officers revived the old accusations that Housing shirked its duties, leaving "Big Blue" to pick up the pieces. Matters came to a head just a few days after the murders when two squad cars, one from Housing and one from NYPD, traveling in opposite directions encountered each other in a narrow street near Brooklyn's Fort Greene Houses. Both sides, predictably and stubbornly, refused to yield to their rivals. The officers exchanged increasingly barbed racial insults before finally drawing their weapons on each other. A radioed "assist patrolmen" signal soon filled the street with cops from both departments in a mass blue-brawl that their superiors struggled to contain. Similar melees followed throughout the summer. So serious, in fact, did the interforce hostility become in the wake of the Jones and Piagentini murders that the mayor had to intervene, ordering the chiefs of both departments to a peace conference in his office.[62]

Perhaps HAPD officers would have joined the other uniformed service unions in attacking the Model Cities CSO plan in any case. But as the Black Power connections to the murders in the Colonial Park Houses became clear in the course of a nationwide manhunt, anything other than full solidarity with NYPD officers became nearly impossible for the largely minority Housing Police. Indeed, backing the CSO recruitment program might have undermined the

HAPD's union by lending credence to the charges that the department's standards were lower and its loyalties misplaced. So despite the HAPD officers' previous support for the HACSO project, the Housing Patrolmen's Benevolent Association now threw its weight behind the legal assault on Model Cities' expanded CSO program.

Days after the line organizations joined forces to challenge the Model Cities plan in court, Joe Balzano, the HPBA president, attempted to explain his union's about-face. Aiming squarely at the CSO program, he denounced the "appointment of unemployed civilians to police positions." Balzano demanded that New York City's elected officials "investigate the federal moneys [*sic*] funneled into the city for police purposes." The safety of New York's streets could be secured, he argued, only by using Washington's dollars to hire "fully qualified, trained police officers."[63] And *that*, Balzano implied, did not include residents of impoverished neighborhoods joining New York's police departments under a federal antipoverty program.

"The city's regular line organizations won. Disadvantaged residents lost," concluded the *Amsterdam News* after a New York Supreme Court justice ordered that the Model Cities CSO exam be canceled just days before it was to have been given. Robert Lowery—the city's black fire commissioner, who had joined the department three decades earlier when only whites could touch a stationhouse's kitchen utensils—was even more blunt. "This is another instance of line organizations thinking it's the eighteenth century," he observed bitterly. Despite legal appeals by the city, the unions eventually succeeded in denying civil service benefits or departmental status to the CSOs.[64]

By blocking the ability of Model Cities programs to create residentially specific hiring practices in police departments, New York's uniformed service unions sealed the program's fate. The project limped along in the city for another decade as a poorly funded community-relations and educational program, but the CSO plan ceased to be a policy tool that might have created urban police precincts more reflective of the communities they served. The impact of the episode, however, was felt nationwide. Numerous municipalities abandoned or, as New York had, watered down their CSO plans following court victories won by Gotham's line organizations, thus slowing the entrance of African Americans and Latinos into big-city police departments throughout the country.[65] Locally, NYCHA residents, too, took note of the decision by Housing's rank and file to kill a program designed to help poor neighborhoods. "Suddenly," one tenant recalled of the HAPD, "you knew they didn't walk the talk. They weren't so much on your side as you thought."[66]

NYPD bitterness over the Jones and Piagentini murders persisted as unfolding events kept the story in the news. One suspect from the Colonial Park Houses ambush was briefly thought to have been responsible for a dramatic skyjacking of a commercial jet to Cuba, while the other suspect repeatedly called the *Amsterdam News* to identify specific police officers and their families on his "to-be-killed" list. Even more Black Liberation Army members became linked with a nationwide murder spree of police officers, events that seemed to confirm many cops' suspicions of Black Power. (For its part, the Black Liberation Army justified such executions as both retaliation for and legitimate defense against police violence in black neighborhoods).[67]

By the summer of 1973, the occasional fistfights between the feuding departments of the previous year became a regular feature of police life in New York. The disdain that NYPD's rank-and-file officers still had for Housing became palpable that August. The NYPD's top brass, during a rapid (if short-lived) expansion of their department in 1973, turned to Housing's civil service list for new men because their own list had been severely depleted during Lindsay's two-year hiring freeze. The PBA, however, denounced the move. As the union's truculent new president, Robert M. McKiernan saw it, hiring from Housing's list would broadcast the fact that the two forces now had identical standards, leveling the difference in prestige between his overwhelmingly white organization and the heavily minority Housing PBA. Indeed, the list of HAPD eligibles from which the NYPD was considering hiring was roughly 65 percent black or Latino. McKiernan, however, did not publicly point to the race of the eligibles; rather, he took a swipe at the entire Housing Police Department. Housing's candidates could not substitute for NYPD's, McKiernan publicly insisted, because the Authority's officers were not really cops at all: they were mere "housing guards." Underscoring the point, he threatened to sue the city if the NYPD's ranks were "corrupted" by the addition of the "unqualified" HAPD eligibles. The HAPD, despite parity in contracts with the NYPD and cooperation in labor battles against City Hall, had clearly not won the esteem they sought from "Big Blue."[68]

Tenants and Supervisors versus Community Policing

Matters improved little for Housing in 1973. The red ink washing over City Hall also pushed HAPD officers and NYCHA residents further apart. Lindsay's 1970 hiring freeze had left the Authority's officers in no mood to see public funds support tenants' anticrime efforts at the expense of their own department's needs. Sharpening their pencils over the mayor's proposed 1973–74 capital budget, the HPBA uncovered a million-dollar earmark for unspecified "community-based crime prevention activities" in public housing. Perhaps, in flusher days, Housing officers might have applauded the financing of tenants as partners in the maintenance of community order in NYCHA's complexes. But with police coverage stretched thin in the projects as attrition outpaced appointments, the HPBA feared, as its president acknowledged, that tenant groups might opt to "hire private guards" with the city's cash—undercutting the position of their union of "full-time, trained, professional officers." This fear was not unfounded. Both NYCHA and its tenants had, in fact, started to contract such private services. Residents in the Alfred Smith Houses, for example, had recently borrowed a page from middle-class developments by chipping in to hire private guards who could provide armed, uniformed patrol for half of the cost of HAPD officers. Meanwhile, the Authority—under HUD pressure but also with tenant approval—had started to replace Housing patrolmen with private guards on a two-to-one basis in a number of complexes for the elderly. Defending their own job security, the HPBA fired off press releases to local newspapers and telegrams to the mayor's office attacking funding for tenant anticrime efforts. Confronted with such political mobilization by HAPD officers at a time when contracts were up for renegotiation, City Hall eventually halved the budget for "community-based crime prevention activities," gutting efforts to deepen residents' involvement in their own security.[69]

Despite the advantages of hiring private guards for their complexes, many tenant organizations also opposed community anticrime efforts. For the many residents who simply wanted more police who responded more quickly, the Authority's efforts to encourage both community cohesion and community policing seemed like money wasted, so the target of several tenant associations' budgetary ire was, surprisingly, tenant patrols. NYCHA had formally launched tenant patrols in 1968, as had city police departments nationwide in the wake of civil disorders; unlike many others, however, the Authority's programs endured.[70] There had, on occasion, been cause for concern over the patrols. Some had decided not just to combat neighborhood criminality but also to enforce community morality by harassing public housing's gay residents. But NYCHA believed the groups reduced crime and built a sense of neighborhood, and so generally backed the tenant patrols. Moreover, the Authority took an expansive view of the role of tenant patrols that went well beyond security to embrace beautification, sports, and social programs.[71] But dollars going to tenant patrols could also conceivably be used to hire more police officers instead, and public hearings soon revealed that tenant groups often preferred the latter to the former.

The hearings sprang from tenants' political mobilization. NYCHA's Harlem residents besieged Frederick Samuel, their immensely popular city councilman, with concerns about increased crime in their communities. Samuel responded by using his status as chair of the Council's Public Safety Committee to call for an investigation into the effectiveness of the Housing Police. Attending the hearings were elected tenant representatives from upper Manhattan's Dyckman Houses (1,167 units), Brooklyn's Marlboro Houses (1,765 units), and Harlem's Drew-Hamilton Houses (1,217 units). As the proceedings unfolded, the tenant representatives learned that NYCHA had directed somewhere between five hundred thousand and two million dollars of federal security funds toward tenant patrols—enough to hire as many as forty Housing officers, as the HPBA president was quick to point out in his remarks.[72] The anxious tenants weren't pleased.

The tenant association president from Dyckman Houses announced that he was "shocked to hear" that "funds that were provided for the tenant patrol were funds earmarked for our police department." Tenant patrols might have been useful in the past, the tenant leader argued, but "with the type of crime we have today all funds that are earmarked for police protection should be used to help strengthen our police department." The president of the Marlborough Houses tenant association echoed the sentiment. "We were all unaware," Sally Hart complained, that money for the "tenant patrol was coming from the police fund" and "we would rather see that money go back to the police fund rather than the tenant patrol." Even the former tenant patrol supervisor of the Drew-Hamilton Houses (and current tenant association president) was astonished to learn the source for nearly a decade of her tenant patrol stipend: "I didn't know I was getting money that they should get . . . I didn't know how you pay police salaries." And although at a subsequent hearing the next month a number of tenant patrol leaders defended both the services they provided and the small stipends they received, the damage had been done. The hearings had exposed sharp divisions among residents over the value of "community-based crime prevention activities." However inexpensive such programs might have been on a per-person basis, they could seem like a big-ticket item when totaled across of all NYCHA's developments at a time of tightening budgets.[73]

When tenants at the hearings expressed a preference for funding police officers over community programs, they voiced a sentiment that many public housing residents nationwide shared—as HUD itself had recently learned. As part of the agency's Management Improvement Program (MIP), HUD hired social scientists to survey in 1972–1975 two thousand residents of Delaware's Wilmington Housing Authority (WHA) in an effort to upgrade services. HUD's researchers, steeped in the era's ethos of social programs and therapeutic measures, had expected to find residents struggling to acquire "much 'needed' social services," as they contended with the pathologies and inadequacies of the "federal slum" the researchers believed public housing to be. The residents, however, saw things differently. Indeed, residents reported little difficulty in obtaining social services—and even less desire for them. When residents took stock of their troubles, they did not blame a shortage of caseworkers in the projects; they placed their faith in remedies stronger than yet more job training or drug counseling. Nearly every MIP interview revealed that "more than anything else, tenants wanted security for themselves and their possessions." And when, in response to such survey data, the WHA slashed its social service budget by three-quarters, the MIP team found residents actually reported more, not less, satisfaction with their housing. Moreover, in contrast to tenants' manifest disdain for social workers, they expressed near universal approval at the creation of a security force of off-duty police officers (later disbanded amid budget cuts).[74] The MIP researchers, in their tellingly titled study, *Caseworkers or Police: How Tenants See Public Housing*, summarized their findings for HUD:

> We reject all talk about pathology and the culture of poverty. . . . The rational preferences of poor public housing residents can sensibly and effectively inform public housing management—there is no "need" for social services in the attack on any culture of poverty, but there is a need for the personal security all Americans seek.[75]

Urban liberalism may have harbored some ambivalence about law enforcement in these years, often seeing police officers as instruments of state oppression, but when given a chance to speak for themselves, public housing residents made clear their preference for cops over community and social programs.

Community Policing and Police Supervision

HAPD commanders also took steps that unintentionally chipped away at their force's community focus. The department's structure of rewards worked against the goals of community policing by pitting officers' ambitions against residents' needs. As in most police departments, assignments to specialized beats or details often served as stepping-stones in a successful Housing Police career. Rookies soon learned that special postings occasioned more chances than did foot patrol to bulge their personnel files or deepen contacts with influential superiors. But such assignments also pulled Housing cops away from regular beats within projects, depriving tenants of the officers' steady presence and hard-won familiarity with residents' lives.

Housing officers, however, saw their careers with the department as a shot at a middle-class life, and they understandably competed for special details. Their elected officials, in turn, saw advantages in angling to help constituents on the force win such assignments. Manhattan Borough President Percy Sutton, for example, repeatedly wrote NYCHA in the 1970s not only to request special details for particular individuals but also seeking to ensure "minority group persons are receiving a fair share of . . . those special assignments" that might allow them to enter the department's "select circle." Not surprisingly, the number of such assignments became a point of contention between minority officers and the HAPD's commanders in these years. At times, NYCHA attempted to hold back the redeployment of Housing officers in this manner, pointing to the "overriding need for uniformed patrol" in its developments.[76]

Moreover, the Housing Police brass explicitly adopted yardsticks for evaluating both the department and its officers that could, on occasion, discourage community policing. As today's proponents of the strategy argue, if a department rewards making arrests, officers will seek to make more. Effecting arrests, however, might be irrelevant for improving the neighborhood conditions that give rise to crime. Too many "collars" might, in fact, sour relations with potential local allies needed to remedy neighborhood crime problems. As two community policing advocates have argued, "police should become pro-active, interactive, and preventative in their orientation rather than rely solely on reacting and control."[77] Such a prescription was unnecessary for Peter Grymes, an HAPD patrolmen in the Soundview Houses (1,259 units) in the Bronx during the early 1970s. As Grymes recalled:

> Playing ball with the kids, which we used to do a lot, and going to events in the projects, we knew that cut down on robberies because we knew who to go to when there was trouble and it gave us respect because we were giving respect. Or on the four-to-twelve shift, the first thing we did was go to stand on the corner when the people would be coming home from work, they'd see us and feel a little more confident, and those who were up to no good knew we were out there working.[78]

But the HAPD didn't reward, let alone measure, playing basketball with NYCHA teenagers or providing a sense of security to wage earners on their way home from a day's work. In 1972, for example, a psychologist with the Graduate Center of the City University of New York studying the Housing Police's handling of domestic violence cases for the LEAA asked the department's Patrol Commander to rank his "police performance criteria." The "number of offense arrests" topped the commander's list of "most valid indicators" of departmental effectiveness. In contrast, solving "interpersonal disputes, "providing "service duties," and enforcing "Housing Authority Rules and Regulations" all had, thought HAPD's brass, "minimal validity as indicators of effective police performance."[79] Such sentiments did not make the HAPD's Patrol Commander unusual. Indeed, since the 1930s, when popularized versions of Frederick Winslow Taylor's theories of scientific management percolated into police headquarters nationwide, department chiefs seeking to "professionalize" their ranks had employed similar indicators to evaluate officers' performance. But the approach of Housing's brass meant that HAPD supervisors rarely measured what its patrolmen and NYCHA's residents often valued in "*our* police force." And as observers of institutions, particularly law enforcement agencies, have noted, "you manage what you measure."[80]

To Patrolman Grymes, well aware that his approach to policing didn't impress the higher-ups or register in their metrics, supervisors saw him as "just some Joe Schmoe out on patrol." They paid little attention to patrolmen who kept their complexes quiet and failed to see the tactic's significance; Grymes remembered "But why were they quiet? Because we were out there everyday, dealing with tenants. They didn't see the connection."[81] Community policing may have been the key to the HAPD's success, but the department's rank and file often doubted, with some reason, that it would be their key to a successful career on the force.

The Rebirth of the Precinct Model

As New York City stumbled from fiscal austerity to, in 1977, a nightmarish blackout, its largest landlord, the Housing Authority, lost confidence in community policing. Unsupervised officers on foot too often failed to patrol their assigned beats, while economically struggling residents too frequently concealed their community's inner workings from patrolmen when they did come around. Competing interests brought on by the city's fiscal crises meant little remained of the once-functioning partnership between the two groups that had aimed to enforce community norms. Faced with demands from both the Housing Patrolmen's Benevolent Association and a constellation of tenant groups and their representatives, NYCHA's first African American police chief, Benjamin Ward, did away with the department's decentralized structure and reorganized the city's 180 housing projects into 15 precinct-like Public Safety Areas (PSAs). Ward explained his decision before a hearing at the City Council's Committee on Public Safety, at which he and other NYCHA officials had endured withering complaints from tenants that police coverage was too thin and response times too long. "I think," Ward argued of the contemplated reorganization of the HAPD into precincts, "it will greatly improve our ability to deploy available manpower. More importantly, it will bring our available manpower under supervision." What Ward failed to mention was that the HAPD had been down this road twice before—with the Fort Greene Precinct in the 1950s and the Bronx Model Precinct more recently—only to be discouraged by the consequences. But under public pressure to reduce response times, and with community policing undermined in the projects by both the community and the police, a precinct system seemed the only path forward. From 1978 on, nearly all Housing officers, as one study noted, found themselves reassigned to precincts and "got assignments primarily intended to staff and support 911 response in radio cars."[82]

The effects, if not visible overnight, were dramatic enough. Although NYCHA, unlike many housing authorities elsewhere in the country, had up until 1978 largely managed to enforce its various quality-of-life regulations through the use of fines (despite rising legal challenges), the new precinct system made it nearly impossible to continue to do so.[83] The experience of the pilot precinct proved predictive in this regard. No longer walking down hallways or stairwells on regular beats in their assigned project, patrolmen lost daily familiarity with tenants and increasingly dispensed with writing them up. Although NYCHA retained the right to impose fines on tenants for violations of Housing rules, the Authority more or less abandoned the practice when it adopted the precinct system in 1978, and no records of fines for violations appear after 1982 in the Authority's surviving papers.

Tenants recall the transformation with dismay. Mary Alfson, who was able to remember the name of the officer who had patrolled her building nearly three decades earlier, still lamented the changes to her community brought about by the move to a precinct system: "suddenly we don't see [Officer] Smitty anymore. When they took him out of the neighborhood, I think that that was a part of the decline of our neighborhood." Terri Sheeps, president of the tenant association at her own development, likewise attributed what she saw as the downward spiral in her complex to the precinct decision: "with no fines . . . folk were not held responsible for what their children did. They did away with the local police record room so that there was no one "in house" to take care of the kids." Residents who entered public housing after NYCHA stopped enforcing its regulations relied on earlier arrivals' memories to make sense of the new conditions. Sister Gibbs, for example, who moved into NYCHA's Harbor View Houses in 1982, reported that many of her "respectable, working" neighbors in the complex blamed the Authority for no longer "policing up" tenants' daily behavior.[84]

Both HAPD's brass and line officers also remember the 1978 move to precincts as severing the daily bonds that had made policing in New York's public housing distinctive. "We lost our number-one asset, our connection to the people in the projects," concluded Peter Grymes of the decision to move to the PSA system. Assistant Chief of Department Joseph Keeney, although at the opposite end of the hierarchy from Grymes, shared the patrolman's judgment. Keeney spares no words in describing the transformation: "Managers lost the daily observations of individual officers in their buildings while officers lost the sense of commitment to the residents. It was devastating."[85]

NYCHA and the Rights Revolution

In the economically stressful 1970s, as the Authority's residents and officers were increasingly abandoning their commitment to community policing, public-interest lawyers began to mount formal challenges to aspects of these policing strategies in the courts. Although several of the ensuing lawsuits succeeded in expanding individual social freedoms, they had the unintended consequence of frustrating tenants' and officers' efforts to maintain the order of their vertical neighborhoods. Attorneys working for Great Society programs persuaded courts, for example, to recognize greater rights for individuals applying to or facing eviction from public housing. These newly defined judicial protections required policy changes that significantly—and sometimes disastrously—limited NYCHA's earlier ability to screen, fine, and evict unruly residents.

The successful legal assault on the Authority's tenant policies was motivated by a progressive individual-rights ideology supported, at that critical moment, by a well-financed and eager army of earnest young lawyers. The raising of that army was undoubtedly the result of impersonal social and political forces, but it also has a more particular and personal history that begins, improbably, twenty years earlier at Milton Academy, the elite boarding school outside Boston where Robert F. Kennedy met and befriended David Hackett.

Their warm relationship would last the rest of Kennedy's life and briefly propel into circles of high power both Hackett and a particular strategy for redressing inequality that he would come to embrace.

When Kennedy found himself in 1961 serving as attorney general in his brother John's administration, he tapped his old friend Hackett to head the President's Committee on Juvenile Delinquency and Youth Crime.[86] Hackett had no real expertise in the field or even experience in government; his previous interests, in fact, had been largely confined to playing ice hockey. Indeed, the novelist John Knowles identified Hackett as the model for Phineas, the insouciant athlete and campus hero of his 1959 classic, *A Separate Peace*.[87] But Hackett was a good Kennedy man: earnest, loyal, and hardworking. Sharing the confidence in expert knowledge that characterized what historians have dubbed the Liberal Hour, Hackett sought out academic specialists in juvenile delinquency.[88] In short order, he became enamored by the most up-to-date theory of youth crime propounded by Lloyd Ohlin and Richard Cloward at Columbia University's School of Social Work.

The pair's *Delinquency and Opportunity: A Theory of Delinquent Gangs* (1960), rejected the prevailing view that delinquency was a psychological malady requiring clinical treatment. Instead, the two scholars argued, such youths had the same ambitions to get ahead as everyone else but found their paths obstructed by social constraints and persistent poverty. In the absence of legitimate opportunities, delinquents who pursued their aspirations through gangs were acting rationally, not pathologically. The problem, Ohlin and Cloward theorized, sprang not from delinquents' heads but from their environment.[89]

The Ohlin-Cloward thesis, however, was more than a highbrow rendering of the gang members' famous quip to Officer Krupke in *West Side Story* (1957): "I'm depraved on account I'm deprived." *Delinquency and Opportunity* held that the poor were poor because they lacked the political savvy to secure the opportunities the postwar economy provided in ample measure. From this assumption flowed a second hypothesis: the interests of the poor were actually at odds with those of existing local institutions, such as welfare agencies and traditional settlement houses, which, as two advocates phrased it, based their policies "on paternalism, on disrespect and distrust of clients."[90] If the downtrodden were to stand on their own, they must be organized to fight such entrenched local powers. A single phrase captured the policy prescription of the Ohlin-Cloward thesis: "community action."[91]

In the "community action" concept, Hackett believed he had found the comprehensive idea that could shape and animate the White House's approach to poverty. But Kennedy's secretary of labor and secretary of health, education, and welfare did not share his enthusiasm: not surprisingly, they had little interest in undermining their own fiefdoms. Amid such recalcitrance, Hackett and his staff quickly won the ear of the president's chief economic advisor, Walter Heller. Heller appreciated that community action was inexpensive, that it bypassed calcified bureaucracies, and that it seemed, in its iconoclasm, to capture the youthful can-do spirit of the Kennedy Camelot. And so through the unlikely vehicle of Hackett, the Ohlin-Cloward thesis was put into action, cautiously, at first, with the Office of Juvenile Delinquency and then, under President Lyndon Johnson, on a grand scale through the new Office of Economic Opportunity (OEO). As the historian Allan Matusow has written, "community action" went from being "an experimental program to precede the War on Poverty into the very war itself."[92]

For advocates of this new approach, empowering the poor required sweeping aside social and institutional practices that sustained poverty yet enjoyed the protection of law. Although 40 percent of the OEO's legal funding went to support existing local legal services to help the poor handle routine problems, more than half went to new agencies who took reforming the law as their mission. Describing the aims of these new groups, the OEO's first national director of legal services argued in 1966 that "lawyers must uncover the legal causes poverty, remodel the systems which generate the cycle of poverty and design new social, legal and political tools to move poor people from deprivation, depression, and despair to opportunity, hope, and ambition."[93] To accomplish these lofty goals the OEO had surprisingly deep pockets for a new agency. In 1967, the Legal Services program received $27 million in federal funding and employed 1,800 full-time lawyers nationwide—or, by way of comparison, only 200 fewer than the total number working at the Justice Department and all of its regional offices. Merely five years later, the program's budget had ballooned to $71.5 million and its staff to 2,000 lawyers.[94] And there was no shortage of eager applicants for these jobs.

As three prominent legal scholars observed a few years later, "by 1967 it was clear that whereas civil rights law had previously been 'in,' poverty law seemed to some extent to have replaced it."[95] Despite comparatively low pay, Legal Services was able to attract ambitious graduates from prominent schools by offering prestigious federally sponsored fellowships and, perhaps even more appealing during these years, draft deferments.[96] The work of these young idealists was inspired and informed by an idea derived from the Ohlin-Cloward thesis: the law could achieve social progress through the expansion of individual rights.[97] And these activist lawyers quickly racked up an impressive record. Before 1965, Legal Services lawyers had never argued a case before the U.S. Supreme Court. In the next decade, they would bring 164 rights cases to the high court as part of their national effort to expand civil liberties, succeeding in 60 percent of the cases. As the legal historian Laura Kalman has observed of this winning streak, "The [Warren] Court made liberals happy for it dodged the tension between liberty and equality . . . by using liberalism's language of individual rights and freedom to help children, the disenfranchised, non-Christians, . . . minorities, and the poor."[98]

In New York, Mobilization for Youth (MFY), headed by Ohlin and Cloward, was among the most energetic advocates of using the law as a tool of social change for the poor. MFY—a fusion of uptown academics and downtown activists funded by the city and federal governments and the Ford Foundation—opened its doors on the Lower East Side in the fall of 1962. By the next year, Cloward arranged space for MFY's legal services wing at Columbia's School of Social Work.[99] As MFY's program director recorded in a 1964 internal memorandum, the unit quickly decided "to affect social policy and administrative practices rather than to supply legal help to clients in an unplanful [*sic*] way."[100] Pursuing this strategy, MFY settled into a pattern of suing New York's Welfare Department, hoping to bring down what the activists believed was an oppressive and disdainful bureaucracy. As the cases piled up, the city refused to pay for further litigation against itself. City Hall also demanded an investigation into MFY's legal unit. In the ensuing tussle, the unit largely separated itself from MFY to become MFY Legal Services, Inc.—just in time to start receiving more secure and generous funding from the OEO.[101] MFY Legal Services was now also at liberty to pursue litigation on behalf of the poor without first enlisting the backing of communities whose liberties they aspired to protect. Unlike MFY's neighborhood-based campaigns (including the rent strike for additional Housing Police addressed in chapter 2), legal action did not require broad support, only the signature of an individual seeking redress for himself or herself. Advocating for their clients, the attorneys understandably—and appropriately—fought for the rights of the persons they represented; their role did not include soliciting or responding to the collective voices of the communities in which their clients lived. Neighborhood sentiment and shared welfare remained largely outside the calculus of MFY lawyers, who were willing to take up even unpopular causes. The loose relationship between community aspiration and MFY litigation reflected the particulars of Legal Services' policy origins. The OEO, after some early disappointments, had concluded that not all neighborhoods were up to the challenges of creating their own community action plans—in some instances, social change would have to come from above. As the White House's leading advocate of community action said at the time, the OEO was eager to get something "highly visible and action oriented before the American public and Congress," so the agency created its own preplanned antipoverty projects known as national-emphasis programs. These would, the hope went, serve as catalysts for more "indigenous" antipoverty efforts in the future. In the original community action model, projects originated within communities and were guided by local citizens. National-emphasis programs, in contrast, originated in Washington and were guided by the ideology of their own national leadership. Legal Services was one such national-emphasis program; although it had hundreds of offices across the country, these branches were under no obligation to be responsive to particular neighborhoods or constituencies.[102]

MFY Legal Services soon picked battles over issues that had previously provoked only occasional or muted grumbling from New York's public housing communities: NYCHA's policies for screening, fining, and evicting troublesome tenants. To MFY's poverty lawyers, many of whom had chosen their public-service careers at least in part because of their faith in personal liberation and their abhorrence of social injustice, the Authority's tenant policies appeared to be state control of an oppressed population.

NYCHA's policies—formulated by social workers in 1957—had originally become a concern for progressive organizations partially through the writings of a new, maverick school of journalists finely attuned, in the era of *The Man in the Gray Flannel Suit* (1955), to institutions' power to compel conformity.[103] Screening potential tenants for past behavior or ability to pay, for example, struck one *Harper's* magazine reporter as the "blank, ugly" face of a bureaucracy that "couldn't see . . . in human terms." Likewise, NYCHA's rules for order in its complexes made public housing "not a home, but a cheap hotel" for its residents who could be sent packing "with a mimeographed notice" from the Authority. The famed *New York Times* war correspondent Harrison Salisbury speculated that delinquency grew in public housing precisely because "warm hearts" cooled and "civic responsibility" evaporated amid the "subordination of personality and ideas to institutions." Indeed, for Salisbury, the "blind enforcement of rules" had left some public housing complexes in New York "worse than anything George Orwell ever conceived."[104]

The tenants themselves, however, did not always share this dystopian view of NYCHA's practices. Apparently differing with elite commentators such as William H. Whyte (author of *The Organization Man*), who saw the Authority's "sterile, bleak towers" as "no better than the slums they replaced," many more of New York's poor wanted to get into public housing than were willing to move out.[105] And once there, they seemingly approved of the social order enforced in the complexes. Certainly, as discussed in chapter 2, some tenant activists pressured NYCHA in the 1960s to be more aggressive in ejecting unruly residents, believing their communities had a civil right to both safe neighborhoods and responsive municipal agencies. But such tenant pressure—expressed in basement community centers and behind the doors of managers' offices—remained largely invisible. When the Authority went to civil court to dispossess a resident, it went without apparent tenant backing. That struggling New Yorkers sized up life in public housing differently than did elite pundits did not escape notice at the time. As Patricia Cayo Sexton, one of Spanish Harlem's best-informed chroniclers in the early 1960s, observed, "for writers, social workers, and architects, the city and its projects are the villains." But "the poor," she noticed, "don't seem to agree." Instead, to New York's needy, "the villain is more often the slumlord," while NYCHA's complexes were a source of "both stability and continuity." More recently, historian Nicholas Bloom, surveying the agitation over NYCHA's tenant policies in these years, concludes that the city's "well-intentioned" had simply "fallen far behind the realities of life in the developments."[106]

By 1966, the growing number of poverty lawyers brought the campaign for personal liberation to NYCHA's tenant policies. They objected that the Authority was free to decide who qualified for an apartment or got ousted from one; that NYCHA need not supply the rebuffed applicants or evicted residents with stated reasons or fair hearings; they complained, in short, that the Authority behaved much like the era's private landlords. And that meant, as one MFY staffer argued in the revealingly titled *Housing for the Poor: Rights and Remedies*, the "arbitrary" policies of management undermined public housing's "potentials for social engineering." NYCHA's projects, lamented the legal activist, could and should have "provided a haven for individualists." Instead, the Authority had chosen to "enforce a strict social conformity." MFY, believing such constraints sustained privation amid plenty, concluded that curtailing NCYHA's power to demand "middle-class" behavior from its residents represented a worthy new front in the War on Poverty. And for these lawyers, this was a battle best fought with the ammunition of individual rights. Here, in fact, was a golden opportunity to use their professional skills as attorneys to help liberate the dispossessed.[107]

At the center of this new legal assault on NYCHA was a young New York University law student, Michael Rosen. As a Fellow at the school's Social Welfare Law Project, Rosen worked under MFY's guidance and with OEO funding. Rosen, by his own acknowledgement, had "almost no experience with public housing" and had made "no concerted effort to reach out to tenant groups." Undeterred, he quickly concluded that the surest way to improve conditions in NYCHA's complexes was to expand the rights of its residents while circumscribing the discretion of its managers. He perceived, as he recollected years later, "no distinction" between "greater personal freedoms for residents" and "the needs of public housing communities."[108]As Rosen saw it in 1967, the courts' practice of deferring questions of public housing tenancy to the "moral and social judgments of [NYCHA's] managers and administrators" clashed with the War on Poverty's ambitions to empower the disenfranchised. Indeed, Rosen detected "paternalism" in the agency's "attitude," that its "reasonable standards for admission or continued occupancy" constituted mere "favors, not rights." Rosen decided that bringing something akin to the rule of law to the city's public housing bureaucracy required redefining occupancy of a publicly subsidized apartment as a form of private property protected by the Fourteenth Amendment.[109]

Rosen aimed first at NYCHA's admissions policies. And here the Authority had, indeed, made itself something of a target. Despite federal requirements that local housing authorities "promulgate by publication or posting in a conspicuous place" their eligibility requirements, NYCHA had avoided doing so in the hopes of foiling those it feared might game the admissions process. The Authority maintained a twenty-one-point list of "Desirability Standards for

Admission of Tenants" that detailed grounds for rejection (including "use of narcotics," "birth of out-of-wedlock children" and "poor housekeeping"), but neither spurned applicants nor Legal Services lawyers could ferret it out of NYCHA's managers. Only through discovery procedures as part of MFY's litigation did the relevant documents surface.[110] Ultimately, however, the Housing Authority's efforts to conceal its policies troubled MFY far less than the content of those policies did. The "Authority's criteria," explained Rosen in 1967, were actually a "thinly disguised form of condemnation of status." Permitting the Authority to exclude applicants on any basis beyond economic need empowered bureaucrats to "sit in judgment on the moral worthiness of entire families." In order to strike down what it saw as NYCHA's efforts to coerce conformity to outdated social conventions, MFY filed a series of suits (employing Rosen's briefs) challenging the Authority's use of past behavior as a basis for selecting future residents.[111]

Explaining the goal of one such 1966 case—*Manigo v. NYCHA*—Nancy LeBlanc, MFY's associate director for legal services, declared that the Authority's methods for screening applicants wrongly made "public housing a reward for social desirability." MFY contended that NYCHA apartments should go to those with "low income and poor housing" regardless of what the Authority thought of their "personal conduct."[112] In the instance of Gilda Manigo, MFY objected to the fact that the Authority had rejected her application on the basis of her husband's behavior. Raymond Manigo, however, made for a surprisingly unsympathetic character in a legal test case. The police had arrested him seven times as an adult for a variety of charges, including narcotics possession, and several more times as a minor—once, notably, for assaulting an NYCHA guard. As a juvenile, Manigo had served two years in a reformatory school for purse snatching; as an adult, he had been sentenced to ten days in the workhouse for resisting arrest. Nevertheless, in their effort to compel the Authority to give the Manigos an apartment, MFY's attorneys condemned NYCHA's concerns over Raymond's conduct as "arbitrary, capricious, and unreasonable." Invoking the original legislation creating public housing, MFY insisted the program existed to eliminate injurious housing conditions, not "maintain the moral fabric of the Nation." And so, argued MFY, NYCHA's actions to preserve the order of its developments by rejecting potentially disruptive applicants like Raymond Manigo were "extraneous" to the Authority's proper role.[113] The New York Supreme Court disagreed.

In his decision, Justice Francis Murphy, in fact, found little in NYCHA's procedures that was capricious or arbitrary. Upholding the Authority, Justice Murphy agreed that "without a proper screening of prospective tenants the dangers to those residing within would be multiplied many times over." But MFY persisted with a fusillade of cases assailing NYCHA's policies from multiple angles, hoping to locate the Authority's legal soft spot that, once breached, could open the way to expanding residents' freedoms. In the 1968 case *Holmes v. NYCHA*, MFY won a minor victory, compelling NYCHA to adopt "ascertainable standards" in their tenant selection procedures. But MFY initially made little headway in three other eviction-related suits (*Escalera, Rolle*, and *Humphrey et al. v. NYCHA*) that sought to recast public housing tenancy as a form of private property warranting protection under the Fourteenth Amendment. Pivoting on constitutional issues, the cases ended up being consolidated before a federal court. There, MFY's arguments again fizzled. Reviewing the evidence, Judge Sylvester Ryan of New York's Southern District concluded in October of 1968 that the Authority's residents faced eviction only as the "final step in sequence of procedural steps taken with the fullest regard for the tenant's rights and those of the other tenants."[114] That ruling, it appeared, ended matters

But just as their legal challenges to NYCHA's policies seemed to have collapsed in the courts, MFY's lawyers benefited from a stroke of judicial good luck that lifted their cases' prospects. In March 1970, a landmark Supreme Court case, *Goldberg v. Kelly*, seismically altered the legal status of nearly all government benefits. Although decided shortly after Warren Burger replaced Earl Warren as chief justice, the case is often said to represent the high-water mark of Warren-era liberalism before the Court's conservative turn. And the decision did, indeed, extend under Burger the previous Court's "procedural revolution" (best known for establishing *Miranda* rights) from criminal to civil matters.[115] But *Goldberg v. Kelly* would also, somewhat ironically, help make the world of New York's public housing residents more difficult and dangerous.

The Kelly of *Goldberg v. Kelly* was John Kelly, a twenty-nine-year-old disabled black man and MFY client whose welfare caseworker had yanked his benefits (and sole source of income) after discovering Kelly had used a false address to collect the checks. OEO-funded poverty lawyers persuaded the justices that New York's commissioner of social services, Jack R. Goldberg, could not purge Kelly and nineteen others accused of fraud from his rolls without first satisfying the same due process requirements afforded to property owners and contract holders.[116] At first blush, this might not seem the stuff of a revolution in American jurisprudence. But it was. The decision expanded the law's earlier blunt binary of property and nonproperty with a middling, third class of "property interests" covered by some intermediate (and undetermined) measure of constitutional protections. Welfare recipients might not have a legal right to benefits, but once such largesse had been doled out, the state could not deprive "property interest" owners of their entitlements without due process. That meant, as a practical matter, every individual case of suspected welfare fraud would have to be litigated in a full evidentiary hearing that provided defendants with rights to representation by counsel, cross-examination of adverse witnesses, and appeal to the federal judiciary. This scenario envisioned by *Goldberg v. Kelly* turned out to be well-nigh impossible to enforce given the city's dwindling treasury and overwhelmed agencies: nearly all of New York's welfare recipients kept their benefits unchallenged, and what had previously been a gratuity transformed functionally into a right. The legal consequences of the decision quickly rippled beyond the narrow confines of suspected welfare fraud. In what has been called the "due process explosion," courts rapidly transported *Goldberg v. Kelly*'s subtle but straightforward line of reasoning regarding welfare hearings to other forms of proceedings—including the Tenant Review Board hearings NYCHA held before evicting residents.[117]

A month after *Goldberg v. Kelly*, the U.S. Court of Appeals reversed decisions from the previous year in MFY's housing cases by applying the *Kelly* precedent to them.[118] In *Escalera v. NYCHA*, the case into which the various cases had been consolidated on appeal, Rosen and other MFY lawyers argued that NYCHA's Tenant Review Board hearings failed to meet the Supreme Court's new and higher due process bar for protecting tenants' property interests in their leases. In particular, the Authority's proceedings had shielded its witnesses, usually fellow residents, from a direct confrontation with the tenants against whom they were complaining. To NYCHA, this aspect of Tenant Review Board hearings seemed a reasonable safeguard to prevent retaliation by vindictive troublemakers; to MFY, however, it was a license for eviction by neighborhood hearsay and bureaucratic capriciousness. As expected, the federal Second Circuit Court of Appeals found NYCHA's procedures wanting in light of *Goldberg v. Kelly* and remanded the case. Acknowledging the reshaped legal landscape, NYCHA in 1971 acquiesced to a consent decree prior to trial. As with most such arrangements, this negotiated settlement would be enforced with the court's power, giving it the authority of a judicial decree and the durability of a long-term contract.[119]

Balancing the safety of wary public housing communities with fairness for their allegedly rule- and law-breaking neighborhoods was, to be sure, a delicate proposition. But the resulting *Escalera* consent decree was not a delicate instrument. *Escalera* imposed on the Authority an elaborately detailed eviction process, with nine major steps and four levels of review. The stipulations provided public housing residents with protections that went well beyond what a private renter could expect in Housing Court—even in famously tenant-sympathetic Gotham.[120] The decree required NYCHA to provide complete disclosure of the charges against the tenant, access to the tenant's file, and—much more substantially—a full evidentiary hearing before an impartial hearing officer. *Escalera*, moreover, prevented NYCHA from serving in the proceedings as a barrier between neighbors who reported disruptive conduct and the tenants facing ouster for that behavior. The decree guaranteed public housing residents the opportunity to confront and cross-examine individuals providing information that might be used to justify their eviction.[121] If NYCHA wanted to preserve order in its complexes by ejecting disruptive tenants, it could no longer anonymously employ the "eyes and ears" of public housing communities that had been at the heart of its distinctive style of policing.

New legal rights are often meaningful, however, only if there are lawyers there to assert and defend them with successful courtroom tools. And in the immediate aftermath of *Escalera*, struggling public housing residents facing eviction enjoyed a surprising embarrassment of litigious riches. The consent decree entitled tenants to make their own tape recordings of the *Escalera* proceedings, rendering such hearings uniquely valuable for what was then an emerging pedagogical approach in law schools: clinical legal education. Progressive law faculty in the city, recognizing a teachable moment, soon agreed their seminars would take every *Escalera* client who walked into a Legal Aid office. For a brief but critical period, entire courses at Columbia Law—with Ford Foundation support—transformed themselves into Ivy League think tanks for developing winning strategies in *Escalera* cases.[122]

Outgunned, NYCHA all but abandoned pursuing evictions. Unsurprisingly, tenants had become unwilling to brave presenting evidence against disruptive neighbors in adversarial hearings. The Authority moved forward in the few instances where it had sufficient evidence from sources other than the project community, but even these cases proved astoundingly expensive with the new *Escalera* stipulations. By the late 1970s, NYCHA was able to evict, on average, fewer than eighty-five families a year for "undesirability"—a figure that, relative to the total number of families, was merely one-twentieth of the share ejected two decades earlier and .06 percent of all non-elderly households. With Legal Aid assistance available at no expense to the tenant, the protracted administrative rituals could stretch out as much as a year and half. No surprise, then, that in this decade NYCHA spent an average of $1,500,0000 (nearly $4,000,000 in 2009 dollars) every year battling even the small number of disruptive residents it did manage to evict. The Department of Housing and Urban Development concluded in an external evaluation of NYCHA that the "courts had produced an anomalous situation where the rights of the majority of law abiding tenants are not balanced against the need to protect the due process rights of the disruptive tenants." The consequence, both HUD and the Authority believed, was an "almost total paralysis [of evictions] in the face of seriously disruptive tenants." Even a former MFY staffer and civil rights activist who left MFY to become NYCHA's public affairs officer recalled that "after *Escalera* we couldn't have evicted Jack the Ripper."[123] Exaggeration aside, NYCHA's policies for maintaining the order of its communities had fallen prey to a conflict born of a larger shift in progressive ideology.

The Housing Authority was the proud creation of New Deal liberals who believed in state solutions to society's problems; it was now, ironically, under assault by a new generation of activists devoted to individual rights. Railing not simply against capitalism's failure to distribute its benefits fairly or widely, the New Left now also warred against what it believed to be the overly bureaucratic organization of American life.[124] Expanding personal freedoms in opposition to government institutions that had come to seem repressive and backward-looking struck MFY's activists as a critical step in such a movement. But MFY's campaign for liberation failed to generate much support, let alone ignite an uprising, in the Authority's developments. Indeed, New York's public housing residents soon mobilized their political resources in an effort to reverse the consequences to their communities of MFY's victories in the courts. The tenants would not succeed, however, until the late 1980s—a story told in the next chapter.

MFY's campaign for expanded personal freedoms was part of a national poverty-law movement that federal funding had made possible, and the effects of this campaign were not limited to the decline of evictions in public housing. As sociologist Richard Arum points out, litigation over discipline in public schools also had unintended consequences in terms of social control. While legal challenges between 1965 and 1975 helped protect students' rights, maintaining order in the public schools—as in public housing—inevitably became more difficult. Individual-rights litigation arose in this period across the country "neither spontaneously from private citizens" nor indirectly from "public interest law firms, such as the Children's Defense Fund."[125] Instead, it was poverty lawyers funded by the OEO who brought more than 1,200 court challenges to schools' disciplinary practices. This legal activism created important procedural protections for students that, like the *Escalera* consent decree, proved so cumbersome in real life that exercising control often became impossible. Surveying thirty years of data on schools, Arum concludes that administrators and teachers—with procedural constraints tying their hands and the threat of lawsuits on their minds—found themselves abandoning not simply outdated authoritarianism but also more progressive ways of managing school disorder the public would have supported.

While the wide discretion NYCHA enjoyed before *Escalera* certainly permitted abuses, many tenants quickly concluded that the medicine of expanded rights for tenants facing eviction was worse than the disease of the occasional arbitrary manager. Indeed, public housing activists placed the development of a cohesive community above any single resident's right to due process. Tenant leaders complained bitterly to the Authority about the new policies, believing NYCHA had abandoned its earlier commitment to "decent project living."

The Authority's new inability to impose fines proved troubling to residents hoping to preserve the safety of their communities. *Lockman v. NYCHA*, an earlier MFY lawsuit about service charges for violations of housing rules, had been consolidated with *Escalera v. NYCHA* on appeal, and the subsequent consent decree had limited managers' hands in imposing fines much as it had their ability to evict residents. As noted in chapter 2, these legal changes halved the frequency with which NYCHA imposed service charges on tenants who broke its regulations. Tenants unhappy about what seemed a loosening of the rules they believed to be essential for project order turned to their elected representatives on the newly formed systemwide Residents Advisory Council (RAC) to complain to the Authority. RAC chairperson Harold Pinkney—seen in an official NYCHA photograph sporting the Afro hairstyle popularized by the era's black pride movements—explained the Council's sentiment in a strongly worded 1976 letter to NYCHA's chair. Noting that the residents they represented could "no longer tolerate" the "deterioration and destruction" of their buildings, the Council demanded that "any tenant that violates the rules and regulations, which they signed when they initially entered public housing, must be dealt with promptly and all service charges should be enforced for any violation of the rules and regulations."[126] Throughout the 1970s and early 1980s, outspoken residents made sure that NYCHA officials attending tenant association meetings heard the same message. When the staff of the Authority's director of community affairs, Blanca Cedeno, for example, met with tenant groups in 1977, resident leaders demanded to know why NYCHA no longer "adequately dealt with tenants who were poor housekeepers." Indeed, such complaints from tenant groups began to swell NYCHA's files as residents demanded the eviction of disruptive neighbors as had been past practice. Veteran NYCHA administrator Cyril Grossman, interviewed in 1990, recalled residents' frustration with what seemed to be the Authority's new laxness: "Almost invariably we'd go to a meeting in the seventies [of] a tenant organization . . . You would have them come up at you with: when I moved into the project you did this, that and the other thing. Why aren't you doing that now? Why aren't you as strict as you were when we moved in?"[127]

But it was *Escalera*'s near freezing of evictions that most troubled tenant groups. Dismayed at the disruptive families who had dodged removal in the year after the consent decree, the RAC's Pinkney said of the pending ouster of one mother for her son's criminal conviction, "It should be a very tough policy in public housing. The undesirables—they have to be evicted." Elected tenant representatives testifying before the City Council Committee on Public Safety in 1978 echoed much the same sentiment. Spokesperson Gladys Johnson argued bluntly, "People should not live in [public housing] after they commit any crime." Tenants also took their concerns about the post- *Escalera* conditions in their communities to elected officials. Congressman Charles Rangel, for example, soon heard grievances from his constituents in Harlem's public housing complexes about the new ability of disruptive tenants to remain in NYCHA apartments. Rangel, in turn, pressed the Authority to explain its policies regarding "felons or families of felons being allowed to reside in public housing projects." NYCHA could do little more than point to the new *Escalera* stipulations that required proceedings before "an impartial hearing officer."[128]

NYCHA tenants connected the rising crime in their midst (addressed in detail in the next chapter) to the declining number of evictions. At one tenant association meeting at Brooklyn's Williamsburg Houses (1,630 units), NYCHA's chairman, manager, and a host of police and elected officials heard residents explain their belief that the "overall security problem" in their complex stemmed from management's failure to "pursue terminations sufficiently and vigorously against multi-problem anti-social families." But as the Authority's chairman and general manager explained to the anxious tenants, with "court decisions and changes in the law . . . evictions have become more cumbersome than ever before," particularly since tenants were understandably "reluctant to testify for fear of reprisal and intimidation."[129] Looking back on these years, tenant leader Terri Sheeps likewise attributed what she saw as her development's decline to the consequences of *Escalera*:

> I think it's due to the *Escalera* consent decree . . . allowing folk to remain in public housing when under a different time they would have been asked to leave or be evicted from public housing. So I think the law has a great deal to do with it. Over the years, there was an upsurge of groups who wanted to promote the civil rights of people and they felt that the government itself, and the government agencies were too hard on people, actually, they would have said that we were exploiting, and I was trying not to use the word exploit, but they were saying that we were exploiting people by asking them to pay fines and . . . be responsible for what they did . . . but that's what kept public housing decent.[130]

Residents, drawing on their firsthand experience, linked tenant behavior and the possibility of eviction.

Circumstances briefly transformed NYCHA's developments into an unintentional laboratory of sorts to test the theory that conditional tenancy powerfully regulated residents' behavior. One of the key facts of the *Escalera* case was that Rose and Pedro Escalera kept a dog in their NYCHA apartment in breach of the Authority's rules, despite multiple warnings, and in opposition to the sentiment of their neighbors. RAC polling revealed that the vast majority of residents opposed dogs in public housing, but MFY had pushed hard on a number of such cases, believing in tenants' rights to keep dogs.[131] While the case was being litigated in 1970, NYCHA suspended evictions for that particular violation—pending the court's decision—while continuing to pursue evictions in other cases. Once word of the policy change got out, NYCHA noted that almost instantly "dogs began to appear in the projects in large numbers"—and with dangerous consequences. Dog bites on Authority grounds jumped 70 percent, sending eighty-five people to the hospital, including forty-six children. The next year, when NYCHA reinstituted the policy after the court's decision, the number of dogs—and dog bites—returned to nearly their previous levels. It seemed residents did keep a close eye on just what management would and would not tolerate, and some tenants adjusted their lives accordingly. As one resident recalled, "Everyone knew everyone's business back then and if someone got evicted, Lordy, you thought a little bit harder about doing that yourself."[132] Little wonder, then, that tenant leaders seeking to maintain order in their communities begged the Authority to exercise a firm hand in evictions.

Black New Yorkers exhibited a similar concern for order when, in the early 1970s, many backed a push for more punitive drug laws in New York state. As political scientist Vanessa Barker has recently demonstrated, despite opposition from the New York branch of the American Civil Liberties Union, many African American community groups, church leaders, and social activists voiced full-throated and crucial support for the infamous Rockefeller drug laws that mandated even nonviolent narcotics offenders be locked away. Dr. Benjamin W. Watkins, long known as Harlem's "honorary mayor," insisted at the time that only the threat of lengthy prison terms for drug dealing could "remove this contagion from the community." Another Harlemite explained that she was "a militant most of the time, but in terms of what he's [Rockefeller] advocating, I'd like to see it happen." The *Amsterdam News* similarly backed Governor Rockefeller's proposed legislation while Harlem parents groups staged raucous protests to demand that NYPD officers be assigned to neighborhood schools in order to root out drug use. Taking explicit aim at civil libertarians, leaders of five Harlem community organizations denounced the "bleeding hearts" opposing Rockefeller's proposed legislation and called for life sentences for drug pushers at a press conference. With the benefit of hindsight, such sentiments can seem naive, but the desire to bring the government's coercive power to bear on crime in black neighborhoods clearly resonated broadly (although not universally) among New York's African American leaders.[133]

Tensions between the era's civil liberties agenda and struggling tenants' aspirations to "keep public housing decent" helped hobble community policing in the Authority's developments during the 1970s, but so too did the thicket of deeply local municipal labor politics that drove HAPD officers to demand changes in the nature and structure of their duties. Community policing in NYCHA struggled though the decade, increasingly abandoned from within by both residents and the police, and under assault from without by a well-meaning army of activist lawyers. Formerly shared interests between officers and tenants splintered, seemingly irreparably, under economic pressures. Tenants wanted more, and more visible, police in their complexes but also sought to shield a new economy of shady deals (and the sustenance it provided) from the Authority's management. Officers wanted greater professional recognition, more opportunities for advancement, and continued job security amid municipal austerity—even, sometimes, at residents' expense. Federally sponsored, but largely untested, tonics hurriedly formulated to vanquish poverty "in our time" unwittingly widened the gulf between struggling tenants and the officers they once viewed as "our cops." Collectively, these political, economic, and ideological forces left the Authority, its residents, and its police force unprepared for the rising crime and changing tenant demographics that pressed hard upon the city's public housing in the second half of the 1970s and beyond.

FIGURE 4.1 Mayor David Dinkins and NYCHA Chair Laura Blackburne (November 1, 1990–February 21, 1992). Photograph courtesy of the New York Housing Authority and La Guardia Community College, CUNY Photograph © New York Housing Authority.

4

The End of Community Policing, 1980–1995

The most extensive and sustained experiment in community policing in urban America would not survive the 1980s. An outside study of the New York City Housing Authority (NYCHA) drew a conclusion that many residents had already arrived at for themselves: community policing as it had been practiced for years in the Authority's complexes was now merely, in the report's words, "an empty dream." As the strategy broke down, crime soared. In a single year, 1985, NYCHA's crime rate jumped 21 percent. Indeed, in the mid-1980s, public housing became less safe than New York City as a whole for the first time since the Authority's inception a half-century earlier.[1] A burgeoning informal economy, the 1971 *Escalera* decree, the 1978 move to precinct-style policing, and Housing officers' individual and collective ambitions had all contributed to this deterioration. But the changing demographics of NYCHA's residents and the HAPD's ranks further undermined community policing efforts. These shifts stemmed from larger economic forces, but they were also the result of public policy decisions that had far-reaching—and often unforeseen—consequences.

"Everything got worse at once, like God was wrassling us all down," recalled one resident of her Bronx public housing complex in the late 1970s and early 1980s. Sheaves of yellowing Housing Authority records confirm her memories of worsening conditions in the projects. By nearly every index, New York's public housing population grew ever more troubled in the 1970s and 1980s, bearing diminishing resemblance to what scholars dubbed the "submerged middle class" that had called NYCHA home in preceding decades.[2] Court decisions and political pressure pushed a reluctant Authority in 1968 to revise its paternalistic admission criteria, and the city's public housing—designed for the working poor—began to fill instead with tenants who lacked, as residents liked to say, "the honest eight" of a stable job.

Increasing, as well, was the share of heads of household struggling to raise a family without the benefits of a nearby partner's watchful eyes, second paycheck, or steadying example.[3] Then, in 1971, City Hall compelled NYCHA to start accepting what proved to be ever-larger numbers of residents who had spent time in New York's homeless shelters and welfare hotels. Finally, the city's declining stock of affordable housing (down 358,000 units between 1970 and 1984) gave rise to a growing practice of "doubling up" in often already overcrowded NYCHA apartments. As many as 100,000 people had, by 1983, taken up residence in the city's public housing without the Authority's permission and, generally, knowledge.[4] Eager to avoid the speedy eviction meted out to non–lease holders, this ghostlike population of boyfriends, boarders, and down-on-their-luck adult children often sought to evade detection—compounding the ill effects of both the "shady deals" economy and the newly exploding narcotics market. Indeed, the well-chronicled crack cocaine wave that swept across urban America in these years broke hard upon New York's public housing developments, many of which became, as NYCHA acknowledged, "a new kind of 'slum' fueled by drugs."[5] Daily encounters persuaded older residents who had moved into NYCHA before the late 1960s that the new tenants were to blame for the rising disorder in their communities; management shared that view, relying on consultants' number crunching that correlated levels of crime in developments to their share of residents on welfare. No surprise, then, that tenant leaders and building managers consistently protested NYCHA's newly liberalized admissions policies.

At much the same time, a changing Housing Police force lost a good deal of its earlier personal connection to the population it served. As detailed in chapter 3, Housing no longer assigned officers to particular complexes, so they were less likely than in the past to walk the stable beats essential to community policing. Equally important, though, were the demographic transformations undergone by both NYCHA's police and its residents. When New York's uniformed services started hiring again in 1979 after the worst of the fiscal storm had passed, shifts in how City Hall allocated police appointments made the HAPD's ranks both whiter and more suburban. Over time, these changes reversed earlier practices and patterns that had made the department distinctive in American law enforcement and encouraged residents to see the HAPD as "our cops." Moreover, many of the officers hired under the new policies had not actively chosen careers in public housing—most had aimed instead for the NYPD. As a result, more than a few nursed grievances over their appointment to what they saw as a second-class department policing third-class neighborhoods.[6] All of these transformations in the overlapping worlds of the Authority's tenants and officers took their toll on community policing.

In the 1980s and 1990s, New York's public housing was also losing the battle for enlightened opinion, even among earlier sympathizers. The Authority's sprawling and isolated complexes became a shorthand image for the sum of problems attributed to an urban "underclass" mired in a "culture of poverty." "Hell in a Very Tall Place," a 1989 article on crime-ravaged NYCHA projects in the liberal *Atlantic Monthly*, made clear that few anywhere on the political spectrum still had faith in public housing as wise social policy. But New York City's public housing, lumped together in the popular imagination with profoundly distressed programs elsewhere in the country, has a history of its troubles being journalistically overstated and the resourcefulness of its tenant leaders undersold.[7]

Studies of NYCHA did make clear that tenant participation in their own security in the 1980s and 1990s fell far short of the active engagement that had marked previous decades. Residents' anticrime activism, however, never died out completely. Certainly, some programs pushed by residents in these years had little visible impact. But others did. Tenacious tenants applied pressure on NYCHA to "do something" about their unruly neighbors and the Authority, in turn, leveraged residents' political voices to win important legal changes in the late 1980s and 1990s. These victories undid weaknesses in the eviction process that *Escalera* had introduced a decade and half earlier, enabling NYCHA to start ousting more swiftly the drug-dealing tenants who had long given rise to residents' complaints.

Looking closely at how these expedited evictions for drug dealers came about sheds fresh light on the origins of the aggressive tactics that increasingly shaped policing in both public housing and the city at large in the 1990s. NYCHA's new practices relied on asset forfeiture laws that commentators have often decried. Forfeiture, from this perspective, is a blunt weapon wielded by an unrestrained police state against passive minority communities in a largely unwinnable war on drugs.[8] But it was, in fact, NYCHA's residents and managers who first pushed a reluctant U.S. attorney for New York's Southern District, Rudolph Giuliani, to use these statutes to evict drug dealers from the Authority's complexes. Indeed, despite Giuliani's law-and-order reputation (cited regularly by detractors, supporters, and Giuliani himself), long-buried internal memos reveal that in this instance the man who would become "America's mayor" did more foot dragging than crime fighting.[9] The use of this strong-armed law enforcement strategy in New York, which helped usher in similar policies nationwide, emerged through the efforts of NYCHA's committed residents and competent technocrats and not—as some have suggested—because of pandering politicians seeking to "govern through crime."[10]

If attempts by NYCHA's tenant leaders and managers to oust unruly and criminal neighbors faced indifference from Giuliani's office, they would later confront outright opposition from Legal Aid advocates when the Authority and elected tenant representatives sought to modify the *Escalera* decree in the 1990s. Similarly, tenant leaders and civil libertarians would tussle over the use of security cameras in NYCHA's complexes. In all of these battles, residents insisted upon what they saw as their community's right to safety, while their opponents invoked the language and logic of individual rights that urban liberalism in New York had emphasized since the 1960s.[11]

Welfare Housing and the Changing Realities of Daily Life in NYCHA

Three forces drove the changing demographics of NYCHA's tenancy from the late 1960s through the 1980s. First, as New York City's welfare system expanded rapidly and massively in the 1960s, NYCHA's practice of cherry-picking tenants increasingly struck many as a form of social injustice: the neediest were denied a valuable municipal service while those with more resources received assistance. In response to mounting political and legal pressure, NYCHA reluctantly dropped the eligibility restrictions that had often barred from its complexes both applicants without jobs and mothers without husbands. The consequences of that shift were accelerated and intensified by a second force, brought about by a piece of seemingly reasonable federal legislation. The 1969 Brooke Amendment, discussed later in this chapter, protected low-income earners from local housing authority rent hikes, but also unintentionally pushed working families out of public housing. The third force stemmed from repeated efforts by City Hall to limit the political fallout of New York's expanding homeless population by obliging the Authority to house such families. From 1971 until the mid-1990s, New York's public housing communities found themselves receiving waves of new neighbors who seemed overwhelmed by the struggles and pressures of life on the margins.

Changing Eligibility Requirements

As historian Nicholas Bloom argues, by the 1960s NYCHA was out of step with the "two-tier" social welfare state that elsewhere in America provided either generous entitlements to the middle class or tightfisted assistance to the destitute. NYCHA occupied an increasingly tenuous middle ground between the two positions. It provided model housing for the working poor, not mortgage guarantees for middle-class homebuyers or shelter of last resort for the impoverished. Indeed, the Authority worked to keep its complexes from becoming modern-day almshouses—in contrast to the programs in Chicago and St. Louis, which rapidly sank as their projects swelled with the jobless indigent during the 1950s. Likewise, NYCHA chose its tenants carefully, with an eye to the interests of existing residents. Critics, however, started to ask if public housing was for the truly needy why so many blue-collar workers lived in NYCHA apartments while the unemployed found themselves locked out. What, besides punitiveness, could explain the Authority's looking askance at what it called "morality factors" in applicants, such as a record of arrest or alcoholism? Under pressure to house the poorest of the poor (and withhold judgment about their likely quality as tenants), NYCHA would reluctantly revise its admission policies.

The political push for these changes started in 1965 when the city's welfare commissioner announced it would be impossible to help the "city's impoverished" until they "first have new housing"; he challenged NYCHA to abandon its criteria for screening out "undesirables." A few years later, Mayor John Lindsay's new commissioner of social services (and former Mobilization for Youth board member) Mitchell Ginsberg renewed the demands, going so far as to testify before the federal government that New York's "welfare recipients are not getting their fair share" of NYCHA's apartments. "Of the 600,000 welfare clients in the city," he pointedly observed, "only 8 percent live in public housing."[12] This campaign by Social Services for more housing for its recipients reflected the new bind in which the agency found itself. Despite the thriving metropolitan economy, welfare rolls had swollen 64 percent since 1960 as the number of low-skilled newcomers to New York grew faster than the city's fading factories could create jobs for them. Racism and limited education often shut what doors remained. Social Services' budget, however, had not kept pace. Closing the fiscal gap by cutting the already none too generous benefits was unthinkable in liberal New York, so the agency sought new ways to meet the poor's growing needs—including housing. NYCHA, which had completed one-third of all new multiunit construction in the city since the war, seemed an attractive solution to this dilemma.[13] Adding to such political pressure, 1967 saw two New York City poverty lawyers and a local attorney in Little Rock, Arkansas, successfully argued in a federal district court that the local housing authority's policy of rejecting applicants with out-of-wedlock children was unconstitutional.[14] NYCHA saw the writing on the wall.

In May of 1968, the Authority's chairman announced that NYCHA was abandoning its twenty-one "potential problem" criteria for selecting tenants and would no longer "exercise moral judgment in determining eligibility." While removing what had been a partial bar on single mothers and the unemployed attracted the most attention at the time, the new policy pushed NYCHA's doors open in other ways as well. Applicants who had been convicted of crimes or joined violent gangs more than five years earlier would now be eligible. So, too, would drug addicts and alcoholics if they claimed to be under treatment. Even those who exhibited "obnoxious conduct during interviews" with NYCHA's staff were now allowed.[15]

The Brooke Amendment

Given NYCHA's low turnover, these changes on their own might not have transformed very much with any speed. Indeed, NYCHA announced it expected the new rules would have little affect for some time.[16] But the next year, progressive reformers at the national level pushed Congress to enact changes to the original 1937 Housing Act. The Brooke Amendment—named after its chief sponsor, the

African American senator Edward Brooke (R-MA)—aimed to help the neediest in federally assisted public housing by pegging tenants' rents to their incomes, which would prevent local housing authorities from passing on increasing costs to residents. More precisely, the law mandated that households in public housing pay no more than one-quarter of their income in rent. Functionally, however, this arrangement meant nearly all would also pay no less than that quarter. And from that new calculus sprang unintended consequences. Rents skyrocketed for working families. Worse still, their rents had become in effect a whopping 25 (later, 30) percent tax on whatever extra earnings a better job or raise might bring. Such families increasingly moved out of NYCHA; they could now do better in the private market. At the same time, the empty apartments they left behind became even more attractive to those on public assistance; they would pay very little under the new policy.[17]

The loosened admission criteria and new rent formulas quickly had a measurable impact. By 1971, nearly 60 percent of all families moving into NYCHA's federally assisted projects were welfare recipients, and just under half were single-parent households. The arrival of these newcomers meant that by 1973, 34 percent of all NYCHA tenants were on welfare—more than double the tenant welfare rate in 1968, the year the Authority liberalized its admission policies.[18]

NYCHA and the Politics of Homelessness

Three years after modifying eligibility standards, NYCHA made an even greater departure from past practice when it bowed to City Hall and began accepting the homeless families that were both crowding New York's welfare hotels and creating political headaches for its leaders. Housing abandonment was largely to blame. In the late 1960s, white flight and growing poverty had led to declining rental incomes that no longer justified maintaining or even owning aging buildings when better uses of owners' capital could be found elsewhere. The buildings may have been habitable, but they were no longer profitable, and between 1965 and 1968 landlords walked away from what amounted to housing for 300,000 persons.[19] As Lindsay readied himself in early 1971 for his ill-fated White House run, he was stung by press revelations that welfare officials, hard-pressed to shelter their growing homeless caseload, had placed a family in the Waldorf-Astoria Hotel on the city's dime. The widely reported story seemed to bolster opponents' "limousine liberal" accusations from the mayoral campaign two years earlier. A chagrined Lindsay publicly declared hotels off limits for such families and quickly extracted an agreement from the Housing Authority to help absorb the homeless—1,000 families a year "until," NYCHA's chairman promised, "the present hotel population [of 12,000] is all adequately housed." The Authority even agreed to offer these new residents jobs with NYCHA "on a preferential basis." Although the records are somewhat unclear, it is likely that just under 10,000 homeless families moved into public housing between 1971 and 1977.[20]

Lindsay's dilemmas (and solutions) proved to be a dress rehearsal for Mayor Edward Koch's administration. By the mid-1980s, another housing crisis gripped the city, brought on this time by gentrification, deinstitutionalization of the mentally ill, and declining social services.[21] The number of homeless swelled to 21,000 by 1985—seeming to grow in tandem with the city's expanding shelter system.[22] The year 1988 delivered Koch his own political embarrassment over homelessness: the public was scandalized by reports that the city was spending $1,800 a month to house families in derelict welfare hotels when apartments rented for a fraction of that cost. Meanwhile, the federal government threatened to cut off emergency housing aid if the practice continued. Confronting a tight primary race with David Dinkins in which polls revealed homelessness was voters' third-most-mentioned concern, Koch hatched a plan that replicated many aspects of Lindsay's. Under pressure from the mayor, the Authority again agreed to house homeless families: 2,000 annually, or twice the number it had agreed to under Lindsay. Koch lost the primary to Dinkins, and the homeless continued to pack into the city's public housing—but this time without the social services and job opportunities NYCHA had provided the newcomers, however briefly, in the early 1970s.

Although this new population was sometimes profoundly troubled (voluntary urine tests of family shelter residents in 1991, for example, had revealed one in six had used crack cocaine in the past forty-eight hours), NYCHA was now too broke to offer much of anything in the way of needed services.[23] A near decade of federal apathy under President Ronald Reagan meant that public housing in New York, as elsewhere, was soon both short of friends and shorn of funds. Reagan's indifference to urban issues was anecdotally epitomized by his failure at a Rose Garden gathering to recognize his own Department of Housing and Urban Development secretary, referring to his only black cabinet member as "Mr. Mayor." More quantifiably, Reagan's administration slashed HUD's budget from thirty-three to fourteen billion dollars between 1981 and 1987. Boxed in by shrinking subsidies from a conservative Washington and diminishing rent revenue from an increasingly impoverished tenantry, the Authority found itself making relentless cutbacks. Despite the lack of services for the homeless, when the Authority finally ended the arrangement in 1992, one in four newly rented NYCHA apartments went to such families, who were able to leapfrog to the front of the Authority's huge applicant waiting list.[24]

Mounting Consequences

Both NYCHA's management and its tenants came to believe that welfare recipients and the formerly homeless drove crime up in their communities. In 1975, outside consultants used data from the Authority to compare the share of welfare recipients in each of NYCHA's complexes with their respective crime rates.

The analysts concluded that across all of the Authority's complexes, "the most significant social variable to correlate with crime rate was 'the percent of population receiving welfare.'" Higher welfare rates, in other words, went hand in hand with higher crime rates.[25] In-depth surveys of New York public housing tenants a few years earlier point to why this might have been the case—without demonstrating, however, that welfare recipients were necessarily more likely to commit crime.

In 1972, Morton Bard of the Graduate School of the City of University of New York (CUNY) extensively surveyed more than 400 tenants in four of NYCHA's Manhattan complexes: Grant (1,940 units), Jefferson (1,493 units), Manhattanville (1,272 units), and Wagner (2,154 units). Bard's study aimed to evaluate how effective police training might be in improving officers' performance in "family crisis interventions." His surveys, however, had also asked residents what they would do if they witnessed from their window a variety of crimes or signs of disorder, such as "somebody being mugged," "a kid shooting dope," "a man and a woman fighting," or "a fire in another apartment." Respondents had numerous choices, including "call city police," "call housing police," and "do nothing." Their answers help explain some of the changes in project life in these years. The higher a NYCHA development's welfare rate, the more likely its tenants were to report they would "do nothing" after witnessing a crime or observing disorder.[26] Bard's data suggested that in those NYCHA complexes with larger numbers of welfare recipients, residents were less likely to engage in precisely the sort of informal social control or cooperation with law enforcement that is central to community policing.

It didn't take long for NYCHA's long-term residents to reach conclusions similar to those of academic researchers and building managers. Tenants may not have been aware of the inner workings of federal housing policy or the twists and turns of municipal politics, but they readily identified what they believed to be the source of their communities' decline. The manager of Brooklyn's Whitman Houses (1,636 units) reported in 1970 that "many of the long-term tenants are complaining that 'these welfare families' are increasing the problems of maintenance and security." That same week in Queens, resident leaders of the Redfern Houses (604 units) reported to their building manager that the development's "deterioration of the quality of life" stemmed from the fact that "most of the new tenants are welfare families." Similarly, the all-black tenant association of a development in Brooklyn complained in 1972 about the "lower living standards" of recent arrivals to the development. The chairman of the elected citywide Residents Advisory Council, Harold Pinkney, complained to a reporter on behalf of tenant leaders, "They let in almost everyone and we're the ones who have live with them." Building managers, too, noted that the new tenants disrupted building life. Between 1970 and 1972, the regular "potential tension situation" reports from the manager of the Van Dyke Houses

(1,601 units) in Brooklyn painted a picture of growing problems, which he connected to the rising number of welfare and formerly homeless families in his development. These newcomers, he believed, had led to the "demoralization" of Van Dyke's residents. Soon, the "tenant patrols . . . ceased to function," and showed so little prospect of coming back to life that he requested the removal of the phone jacks from their station. The lapsing of tenant patrols became a frequent lament of project managers in the late 1970s.[27]

By the 1980s, NYCHA residents, alarmed by how wide the Authority had flung open its doors, had started to demand the right to screen their future neighbors. A largely black and Latino tenant group associated with National Congress of Neighborhood Women and representing six Brooklyn developments—Borinquen Plaza (934 units), Bushwick Houses (1,221 units), Independence Towers (744 units), Cooper Park Houses (699 units), Hylan Houses (210 units), and Williamsburg Houses (1,622 units)—protested to NYCHA that "we have the right to choose our neighbors" in order to exclude "undesirable and basic menaces to our community." Believing it was their due as "citizens" to "be confident and comfortable with our living conditions," the women demanded "going back to the old system of screening by the Housing Authority." The depth of their frustration emerged in their description of potential applicants: "breeding shows," the women explained, and so "a judgment can be made properly when screening." Invoking both their own roles as mothers and the rhetoric of neighborhood caretaking, they insisted that the Authority start excluding "people who don't disapline [*sic*] their children" as a "first step toward up-lifting" the community. The women's arguments carried weight: NYCHA did eventually, albeit on a limited basis, give a number of resident groups a voice in the screening process, a practice that continues today.[28]

Complaints by tenant leaders continued through the 1980s, and by 1990 there were protests at City Hall. "Stop Dumping on Public Housing," chanted the throngs of marchers, who expressed fears that families from welfare hotels would bring "vandalism and drugs" to their complexes. Violet B. Hamilton, a middle-aged African American mother and executive director of the Tenants Advisory Council (the elected representatives for NYCHA's residents throughout the city at the time), explained to a reporter her constituency's position as she saw it: "Unless stopped," the flow of "homeless and welfare families" into NYCHA would leave "the projects unstable and make the working class leave." She bluntly echoed the larger society's judgments of such families: "We've already taken enough garbage in our public housing."[29]

Hamilton's intemperate words certainly ignored the larger political and economic contexts that had given rise to growing number of profoundly impoverished New Yorkers, but subsequent academic research seems to have partially confirmed aspects of the concerns that she and other NYCHA residents shared. Studies conducted in the early 1990s reveal a strong correlation between the number of the formerly homeless living in a building and the ability of its tenants to maintain the dwelling's safety and order through personal interactions—what criminologists like to call a community's "collective efficacy."[30] Researchers, again at CUNY's Graduate Center, surveyed 2,985 low-income Brooklyn residents living in *in rem* housing (buildings acquired from tax-delinquent landlords that the city rehabilitated and then, with mixed results, attempted to manage).[31] These surveys were then matched to the locations ("geocoded") of six months' worth of crimes in 1995 as recorded by the NYPD. Cross-referencing these two sets of data made it possible to chart the relationship between neighborhood disorder and a building's demographics. The researchers discovered that even after controlling for a variety of factors, the more of the once-homeless who lived in a building, the more crime got committed there—much more, in fact—although not necessarily by the residents themselves.[32] The formerly homeless and their neighbors, it seemed, simply had trouble getting along in ways that could deter crime, let alone give rise to organized tenant patrols. That lack of collective efficacy matters, criminologists explain, for the location and volume of crime. As recent in-depth ethnographic research with drug dealers and routine robbers has revealed, although these offenders rarely rely on a neighborhood's physical signs of disorder when choosing where to ply their trades, they are highly attuned to the "capacities for action with local social networks." In other words, from the criminal point of view, broken social networks matter far more than "broken windows."[33] And NYCHA's changing eligibility policies and agreements to house homeless families had unwittingly helped shatter such networks, as building managers' reports and the Tenants Advisory Council's opposition to the newcomers make clear.

For some older residents, making such social distinctions offered a way to navigate the growing stigma of public housing, even as it complicated their ability to regulate behavior in their communities. As historian Rhonda Williams found in her study of Baltimore public housing, the newcomers arriving in the wake of lowered admission barriers provided long-term residents with a "visible and tangible explanation for, as well as a way to distance themselves from, disrepute." Older residents "developed their own explanations for the changes they perceived in the social and political landscape of their communities" that focused on the "influx of new tenants."[34] The same held true in New York. Listen, for example, to former NYCHA resident Mary Alfson recalling the world of the Bronx's Millbrook Houses (1,255 units) during the 1970s.

> They [NYCHA] were letting in just anybody, you know, so the old residents stuck with the old and the new with the new . . . before the new residents, parents could say something to your child, not to do something and it was alright. But . . . you know with the new people coming in, oh Lord. . . . We couldn't say nothing to them.[35]

Alfson's daughter, Tricia, underscored what she saw as the impact of public housing's new social divisions on informal social control:

> The new residents, their behavior, you knew you couldn't scold them. They weren't friendly, you know, they just weren't approachable.[36]

NYCHA residents did furtively welcome some newcomers to their complexes, dubbed by frustrated management and police officers as "ghost tenants." As the city's supply of affordable housing dwindled, many who could not afford shelter on their own moved into the NYCHA apartments of willing family or friends in an illegal practice known as "doubling up." Using school and utility records, NYCHA calculated in 1983 that roughly 50,000 people had doubled up in its complexes. By 1990, not only had the number of the doubled up itself doubled, but also the practice had spread to many more families. That year, the Authority estimated that one in five of its apartments housed residents who were not "the tenant of record." These new tenants placed the Authority in a difficult position. On the one hand, NYCHA was in violation of federal and local laws if it allowed them to stay; moreover, the increased use of utilities badly burdened NYCHA's already strained budget. On the other hand, as NYCHA's general manager said of the situation, "we respect [tenants'] privacy," and the Authority was not about to "sneak into people's apartment finding out who lives there." Nor was it obvious to anyone where 100,000 impoverished individuals might find affordable housing in the city. Such reluctance cost the Authority millions of dollars in the 1980s because NYCHA feared that if it asked for a larger federal subsidy, the Reagan administration would demand the eviction of thousands of informally housed families. Splitting the difference, the Authority moved to evict ghost tenants only when "discovered by maintenance men . . . or when a crime is committed."[37] But this policy inescapably complicated community policing as it provided yet another reason for tenants to shield their lives from the HAPD and to hesitate before reporting a crime.

Recalling the adult sons who had doubled up in their mothers' NYCHA apartments in the 1980s, one exasperated former Housing officer resorted to stereotypes: "You couldn't get those clowns to tell you nothing about nothing. Where they were when, where their associates lived—always silence. It was very frustrating."[38] NYCHA's management noticed the crime-generating ("criminogenic" in sociological parlance) aspects of the doubling-up phenomena as early as 1979. The building manager of Brooklyn's Williamsburg Houses for example, reported that the Tenants Association added little to the complex's security or stability, staffed as it was by residents who were themselves in violation of Authority rules and who often sheltered doubled-up adult children suspected of a variety of crimes. Indeed, within months of raising this concern, one ghost Williamsburg resident who lived with his mother—and whose rap sheet of sex crimes and grand larceny would otherwise have kept him out of public housing—was arrested (and later convicted) for the rape and murder of a fourteen-year-old neighbor.[39] Similarly, tenant leader Terri Sheeps recalled how ghost tenants eroded the effectiveness of the tenant patrol at the Castle Hill Houses (2,023 units) in the Bronx in the 1980s. Fewer and fewer responsible residents wanted to serve because "a lot of their children living with them were involved in the whole drug trade, so it was better for them not to be involved in the tenant patrol so they wouldn't have to answer any questions or have fingers pointed."[40]

Ghost tenants also drifted into NYCHA from an unexpected institutional source: the New York State Division of Parole. Although regulations at the time forbade paroled felons from living in public housing for five years after leaving prison, parole officers routinely released convicts to NYCHA addresses and then withheld that information from the Authority. It wasn't that officials didn't know where their parolees lived. They did. But as journalist Jennifer Gonnerman reported of the practice, "a parolee with a stable home is easier to keep tabs on—and less likely to return to jail—than a parolee who is sleeping in a shelter." However useful the Division of Parole found dodging NYCHA's policies to be for easing prisoner reentry, the practice also held real consequences for community policing in the city's public housing. As one former Housing officer reported, "it was just one more reason for even decent tenants to conceal shit from us."[41]

The swelling population of ghost residents, the repeated waves of formerly homeless newcomers, and the surging ranks of tenants without "the honest eight," all reflected larger economic crises and accumulated political failures that bedeviled postwar New York. To be sure, such residents are far better understood as symptoms rather than causes of the city's woes. But as much as these residents' arrival at NYCHA symbolized critical social breakdowns, their growing presence in public housing communities also helped destabilize the world of more-established tenants as mounting needs, sufferings, and disorder pressed hard against dwindling financial, political, and social resources.

Affirmative Action and the Whitening of HAPD

Court decisions and city politics also reshaped the demographics of the Authority's police department in the 1980s, leaving behind a force both whiter and more suburban than it had been throughout the previous two decades. Critics on and off the force blamed these shifts for widening the gulf between NYCHA's police officers and its overwhelmingly minority tenants. In another case of unintended consequences, however, the growing number of white cops patrolling the city's public housing came about through both a landmark civil rights case and antidiscrimination litigation pushed by black and Latino officers' fraternal organizations.

As described in chapter 2, Housing had become an increasingly black and Latino department during the 1960s. In the ten years after 1965, for example, the percentage of white officers in the HAPD dropped from 65 to 40.[42] The NYPD was a different story: nine out of ten city officers were white. The "long, hot summers" of black rioting in more than two dozen cities in the late 1960s, however, rocked the nation and led to a chorus of calls for big-city police departments that more closely reflected the population they served. A series of lawsuits sought to force change in departmental hiring policies, but with uncertain results until a pivotal 1971 Supreme Court case filed not by urban police officers but by laborers in North Carolina.[43]

In the wake of the 1964 Civil Rights Act, a dozen black employees of Duke Power—which hired African Americans only as laborers—asked to be transferred to the company's better-paid mining division. But Duke Power had implemented, on the very day it was legally required to drop its long-standing segregation policies, a new requirement that miners (black or white) produce a high school diploma or pass an aptitude test. The black applicants met neither hurdle (only 12 percent of North Carolina's black males had graduated from secondary school in 1960). With the help of NAACP lawyers, Willie Griggs and eleven other African American employees filed suit, pointing to Title VII of the Civil Rights Act of 1964, which banned preferential treatment. The NAACP argued that tests were unrelated to job performance and so amounted to "thinly veiled racial discrimination." The case wound its way in 1970 to the Supreme Court, which sided with the black workers the next year. In handing down *Griggs v. Duke Power*, the justices extended the scope and reach of the 1964 Civil Rights Act by holding that hiring practices leading to racially disparate impacts must be specially justified, even when intentional discrimination is not alleged. *Griggs* would define affirmative action for the next two decades, encouraging institutions to seek the legal safety of the "bottom line defense" of representative racial percentages.[44] *Griggs* also inspired the black and Latino fraternal organizations of the NYPD to challenge the city's civil service examinations, which, like Duke Power's aptitude test, qualified many more whites than minorities for employment.

Less than a year after *Griggs*, the Guardians Association (the African American police fraternal order in New York) and the Hispanic Society of the NYPD filed a joint lawsuit in federal court against the city's Civil Service Commission. Jack Greenberg, an NAACP lawyer who had helped win *Griggs*, argued their case. Pointing to *Griggs*, Greenberg alleged discrimination at the NYPD on the grounds that "existing entry level and promotional examinations had a racially disproportionate impact, were improperly prepared, and were not job-related."[45] The suit was part of larger campaign by the organizations for increased minority hiring in the city's police departments. The Guardians and Hispanic Society's brother organizations at the Housing Police, for example, had filed a complaint with the New York State Division of Human Rights the previous year, alleging "discriminatory practices relating to employment." The basis for that charge was somewhat convoluted: a 1968 civil service list of eligibles for Housing sergeant was set to expire in early 1972, leaving stranded twelve black and Puerto Rican officers whose scores had placed them toward the bottom of the eligibles pool. In January of 1971, the Civil Service Commission did what it had done in the past: it scheduled a new test in anticipation of the existing list's expiration. But the Hispanic Society and Guardians claimed "the new exam is a ruse to negate the 1968 list" and NYCHA "would not have run a second exam if all or a majority of the existing eligibles were Caucasians." The organizations, however, did not challenge the exam's legality on disparate impact grounds. In fact, in a confidential meeting with Lindsay aide Carl Irish (who leaked the information to the Authority) the organizations had admitted that their complaint to the Human Rights Division was as much "gimmick" as grievance. The Hispanic Society and Guardians hoped it might "bring pressure to bear" on NYCHA in order "to get an increase in the sergeants quota" before the existing eligibles list expired (and, with it, their chances for promotion). Securing that change would, of course, have required "a corresponding increase in lieutenants, captains, etc." throughout the largely black and Latino department. After several hearings, the Division of Human Rights dismissed the case in July 1971, six months after *Griggs*.[46]

But the fraternal organizations' 1972 federal lawsuit explicitly invoked *Griggs* in challenging the NYPD's use of exams to hire and promote police officers. The city and the Guardians jointly retained the RAND Institute to analyze the racial impact of the most recent police examinations. RAND reported that 66 percent of the white applicants passed, while only 30 to 40 percent of the black and Latino test takers did.[47]

Moreover, the passing scores tended to bunch near each other, separated by minute quantitative slivers that did not justify a rank ordering of applicants.[48] Upon such evidence, the court required in *Guardians Association v. Civil Service Commission* that future tests and hiring decisions be designed under a protective order with the Equal Employment Opportunity Commission (EEOC). The whole matter, however, soon proved to be largely academic as the city froze all hiring in the uniformed services in 1975.[49]

The city did not offer its next examination for police officers and generate a new civil service eligibles list until 1979. After some legal wrangling, a court-ordered formula required that one in three of those appointed from the list be a minority (passing over, in the process, roughly 11,000 white hopefuls). But avoiding a racially disparate impact with three separate civil service lists for the City, Transit, and Housing police departments—which attracted very different applicant pools—proved unworkable, and the EEOC protective order produced an unexpected result: in 1980, New York adopted for the first time a single "tri-agency" list for the city's three police forces. From that roster of names, City Hall then allocated officers to the three forces using what became known as the "7–2–1 formula." Of every ten new appointments, seven would be assigned to NYPD, two to Transit, and one to Housing. But the recruits could no longer choose in which department they would spend their next twenty years; appointments were now done by lottery, in a system that would prevail until 1991.[50]

These changes had a dramatic impact on the demographics of Housing Police officers. Attrition coupled with the hiring freeze had by 1980 reduced the force to a historic low of 1,457 officers, giving the roughly 800 recruits appointed between 1980 and 1985 an outsized effect on the HAPD's racial makeup.[51] In 1979, only 37 percent of the HAPD had been white; when they could, most whites joined the more prestigious NYPD. But the new arrangement sent a steady, if often discontented, stream of white appointees to NYCHA's police force. Their numbers increased every year, so that by 1985 the share of white officers in Housing had jumped to 56 percent. By the 1990s, white officers made up 78 percent of Housing. A force that had once proudly pointed to being 56 percent black was now—as a consequence of court-ordered affirmative action—less than 16 percent African American. At the same time, the NYPD moved in the opposite direction: the percentage of whites in "Big Blue" fell from 88 in 1979 to 76 in 1985.[52]

More than race distinguished the new Housing force from the old. The post–fiscal crisis recruits were also much less likely than their predecessors to have a personal connection to public housing or even to New York City itself. As Housing PBA President Jack Jordan wistfully observed to a journalist in 1990, many of the earlier Housing officers had grown up in NYCHA, and nearly all had lived in the city. The same could not be said of the recruits Housing received after 1979. The new appointees had, by and large, been raised in the blue-collar suburbs ringing New York; towns that were not only home to a good share of NYPD's officers but that had also produced two generations of fresh recruits for that department—"cop factories," in stationhouse argot.[53] Former Housing detective and NYCHA resident Peter Grymes recalled noticing the difference such a background could make when patrolling public housing:

> A lot of them, they didn't understand the mentality of people in the projects. Everyone in, say, Soundview Houses, is going to look like a criminal to you if you're coming straight from the suburbs. They just couldn't make distinctions, which is half the job. They thought it was all about racing across to respond to "shots fired" and being like NYPD. But that wasn't what we were about. Of course there were going to be conflicts.[54]

The complaints started to come early. A 1983 letter to NYCHA's chairman from a "concerned Housing police officer" detailed the department's decline as seen from the writer's perspective. "The H.A.P.D. is serving none of the goals for which it was originally set up," began the letter. It continued:

> The younger generation of housing cops is ill-suited to its supposed task of policing inner-city housing projects populated overwhelmingly by minority group. The vast majority of recently hired housing police officers are white, from middle-class backgrounds. They shun the projects. If forced to patrol the interior of the projects, they look for trouble, provoking incidents in order to make a "quick collar" and get out.[55]

The letter writer was not alone. Several higher-ranking former Housing police confessed off the record that the department's rapidly changing demographics in the 1980s complicated its mission. "Do the job professionally, and your background doesn't have to matter," explained one. "But we couldn't really absorb that many kids so quickly who had to learn so much."

That job had changed, however, in ways that made learning the world of NYCHA's residents more difficult. Although Housing sought to have as many officers on foot patrol as possible and nearly all HAPD cops walked beats at some point during their careers, the move to precinct-style policing coupled with limited resources inevitably reduced the time officers spent on foot. Instead, officers increasingly patrolled from sector cars—an arrangement that was just fine for many. "Give a Housing cop a choice," former assistant chief of department Joseph Keeney observed, "and four out five times he'd rather be in that car." Unlike policing on foot patrol, however, officers rushing from 911 call to 911 call in Housing's orange-topped Plymouth cruisers predominantly encountered only victims and criminals. Of course, the vast majority of public housing residents, as statistics confirm, were neither. But HAPD officers out on RMP (Radio Motor Patrol) were much less likely to meet them. "How you gonna learn about the projects sitting in a RMP?" wondered former Housing detective Peter Grymes of the later recruits.[56]

The End of Community Policing

By the end of the 1980s, changes in the HAPD's policing culture were visible even to outsiders. In 1992, NYCHA hired an independent consulting group, Wasserman Associates, to assess security practices in the Authority's complexes. After several months of observations and interviews with tenants and officers, Wasserman's analyst concluded "community policing within the HAPD is only an idea, not a reality." One key factor in community policing's decline was that, in contrast to the past, "the [Housing] police do not perceive themselves as employees of the Housing Authority. There is little sense of accountability toward the Authority or residents of the developments, except among some very community-oriented officers."[57]

That the new social chemistry at work in NYCHA's complexes had disruptive effects on community policing became vividly apparent in the spring of 1989. On May 22 of that year, Richard Luke, a twenty-five-year-old unemployed handyman, began to suffer from cocaine intoxication in the apartment he shared with his mother and sister in NYCHA's (and the nation's) largest public housing complex—the sprawling, thirty-acre, 3,200-unit Queensbridge Houses in the Long Island City section of Queens. As the drug took hold of Luke's body, he had trouble breathing and stumbled out of the apartment desperate for more air; his frantic sister called an ambulance. The Housing officers responding to the 911 call encountered Luke in the building's lobby. A violent struggle ensued; it ended with Luke handcuffed in a nearby holding cell for more than thirty minutes. There, the police reported, Luke started to beat his head wildly against the cell's floor and bars. Anxious officers called for an ambulance and backup from the Emergency Services Unit, who placed Luke in a restraining blanket. That decision both led to Luke's death and set off two days of protest and near-riots against the Housing Police.[58]

While encased by the blanket as the ambulance rushed him to the hospital, Luke died either of hyperthermia (a common consequence of drug overdose akin to heatstroke) or of asphyxiation from his own vomit; subsequent medical reports differ.[59] But to many Queensbridge residents and others from the surrounding community, it was the white Housing officers who had assaulted Luke and it was their blows that had killed a young black man. Two days after Luke's death, two hundred protestors—monitored by an equal number of police officers—attempted to block traffic on the nearby Queensboro Bridge. Angry speeches assailing the Housing Police and the "white media" held the protestors' attention. The demonstrators eventually descended upon a local police station where a speaker shouted, "Who do we want?" through a megaphone. "Robocop," came the reply from the restless crowd, using the revealing nickname of one of the arresting officers in the Queensbridge development. "How do we want him?" the speaker asked.

"Dead!"[60]

The protest and its tone captured how much had changed since Edward Troutman's shooting death outside the Marcy Houses two decades earlier (discussed in chapter 2). Although that case had represented a much clearer example of excessive force and occurred in plain view of the residents, tenant leader Eleanor Ford had been able to leverage residents' personal relationships with the Housing police—forged by the daily encounters that occurred as officers walked their steady beats—to soothe neighborhood tensions and, ultimately, get the responsible officer transferred out of the HAPD entirely. But that was before the move to precinct policing, before the rise of the informal economy, and before the demographics of NYCHA's officers and residents changed. This time there would be nothing but bitter acrimony on both sides; as one observer said during the Queensbridge protests, "the image of the police in the black community is nil."[61]

The surviving Housing Police personnel files, although fragmentary, also point toward a growing tension between officers and tenants as evidenced by a sharp increase in brutality complaints. When tenants filed formal complaints against HAPD officers for excessive force or other grievances, Housing Police procedures called for—as they did with all infractions of HAPD rules—the officer to appear before an impartial "trial officer" in a departmental "disciplinary hearing." Tabulations of dispositions from such hearings exist for 1966–1974 and 1979–1983; the timing of the missing years in the paper trail suggest that the chaos of New York's fiscal crisis and Housing's layoffs interfered with departmental record keeping.

For the period before 1975, remarkably few complaints of what might be considered "police brutality" appear. In 1966, one officer at St. Mary's Park Houses (1,007 units) in the Bronx was found not guilty of being "discourteous to tenant's child," although another patrolman that same year was found guilty of being "disrespectful to others" in Brooklyn's Gowanus Houses (1,134 units). No such offenses appear in 1967. The next year, however, Herman Hanshaw, a community-service patrolman freshly hired as part of the Model Cities minority recruitment program, drunkenly struck a patron with a loaded pistol before aiming it at the other customers of Land's Bar and Grill in the Bronx; after a hearing, the HAPD promptly dismissed him from the force. To that case must be added the Thomas Johnson affair discussed in chapter 2. A single complaint ("disrespectful toward public") appears in 1969, but was deemed unsubstantiated. No complaints appear in the records again until thirteen cases of "disrespectful" behavior appear in 1972; all but two of these were found unsubstantiated. In 1974, tenants brought two complaints of "failed to use the minimum amount of force to accomplish his mission" (found unsubstantiated) and a single complaint of "disrespectful behavior" (found guilty).[62]

These are surprisingly low numbers. By way of comparison, a careful RAND Corporation study revealed that nearly six out of ten NYPD officers appointed in 1957 had accrued at least one civilian complaint by 1968. But the comparatively conflict-free relations between the Authority's residents and its officers would not last. Between 1979 and 1983, tenants filed seventy to one hundred brutality complaints annually against Housing officers; the department, however, only considered a handful of these complaints sufficiently substantiated to take formal action against the officers involved.[63] Given the challenges of proving police brutality claims and the minimal detail provided by surviving records, it is difficult to draw conclusions regarding the actual behavior of officers in these years. What is clear, however, is that tenants were much more willing in the 1979–1983 period to accuse the officers patrolling their communities of brutality than they had been between 1966 and 1974. The relationship between NYCHA's officers and tenants had manifestly broken down.

Rising Crime Counts

NYCHA's complexes experienced growing crime in the late 1960s and beyond—but so did New York's streets. Questions about how much more or less crime occurred in New York's public housing than elsewhere, and why, have fueled local and national policy debates since 1957, when the *New York Daily News* ran a series blaming supposed Communists in the Authority for turning the newly built projects into a "criminal paradise" for delinquent teens. Like many statistics, public housing crime data can be assembled and interpreted in a number of ways, providing ammunition for various and often opposing causes and camps. The Authority, keen to defend public housing and its residents, pointed to the consistently lower rates of "index crime" in the projects than surrounding precincts. Housing PBA leaders, angling for more resources, insisted that the official data—once the flaws had been corrected—revealed that HAPD cops faced greater dangers than did city officers. Community activists (black and white), fighting NYCHA developments slated for their neighborhoods, claimed the numbers made clear that public housing delivered criminals to previously quiet streets. Nationally, architects and planners pronounced that violence in the city's developments demonstrated that the modernist project itself had failed. "Towers in the park," envisioned as oases of order in builders' blueprints and futuristic sketches, turned out to be hotbeds of social deviance in the real world—or so went the mantra of a generation of urban thinkers.[64]

Sorting out something approaching the truth about crime in New York's public housing has been neither easy for analysts nor, it turns out, much in demand. Empirical certainty has often seemed beside the point to an American public that has woven crime, public housing, and racial minorities into what historian Wendell Pritchett has called an "unholy trinity." As one criminologist observed recently, "that public housing projects are rife with serious crime is more or less accepted as fact despite a discernible paucity of evidence supporting such a contention." When it came to crime, public housing the place often became obscured by public housing the notion.[65]

Even earnest efforts to make sense of the data face a host of methodological problems. Although having its own police force allowed NYCHA—unlike most local housing authorities in the country—to keep crime records separate from its host city, simply comparing crime statistics from NYCHA and NYPD can obscure real differences in the neighborhoods they patrolled and how crime got measured there.[66] In addition, New York's public housing projects are not randomly distributed across the city. Instead, they tend to cluster in neighborhoods that themselves suffer from high crime. That fact of geography can lead to what statisticians call an "ecological fallacy": inaccurate inferences about the nature of specific subjects (here, projects) based solely upon aggregate statistics collected for the group to which those subjects belong (here, high-crime neighborhoods). Similarly, the "ghost tenant" phenomenon described earlier in this chapter means that official counts of NYCHA's population often were far lower than the actual population, artificially inflating crime rates expressed as offense complaints per 1,000 (official) residents. Finally, although advocates often presented their readings of crime in NYCHA's complexes as a final verdict on public housing's high-rise architecture or low-income residents, wide variation across time and place in crime data render any such judgments incomplete. As criminologists have argued, neighborhoods have "crime careers," often undergoing significant variation in crime rates as conditions change. Likewise, in any given year different NYCHA developments will experience significantly different rates of crime, as a number of studies have revealed.[67]

With care, however, it is possible to trace the broad historical contours of crime in NYCHA from 1967 until 1996, although with greater clarity for the last of those three decades than for the first two. The data not only get richer and more complete for the 1980s and early 1990s, but they have also been subjected to sophisticated analysis by criminologists using statistical tools unavailable or ignored in previous decades. But even the incomplete data for the 1960s and 1970s allow some conclusions to be drawn.

NYCHA developments were safer than the city as whole from the late 1960s to the late 1980s, often providing a refuge from neighborhoods in decline. The Authority's complexes did, however, experience fast-growing violent crime in the second half of the 1970s. NYCHA's violent crime rate largely tracked the citywide rate between 1967 and 1975; both, for example, experienced a crime spike in 1971. But NYCHA's rate of increase was slower than the city's in the first half of the 1970s (13 percent and 21 percent respectively). Violent crime, however, increased much more rapidly in public housing than in the rest of New York between 1975 and 1980 (62 percent and 26 percent respectively). Even with the rapid rise in the Authority's rate of violent crime and despite the projects' growing reputation as "breeding grounds" of pathology, NYCHA's rate never exceeded citywide levels that decade. By the late 1980s, however, the gap in violent crime rates between NYCHA's complexes and the city's streets had dramatically narrowed. Public housing became ever more dangerous between 1985 and 1991, as the mayhem accompanying the distribution of crack cocaine in volatile open-air markets took hold in the courtyards and stairwells of the Authority's developments. Even when citywide violent crime rates dropped in the 1990s, they fell less rapidly in NYCHA, remaining stubbornly high through the decade. As criminologist Garth Davies has exhaustively documented, by 1996 New York's public housing complexes—widely seen as the nation's best—had actually become what opponents had earlier (and inaccurately) portrayed them to be: hotspots of crimes that diffused violence outward to surrounding blocks in a troubling fashion. (A more extensive discussion of the methodology behind this historical summary of crime in NYCHA's developments and its meanings, as well as a graph on page 143 aggregating the patchwork of evidence, appear later in this chapter).

Because of differences between the city's streets and the Authority's complexes, some critics have charged that NYCHA's methods for reporting crime data skewed crime tabulations in ways that made public housing projects appear safer than they likely were. Public housing blocks, critics pointed out, lack New York's characteristic jumble of ground-floor shops. By 1965, for example, the Authority's 150 developments had only 170 stores, leaving NYCHA with enormous numbers of residential apartments but scant retail locations.[68] Moreover, the Authority's superblocks featured sprawling grounds, but not through streets where cars might park. Fewer stores and cars meant fewer opportunities for property crimes. The Housing Police, however, reported crime complaints using the FBI's Uniform Crime Reports (UCR) index, which blended together property offenses with more violent crimes against the person (aggravated assault, forcible rape, murder, and robbery). Such a yardstick, critics have asserted, made NYCHA's complexes appear safer than they really were, as the unusually low level of property crimes pulled down the overall index.

This criticism of NYCHA's crime statistics would reappear in various forms in over three decades of public housing debates. It first publicly surfaced in 1971 during the Forest Hills controversy. That year, the largely Jewish neighborhood of Forest Hills—two and half square miles of quaint Tudor houses and modest apartment buildings tucked into central Queens—launched a furious grassroots campaign against Mayor Lindsay's plans to locate an 840-unit NYCHA development there. The community uproar provoked a racialized rhetoric identifying public housing with crime. The director of the American Jewish Committee's Legal Division wrote, for example, that neighborhood residents opposed the development because they were "not willing to sacrifice their own children on the altar of black revenge."[69] NYCHA, perhaps naively, hoped to counter community anger and fear with an array of statistics drawn from its records. As the controversy boiled over, the Authority issued a press release contending that the crime rate for its public housing was "invariably lower than [in] the surrounding neighborhoods." NYCHA's chairman Simeon Golar described as "conclusive" statistics showing that New York's public housing had an "index crime" rate one-third that of the citywide rate. Taking aim at the Forest Hill opponents, Golar added: "The widely held impression of crime-ridden public housing is destructive nonsense which slanders the working poor."[70] The Authority's opponents were not impressed.

City Council President (and former NYPD chief inspector) Sanford Garelick asked, "How can anyone compare the crime rate in fixed and limited confines such as a housing development to citywide figures? You certainly can't commit a bank holdup or store robbery in a housing development." Garelick, who had just the previous month voted against a NYCHA project in the middle-class Queens neighborhood of Lindenwood, cited Housing PBA President Joseph Balzano's assertion that "crime in public housing had risen 100 percent in five years." Public housing is in "the throes of a crime wave," an adamant Balzano declared when asked for details. The *Daily News* bemusedly noted the irony of a conflict between "the Housing Authority which claims the 190 city-operated developments are safe and the head of its own Police [PBA] who charges that the force is undermanned and unable to cope with soaring crime."[71] It was a charge that Balzano would repeat frequently in an effort to squeeze more resources from NYCHA—and that opponents of the Forest Hills project eagerly redeployed in their own battles with the Authority. At the height of the Forest Hills controversy, Garelick—already distancing himself from Lindsay in anticipation of his own short-lived 1973 mayoral bid—announced he was "alarmed at the rising incidents of rape, murder, assault, and robbery in city housing" and called for a city council hearing on crime in the Authority's complexes. He recruited Balzano to testify; the union chieftain publicly promised to "paint the *true* crime picture in NYCHA."[72] But the HPBA president never got a chance to make good on his promise, as Garelick never got his hearing.

Although the Forest Hills storm had largely passed by 1975, Balzano again charged NYCHA with cooking its crime statistics. Pressed in a local television interview to explain why he thought that an already broke city should pay to double the Housing Police's ranks, Balzano explained, "If you are visiting a project or a tenant of a project chances are twice as great that you will could be a victim of an attack." The union leader then went on to accuse the Authority of "covering up" crime in its developments. "They're dummying the figures up," Balzano asserted. "When I say dummying the figure up they will come out with a crime rate compare to the outside are 30 percent lower—that's not true." Balzano's math and memory were both a bit off, however.[73]

The Authority had actually claimed that UCR "index crimes" in its complexes were one-third that of the citywide rate (which was, in fact, accurate). Likewise, a person's chances of being a victim of a murder, robbery, assault, or rape in the previous year were actually 78 percent greater on New York's streets than in its public housing—the reverse of Balzano's statement on television. The Authority quickly shot back a few days later, releasing the year's crime statistics and slamming as "irresponsible" and "ignorant" those it felt trafficked in falsehoods, "whether it is the *New York Times* describing low-rent housing developments as 'fear-swept jungles' or Mr. Joseph Balzano of the PBA accusing the Authority of a 'cover-up' of crime statistics."[74]

More recently, Nicholas Bloom in his far-reaching and authoritative institutional history of NYCHA took the Authority to task for making "inflated claims about safety" in the 1960s and 1970s by reporting "absurdly low" crime statistics through a "lumping together [of] property crimes and more serious index crimes."[75] But NYCHA's use of the UCR index, which does indeed blend together crimes against property and persons, was neither as calculating nor as concealing as Balzano or Bloom's criticisms might seem to imply.

For the better part of a half-century, the majority of law enforcement agencies in the United States have reported crime figures using the UCR index, which was established in 1930 by social scientists and police reformers in a last hurrah of social progressivism. True to its architects' intent, the index creates a uniform set of national crime statistics. Certainly the UCR has come under criticism in recent years—as every first-year criminology student learns—for reporting only crimes known to police, for including only the most serious offense from multiple-crime events, for excluding federal crimes like blackmail, and for sundry other statistical sins of both omission and commission. But in the 1960s it would have been remarkable for a department the size of the Housing Police not to use the UCR. And for a force eager to establish its professional bona fides in the shadow of the much larger NYPD, it would have been inconceivable to report crime statistics any other way.[76]

Conveniently for NYCHA, using the UCR index did make the Authority's complexes seem safer than they probably were—but the index figures did not overstate the projects' safety to quite the degree some critics have asserted. The Authority did keep records of crimes by type (and reported them when asked), so it is possible to extract the figures for violent crimes—murder, robbery, assault, and rape—from archival NYCHA documents and then compare rates for just those crimes against rates for the same offenses for the city at large.[77] Matching apples to apples in this fashion, however, requires navigating around inevitable quirks in the historical data.

Changes in reporting practices in New York City mean that crime statistics from after 1965 are more accurate than—and so not completely comparable with—those collected earlier in the decade.[78] The first surviving NYCHA records that clearly separate property and violent crimes date from 1967, making that year the first for which real comparisons are possible between NYPD and Housing statistics. Documents detailing the volume of both property and violent crime in NYCHA exist for many of the years after 1967 until 1995, when Housing merged with the NYPD. Only the years 1972, 1973, 1977, 1978, and 1979 lack details about property versus violent crime. Even with these holes in the paper trail, however, more than enough evidence exists to chart trends for the 1970s.

For the 1980s and 1990s, the data situation improves dramatically. Researchers have collected and digitized complete records of crime in NYCHA's complexes, broken down by individual development and specific offense, for the years 1985–1996; the same has been done for NYPD statistics by precinct for those years. Likewise, the Center for Disease Control has tabulated homicide statistics for that period broken down by individual New York City blocks, including those containing NYCHA developments.[79] Collectively, then, for the decade 1985–1995, it is possible to compare violent crime rates for NYCHA to those for the city as a whole as well as to precincts and blocks with and without public housing.

But even this unusually rich assemblage of data poses problems. Scholars have recognized since at least 1995 that if using the UCR index pulled down NYCHA's reported crime rate artificially, using official tenant population statistics likely pushed it up misleadingly. Because crime figures are generally expressed as a rate of complaints per 1,000 persons, the underreporting of doubled-up residents in the Authority's official population figures would inflate the reported crime statistics, making public housing appear more dangerous than it really was. No one knows for sure, however, how many people have actually doubled up in NYCHA apartments, so even scholars attentive to the phenomenon have shied away from recalculating NYCHA's crime statistics in light of "ghost tenants." But the consequences of not doing so are significant. If, as NYCHA estimated, official tallies undercounted residents by 20 percent, the real crime rate would decrease by close to 20 percent. Indeed, NYCHA's estimates may well be conservative; system managers in the early 1990s pegged the undertally at somewhere between 30 and 35 percent.[80] Erring on the side of caution, however, this study uses the lower population figures, which NYCHA estimated based on indirect evidence such as utility usage and school records. Moreover, the graph on page 00 presents separate crime rates calculated from both the official tenant tallies and the estimated actual resident population, including "ghost tenants."[81]

Comparing just violent crime rates in NYCHA's complexes and New York's streets for the first five years of good data (1967–1971), the city at large was 60 percent more dangerous than was public housing. Similarly, the Authority's residents were significantly less likely to find themselves arrested than were their immediate neighbors. In 1968, for example, NYCHA tenants represented 15 percent of all residents in Model City neighborhoods, but only 6 percent of all Model City area residents arrested.[82] Index crime figures might have made NYCHA seem safer than it actually was, but the fact remains that even after dropping property crimes from the UCR's statistical mix, NYCHA's developments were dramatically safer than the rest of the city—despite both escalating national crime rates and the growing stigma of public housing in the late 1960s. But this happy state of affairs was not to last.

Once oases of comparative calm, NYCHA complexes would lose much of their distinctive safety amid the various shocks to the city's public housing and the HAPD's community policing strategies during the 1970s: changing tenant demographics, the informal economy, the growing influx of homeless families,

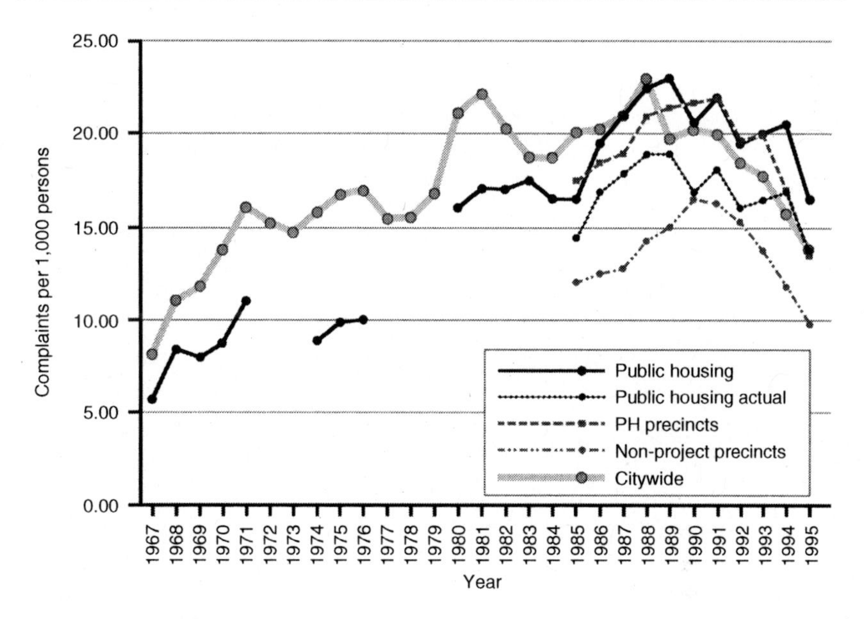

FIGURE 4.2 Violent Crime Complaints: New York City versus New York City Housing Authority, 1967–1995.

NYCHA sources for violent crime complaints before 1985: 1967–1968: "HAPD Annual Report, 1968," folder 1, box 65A6, NYCHA; 1969–1971: "Statistical Worksheet, Part I Complaints," folder 1, box 62C1, NYCHA; 1974–1975: "Statistical Worksheet, Part I Complaints 1974 vs. 1974," folder 4, box 89E6, NYCHA; 1976: "Statistical Worksheet, Part I Complaints 1976 vs. 1975," folder 4, 89E6, NYCHA; 1977: Benjamin Ward to Joseph Christian, 12 October 1978, folder 1, box 91C4; 1980: "The State of NYC Public Housing at a Glance," 12 March 1993, folder 8, box 100B3, NYCHA; 1981–1982: "Crime Index Complaints NYCHA vs. NYV 1982–1981," folder 9, box 91D5, NYCHA; 1983–1985: "The State of NYC Public Housing at a Glance," 12 March 1993, folder 8, box 100B3, NYCHA.

Non-NYCHA sources for violent crime complaints after 1985: Tamara Dumanovsky, "Examining the Neighborhood Context of NYC's Housing Projects" (Ph.D. dissertation, New York University, 1999).

Escalera, and the move to precinct-policing. Between 1975 and 1980, violent crime rates in public housing took off, increasing at more than twice the rate of citywide crimes in the same period. In 1981, however, NYCHA tenants were still less likely to be victims of murder, assault, robbery, and rape than the city's non–public housing residents, an astounding one in fifty of whom fell victim to violent crimes that year.

In the second half of the 1980s, both public housing and the city at large became more dangerous, but again, public housing's rate of violent crime grew significantly faster than did the rate in the rest of the city. Crack cocaine was largely to blame. As extensive scholarship has now chronicled, crack's 1985 arrival in New York drastically increased violence in the city.[83] Despite the media's fondness for stories of crack-addled criminals with superhuman strength, evidence for such pharmacologically induced menace is sparse. Instead, it was the distinctive nature of crack markets themselves that unleashed such carnage in poor neighborhoods. Crack's low price democratized the consumption of cocaine, an expensive "champagne drug" during the 1970s, creating far more customers than existing criminal networks could service. Unprecedented opportunities opened up for new sellers who could enter the game with no more than a modest investment. The crack industry, in other words, had what economists like to call "low barriers to entry." But this entrepreneurial activity came at a price: stability. Unlike the narcotics trade during previous drug epidemics, established gangs could not regulate crack's decentralized distribution, which quickly became violent as rival sellers battled over turf.[84]

The opportunities provided by crack came on the heels of the 1981–82 recession, and while New York, like other urban areas, was in the throes of an economic restructuring that excluded low-skilled and often minority workers from tightening formal labor markets.[85] Little wonder, then, that public housing—where nearly two decades of legal and policy changes had concentrated economic disadvantage and shattered social networks—offered ideal locations for motivated crack sellers and desperate buyers to do business. Forty percent of NYCHA's building managers in 1988 reported drug trafficking in their complexes to be a "serious problem." The crack trade seemed to touch many layers of public housing's world. The Authority, for example, discovered in 1989 that a quarter of its employees at Unity Plaza (462 units) in Brooklyn had sought counseling for addiction to the drug. That same year, two Housing officers were arrested for allegedly trying to rob a man of two kilograms of cocaine at a White Castle restaurant in Jamaica, Queens. Their arrest, in turn, led within days to the resignation of the department's third-highest-ranking officer, Joseph Irizarry, after what Authority officials described as "a private conversation" with HAPD Police Chief Louis Raiford. The chief refused to elaborate, telling reporters only, "'Draw your own conclusions." In a further indication of the extent of the problem, the department transferred four additional senior officers and thirty patrolmen.[86]

The widespread violence that came with the crack trade clustered geographically in and around New York public housing in an unprecedented fashion. In an exhaustive statistical analysis, criminologist Garth Davies found that between 1985 and 1995 "public housing and public housing neighborhoods [were] much more likely than non-public housing areas to be hot spots of particular types of crimes and violence." Hot spots of crime appeared near public housing projects "at twice their expected rate" and "extreme hot spots" appeared at "over three times the expected number." But crime seeped in both directions: poor neighborhood conditions increased the number of assaults inside public housing, while drug markets centered in the developments pushed homicides rates up in surrounding areas.[87]

After peaking in the late 1980s, the violent crime rates for both public housing and New York City declined between 1990 and 1995. Judging how much safer public housing became in these years depends significantly upon which population figures are used: official tenant tallies or estimated population, including "ghost tenants." In either scenario, however, public housing residents did not benefit as much as other New Yorkers during the city's famed crime drop after 1991.

The real story of crime in NYCHA, then, is one in which two dramatic escalations in violence closed the "safety gap" that New York's public housing had historically enjoyed over the city at large. In both of these periods of escalation, 1977–1980 and 1985–1990, NYCHA's complexes essentially amplified broader citywide patterns. The phenomenon of NYCHA complexes magnifying larger trends in city crime, however, was new. Between 1967 and 1977, NYCHA complexes had tracked but did not intensify movements in New York's crime rate. Indeed, the "safety gap" between NYCHA and the rest of the city grew in this period. In 1967, NYCHA's complexes were 42 percent safer than New York's streets; in 1974, they were 78 percent safer. But after 1977, every bump in city crime rates came with a greater jump in NYCHA's. When crime in the city grew 43 percent between 1977 and 1981, NYCHA's crime rate echoed that rise with a 70 percent spike. Likewise, when New York's crime rate floated up 13 percent between 1986 and 1988, NYCHA experienced somewhere between a 30 and 40 percent jump (depending on base population assumptions using "corrected" estimates or official figures respectively).

This broad historical account of crime in NYCHA helps to answer a persistent debate in public housing circles. What matters more for explaining the rising tide of disorder in many NYCHA complexes: the choices made by architects responsible for public housing's much-maligned designs, or decisions by policy makers about how (and how much) to regulate "decent project living"? The timing of NYCHA's upsurge in crime provides a powerful alibi for the architects. The first significant increases in public housing crime occurred some two decades after the city had erected the mass of "towers in the park," so the projects' bleak modernist landscapes, long and widely blamed for many of public housing's troubles, most likely did not propel the soaring rates of crime. Architectural defects may have encouraged or exacerbated the growth in crime, as even some recent studies have suggested, but they did not give rise to it.[88] Rather, it was the unintended consequences of policy choices—and their interaction with New York's restructuring economy—that undermined the order that NYCHA's tenants and police officers had worked to maintain.

Likewise, the timing of NYCHA's spikes in crime debunks a popular narrative that racializes "the problem" of public housing. In these accounts, New York's housing developments became "the projects"—mired in poverty and marred by violence—once the original white residents moved on (and up) and minority tenants poured in. One popular textbook, for example, glibly explains: "[A]s whites moved out, many poor blacks moved in, filling low-income public housing projects. The 'projects' were often haunted by unemployment, poverty, crime, and drugs." Such a telling invites the reader to see the experience of public housing ("a city within the city") as a condensed version of one oft-told parable of New York's "fall" in the 1970s: the once-great metropolis brought low and made mean by newly arrived migrants of color.[89] But New York's public housing was overwhelmingly black and Latino during the two decades it was safer than the rest of Gotham. Indeed, as previous chapters have detailed, black and Latino public housing activists worked hard and successfully to preserve the order they cherished in their neighborhood from the 1950s onward.

Residents and NYCHA Respond to Crime

Neither the Authority nor its residents stood idly by as a rising tide of crime threatened the city's public housing communities. Together and separately, both groups sought solutions to the challenge of disorder. In the 1970s, when they defined the problems to be solved and the range of remedies to be embraced, tenants and management often focused on particular design features of the Authority's sprawling complexes. Buildings were too tall, hallways too long, corridors too isolating. This "physical determinism," as one critic later dubbed the approach, rarely considered the Housing Authority's policies, the HAPD's practices, or the realities of tenants' daily lives—even as all three were transformed in ways that undermined community policing and neighborhood safety.[90] By the late 1980s, however, tenant groups and NYCHA's management had begun to take aim at the collection of legal and policy changes from the late 1960s and 1970s that had remade the social and political landscapes of NYCHA. In particular, they sought to reverse the consequences of the *Escalera* decision, the move to precinct-policing, and the liberalized eligibility policies that they now perceived as impairing the ability of public housing communities to regulate disorder. The welfare of NYCHA's communities required, such advocates argued, that the Authority exercise a firmer hand by screening and evicting tenants as it had back in its more paternalistic days.

These efforts may appear to represent the authoritarian side of a classic debate between collective security and individual rights. But the shifting agendas, needs, and alliances of diverse groups—politicians, social activists, tenants, police, judges—complicate any political labeling. Ideological categories are an especially unhelpful way of understanding how tenant activists understood their own realities and defined their own activism. Labels such as "progressive" or "conservative" shed little light on tenants' experience of public housing or concepts of self-determination against the backdrop of New York's changing economic and social realities in the last three decades of the century.

Defensible Space and the Solutions of the 1970s

Much has been made in public housing histories of Oscar Newman's seminal 1972 work *Defensible Space*, which argued that the physical layout of public housing developments made them more susceptible to crime and disorder by contributing to a sense of alienation among residents. Open space was indefensible space, Newman held, and high-rise buildings led to high rates of crime. Crowded streets peopled by women resting on crates and men lounging around stores had kept the peace in urban neighborhoods in ways that project walkways through patchy and exposed grounds could not. By fixing the worst features of the institutional architecture of the 1950s, Newman argued, housing authorities could help "design out crime." Eliminating "scissors" stairways and "blind" vestibules could remove the barriers that prevented tenants from naturally keeping watch on community order. For urban planners, architects, and other elite converts, Newman's theories of high-rise pathology—which borrowed heavily from Jane Jacobs's notion of "eyes on the street"—proved a potent argument against an earlier generation's doctrinaire modernism. Mirroring the New Left's attack on immense and faceless bureaucracies, the new design and planning philosophy rebelled against architecture that seemingly could not sustain urban life on "a human scale."[91]

Scholars have traced the ways in which Newman's developing theories both shaped some of NYCHA's policies and led to a national moratorium on the construction of high-rise blocks. The underlying concepts behind "defensible space" also inspired tenant activists who placed their own, different meanings on the new design theories.[92] In 1970, the Authority—persuaded by a presentation Newman gave officials—applied for federal funds under the 1968 Safe Streets Act to experiment with defensible space principles at the Bronxdale Houses (1,500 units). Crime had risen relentlessly at the development, encouraging many longtime residents to leave. (The exodus included the family of Supreme Court Justice Sonia Sotomayor, who left that year after living in the complex since 1959, pushed out, her brother Juan recalled, by both crime and an influx of refugees from burnt-out housing, who flooded the development "with people who were strangers to each other."[93]) The federal funding secured by NYCHA paid for a major redesign of Bronxdale's grounds and a $50,000 video surveillance system that, following Newman's designs, allowed tenants to observe the building's public spaces from their home television sets and report "irregularities" to the Housing Police.[94]

This idea appealed to tenant activists elsewhere in the city. In 1977, Mae Miller, the Tenant Association president of Brooklyn's Tompkins Houses (1,048 units), rallied residents in her complex—40 percent of whom subsisted on public assistance—to scrape together their scarce resources to purchase, with the help of city funds, a video surveillance system for the development's eight high-rise buildings. Miller's group commandeered unused storage space to create a tenant patrol room from which three volunteers on six-hour shifts observed the activities of building residents on twelve closed-circuit monitors. "We can always see who is coming and going," Miller smilingly told a reporter. But Mae Miller was no law-and-order conservative: she had renamed her project's community facility the Tompkins African Liberation Center and painted it (to the consternation of the complex's Puerto Rican residents) in the red, black, and green stripes popularized by black pride movements since the days of Marcus Garvey's Universal Negro Improvement Association. Moreover, rejecting modernist design played little part in motivating the efforts of these tenant activists. Instead, they understood their activism as being of a piece with a broader effort by African Americans to secure full citizenship and a dignified life. As Miller said proudly of her group's new equipment, "We've got the same kind of system they've got in luxury buildings." Similarly, a former Tompkins resident, recalling how she felt when the video monitors were switched on for the first time, said "it was like we finally got *ours* after so many years of eating crumbs. It was an equality and rights thing." Because they saw security and dignity as the rights of their community, these activists welcomed video surveillance as a step forward for the welfare of their neighborhood.[95]

If residents had concerns over individual privacy rights, they kept them to themselves. A team of outside evaluators interviewed hundreds at Bronxdale to assess both the cameras' effectiveness and the community's reaction. Privacy, apparently, never came up—as one of the original evaluators confirmed in a recent interview. But two factors eventually ended both pilot experiments in video surveillance: fear and boredom. Many tenants, the evaluators discovered, believed those preying on the complex were their neighbors rather than outsiders. Arrest statistics suggest they weren't wrong; 74 percent of all Housing arrests that year were NYCHA residents, up from 60 percent little more than a decade earlier. Keeping criminals at bay through "defensible space" made little sense when they already lived in the community. It is not surprising, then, that one-third of the sampled residents told the evaluating team they were too afraid of reprisals to report any crime they might see on their television. And they frequently could not see anything at all as an "abnormally high number of bored youngsters" relentlessly vandalized the expensive equipment—requiring over $1.5 million in repairs over several years. Interviews and crime statistics also revealed that the Bronxdale system reduced neither crime nor residents' fear of it. Within a few years, both experiments were abandoned as failures.[96]

This was a turn of events that Oscar Newman would have preferred go unnoticed. He threatened both the evaluators and the *Social Science Quarterly*, the journal that published the evaluation, with a $500,000 lawsuit, claiming that their "dishonest" research had caused his consulting firm, the Institute for Community Design Analysis, "much unwarranted damage" in lost government contracts. In a testy three-part exchange that appeared in a subsequent issue of *Social Science Quarterly*, the editors stood by the article; Newman withdrew his lawsuit, and the authors retorted to the architect turned crime entrepreneur, "[W]e are pleased to learn that the [evaluation] had a significant impact on public policy. In an era of budgetary constraints and scarce resources, crime prevention programs that do not work should be eliminated."[97]

This contretemps did no lasting damage to Newman's reputation as an expert on crime, and his ideas continued to influence professional thinking about public housing crime for another two decades. But the various criticisms that greeted *Defensible Space* over the years pushed crime control research and Newman himself beyond a narrow focus on public housing's physical characteristics to consider the social and economic aspects of life in developments.[98] This shift in perspectives received a push at the federal level with the 1978 Public Housing Urban Initiatives Anti-Crime Program (UIACP). Washington's dollars briefly funded the physical renewal of developments, provided incentives for housing authorities to work with local agencies and organizations to develop comprehensive anticrime strategies, and emphasized the needs of individual developments. The results, however, were underwhelming. The many evaluations of UAICP deemed it a failure. One comprehensive study, for example, found that "the programs in so many housing developments were so manifestly ineffectual that there was no basis for believing that they could have produced any significant impact." Ronald Reagan's presidency brought an abrupt end to the whole effort, and the multivolume studies of UIACP's effectiveness ended up gathering dust on library shelves rather than influencing future policy.[99] But even the ephemeral and apparently ineffective programs that UIACP funded succeeded in encouraging residents and management alike to contemplate the larger structural and social origins of crime in NYCHA's complexes. By the 1980s, NYCHA's tenant policies became the focus of concern in much the same way that its architecture had inspired hand-wringing a decade earlier.

The 1980s and the Politics of Eviction

Residents did not need a professional criminologist to know crack had brought violence and fear to their communities. "Talk to an officer," explained tenant leader Sylvia Velazquez of sharing a building with drug dealers, "and you're gone. They'll put a dead rat in front of your door."[100] What the crack epidemic had not brought, many tenant leaders believed, was action from the Authority. They leveled angry criticisms at the Authority for what they perceived as the agency's passivity in the face of the crack dens that were opening up and unhinging life in many NYCHA developments. Tenant activists pressured the Authority to oust residents who carried the drug trade's havoc to their doorsteps. NYCHA, in turn, pushed the reluctant U.S. attorney for the Southern District of New York, Rudolph Giuliani, to pursue more aggressive actions against lawbreaking tenants. These eviction strategies relied on legal innovations that NYCHA pioneered and that would, in short order, become a template for the harsh policies implemented by the federal government in the Anti-Drug Abuse Act of 1988. In 1993, New York's Legal Aid Society went to court to prevent NYCHA from taking tenants who broke the law directly to Housing Court, arguing that the changes to the *Escalera* consent decree would erode tenants' due process protections. But elected tenant leaders chose to ally themselves with the Authority's management rather than with their purported advocates from Legal Aid.

Distributors and users of crack cocaine appreciated the advantages of moving their business into public housing units and away from scrutiny; the neighbors of such operations did not. Journalist Michael Massing chronicled the 1987 opening and subsequent workings of one such crack house and shooting gallery: apartment 9D of East Harlem's Clinton Houses (749 units). The tenant of record and a ghost boarder charged a two-dollar entry fee to visitors looking to forget their troubles, supplying "works" to the heroin users and, the journalist implied, sex to the crack traffickers. Every day, Massing estimated, two hundred residents, friends, and strangers—all seeking their fix—snaked in and out of the unit. "With so many addled individuals packed into such tight quarters," wrote Massing, "9D became a blight on the entire building and the management file on the apartment soon bulged with eviction notices, court documents, and police reports recording everything from shootings to medical emergencies." But NYCHA, its hands tied by a combination of *Escalera*'s stipulations for due process and tenants' fears of reprisals, could do little. That same year, undercover officers in the Jacob Riis Houses (1,187 units) on the Lower East Side bought an ounce of crack from a tenant who had "installed a steel door to section off the bedroom from which she sold" her product. And in a chilling inverse of Oscar Newman's vision, the officers discovered the dealer had also wired "a closed circuit television system by which she could monitor what her customers did in the hall."[101]

NYCHA's managers soon found themselves facing newly urgent demands from tenant activists for action against places such as the Clinton Houses' anarchic crack den and the Riis Houses' fortified narcotics entrepôt. Residents drew strength from their own traditions as they applied pressure on NYCHA to do something to stem the rising tide of disorder. Consider, for example, a 1987 meeting of more than two hundred residents at the Bronx's Edenwald Houses attended by NYCHA's management director for the North Bronx, Robert McCabe. "The meeting opened," wrote McCabe in an internal NYCHA memo, "with a Southern Baptist style prayer." Then the tenant association president, Hazel Johnson, proceeded to "orchestrate a series of complaints to a crescendo pitch." With each grievance about crime Johnson raised, the tenants called back, "What are you going to do about that, Mr. Policeman, Mr. Manager, Mr. Politician?" But it was the content of the meeting that most caught the NYCHA manager's attention. "It was the first meeting in my entire housing life," reflected McCabe, "that maintenance-janitorial problems were lightly mentioned and almost completely glossed over. The main thrust of the meeting was DRUGS and the related problems. . . . tenants claim prostitution is very prevalent as by-product of the drugs problems." The dealers, residents explained, included NYCHA grounds workers, ghost residents, and even postal employees on their rounds. Just as the meeting was breaking up, "cops with guns drawn ran through the project to raid one of the buildings behind the community center" where the tenants had gathered. The residents, more accustomed to municipal inaction, voiced the jaded conclusion that the "raid was staged for their benefit," wrote McCabe.[102]

Responding to soaring crime and growing tenant pressure, in 1987 NYCHA established an "Anti-Narcotics Strike Force" (ANSF) to explore possible ways to meet the new challenges posed by the crack trade. Although the task force mulled over a variety of options, including "economic alternatives," its focus quickly settled on ways to take advantage of recent legal changes that might make it easier to evict drug-dealing tenants. A 1984 amendment to Nixon-era antidrug legislation had permitted civil forfeiture of real estate connected to felony drug transactions.[103] Why not, ANSF staffers wondered, apply the law to public housing leases as a form of "property interests"? Perhaps federal seizure of tenants' leaseholds could enable the eviction of drug dealers that *Escalera* had essentially thwarted? Even better, because federal law did not require advance notice, residents who fingered their drug-dealing neighbors need not fear reprisals.[104] All NYCHA had to do was persuade the U.S. Attorney Giuliani that such evictions were an appropriate use of existing federal statutes.

That was easier said than done. To NYCHA's surprise, Giuliani showed less enthusiasm for evicting drug-dealing public housing residents than did many tenant leaders. As U.S. attorney, Giuliani had just ridden a wave of populist anger by arresting the head of Goldman Sachs's arbitrage desk, Robert Freeman, on insider-trading charges. Giuliani had made the most of his attack on Wall Street crime, parading his handcuffed white-collar catches before waiting television cameras in the elaborate midday "perp walks." New Yorkers, fed up with the era's deal-making excesses, had applauded the campaign. Indeed, such cases had all the makings of electoral success in traditionally liberal Gotham.[105] But for a politician with an eye to his political future, using the power of his federal office to oust families from public housing was an entirely different matter.

In early December 1987, NYCHA's legal staff presented its forfeiture arguments to the U.S. attorney's office; Giuliani and his team questioned the Authority's interpretation of the statutes and demanded a full brief of the relevant case law. NYCHA did its homework and hand-delivered a detailed response two weeks later, hoping to move forward quickly on the evictions.[106] But Giuliani's office repeatedly brushed off the Authority. In a confidential memo, Manuel Quintana, NYCHA's general counsel, reported that the staff member Giuliani assigned to the project "felt the matter was not important to her personal advancement or of any priority within the office." Quintana revealed his frustration with Giuliani:

> We've gone more than 99.5% of the way in answering all questions, reasonable or otherwise, and the time has come for Giuliani to get moving. If he doesn't have the will to tackle the matter, there are other approaches we can take. But the endless dithering and "please provide me more information" gambit should continue no longer.[107]

But Giuliani did continue to dither on evictions. Indeed, he simply stopped returning the phone calls of NYCHA chairman Emanuel Popolizio. In February, an exasperated Popolizio wrote to Giuliani, "Dear Rudy, I have personally called you on three separate occasions and each time I was told you would return my call and unfortunately I have not heard from you." Popolizio, no political fool, then invoked his well-known friendship with Mayor Ed Koch in an effort to pressure the recalcitrant Giuliani: "I am a little embarrassed because Mayor Koch has been interested in the cases . . . I am at a loss to understand your silence." "Please call," Popolizio wrote, "so that I can respond to the Mayor's request for update." Perhaps leveraging his friendship with Koch helped. In April, Giuliani approved the use of federal forfeiture statues to evict drug dealers from NYCHA. But a bit of political horse-trading might have been necessary to change his mind. In a private letter thanking Giuliani for green-lighting the evictions, Popolizio intimated he would shift his political allegiances from his old friend Koch to the young and ambitious U.S. attorney readying himself to unseat the mayor in the upcoming election. "One of the best things that I have experienced in the last two years of public service is having the pleasure of meeting you and working with you," Popolizio proclaimed, all "dithering" now forgotten. "I want you to know that I am interested in your career and when you call upon the public to assist you, I wish to be numbered among the troops." (Giuliani would later, while attempting to persuade a congressional panel looking into his proposal to merge New York's police forces of his commitment to public housing, inaccurately and more than a little self-servingly claim that he had "initiated for the very first time the seizure [of the leases] of those people in housing developments that were using their premises for the dealing of drugs.")[108]

In late April of 1987, NYCHA—backed by federal law and marshals—evicted its first two drug-dealing tenants under forfeiture statutes. Small fry, no doubt, but the Authority struck again six months later in well-publicized raids on Brooklyn's Red Hook Houses (2,891 units), where they arrested fourteen residents and seized large quantities of crack, tens of thousands of dollars, and an M-16 automatic rifle.[109] Because of the legal innovations pioneered by NYCHA's ANSF staff, which made these successful evictions possible, Congress later that year again amended the original Comprehensive Drug Abuse, Prevention and Control Act of 1970 to clarify that the "real property" subject to forfeiture included leasehold interests; by extension this also allowed public housing authorities to exclude applicants with a record of drug arrests. This legislation, the Anti-Drug Abuse Act of 1988, affirmed NYCHA's civil forfeiture practices and cleared the way for the broad use of such eviction policies in public housing nationwide. The laws, in turn, got sharper teeth with the National Affordable Housing Act of 1990, which enlarged the range of eviction-worthy offenses beyond drug violations to include "any criminal activity that threatens the health, safety, or right to peaceful enjoyment of the premises by other tenants."[110]

The due process protections built into the *Escalera* consent decree ensured that the procedure for evicting public housing tenants was not a swift one. After seizing a lease, NYCHA was required to hold an administrative hearing while the district attorney litigated a separate drug-holdover proceeding in civil court. Tenants could appeal their NYCHA administrative case before the New York State Supreme Court, during which time they could apply for (and generally received) a stay against eviction until the court rendered a ruling—a process that could stretch out for a year and a half. But a 1992 Supreme Court decision (*Rufo v. Inmates Suffolk County Jail*) seemingly opened the door for adapting consent decrees in response to changing circumstances. NYCHA, accordingly, moved the next year to modify the *Escalera* consent decree so that it could use New York's "Bawdy House" Laws—a dusty bit of legislation from gas-lamp era Gotham that had aimed at the urban demimonde—to bypass the administrative hearing and take cases directly to the civil Housing Court. Tenants would be accorded the due process protections of any defendant before that court, but evictions could now be fast-tracked.[111]

Lawyers with New York's Legal Aid Society, however, immediately objected—pointing to the twenty-two-year-old *Escalera* consent decree. They were still, they insisted, the attorneys of record. Claiming to speak on behalf of all of NYCHA's 600,000 tenants, they argued the proposed changes were illegal because they departed from *Escalera*'s stipulations.[112] New York's Legal Aid lawyers, however, were a bit unusual in this intransigence. A number of Legal Aid organizations elsewhere in the Northeast had by this point begun to conclude the gravest threats to their clients might arise not from a misuse of public power but rather from the private abuses inflicted on them by other residents of poor communities. Boston Legal Services, for example, had just the year before sued the local housing authority, demanding that it use the new federal laws to oust drug-dealing tenants. The city's poverty lawyers subsequently stopped taking drug-related eviction cases at all, citing a conflict of interest. The director of Legal Services in Camden, New Jersey, had publicly called for a greater emphasis on the interests of public housing's law-abiding tenants.[113] But recent events had given New York's Legal Aid Society powerful ideological and, perhaps, financial incentives to resist modifying *Escalera.*

The city's unionized Legal Aid attorneys had struck against the society in 1994, demanding, the union's president Michael Letwin insisted, not more money but "a place at the table" and an end to the "alienation" they suffered in a "hierarchical" organization.[114] Unfortunately for Letwin's membership, their cries of alienation fell on deaf ears at Gracie Mansion. Giuliani, now mayor, refused to let the labor impasse freeze the city's courts and offered the strikers an ultimatum: return to work in twenty-four hours or Legal Aid would lose its $80 million in contracts with New York and no striking lawyer would find work with the city ever again. At the eleventh hour, the poverty lawyers voted to save their jobs.

The strike and its aftermath produced two significant changes for New York's Legal Aid. First, a month after the lawyers returned to work, Legal Aid's board of directors selected Mobilization for Youth's longtime managing attorney, Daniel Greenberg, as the new executive director and attorney in charge. Second, Mayor Giuliani—invoking the supposed advantages of a competitive marketplace—moved to break Legal Aid's near-monopoly on indigent criminal defense, shifting such work increasingly to other nonprofits and independent attorneys.[115] Both of these consequences mattered for Legal Aid's response to NYCHA's efforts to modify *Escalera*. As New York Legal Aid's new director, Greenberg had deep ideological and historical commitments to the original 1971 consent decree. MFY had long cherished the case as essential to its legacy; *Escalera* symbolized the poverty-law movement's strategy of deploying rights litigation to tame oppressive institutions and so liberate the vulnerable caught in their impoverishing grip.[116] But financially, Legal Aid also needed to maintain its presence as the preeminent provider of legal services to the poor amid Giuliani's threatened defunding. Their own litigation strategies soon made keeping that privileged position more difficult.

In resisting the move to modify *Escalera*, Legal Aid argued—notwithstanding NYCHA's spiraling crime rate—that crack had actually created conditions no worse than had existed at the time of the original consent decree two decades earlier. There was, accordingly, no reason for the court to change *Escalera* now. Legal Aid brought in expert witnesses to testify why, contrary to common misconceptions, living next door to a crack dealer did not increase the risk of criminal violence. And even if crime had, perhaps, somehow increased in NYCHA complexes, the attorneys argued that a "more suitable" solution would be to expand the number of Housing Police officers rather than speed the evictions of alleged drug dealers. None of this sat well with the representatives for NYCHA's elected tenant organization, the Interim Citywide Council of Presidents, who had—like their predecessor organizations the Residents Advisory Council and the Tenants Advisory Council—long pressed the Authority to be more aggressive in evictions. Incensed at Legal Aid's courtroom arguments, which flew in the face of their lived experience in public housing, the tenant organization hired new attorneys to fight, as two legal scholars wryly observed afterward, "on the side of the Housing Authority and against the lawyers who theoretically were representing them."[117]

The tenant leaders' new attorneys, however, also had their own agenda. Affiliated with the politically centrist American Alliance for Rights and Responsibilities, the tenants' new lawyers presented the *Escalera* case as a political dilemma best understood and solved through the lens of a movement that been had been gaining ground in academia and think tanks: "communitarianism." With its focus on community welfare, this school of thought resonated more closely with the tenant leaders' aspirations than did Legal Aid's emphasis on individual rights, but in trumpeting communitarianism's intellectual innovations, the conservative scholars associated with it—including Amitai Etzioni and Fred Siegel—failed to recognize that NYCHA's tenant leaders already had a long political tradition of locating both rights and strengths within their own communities. The "community mothering" practiced by public housing activists like Mildred Tudy and others chronicled in this book represented a deeper and more original impulse than allowed for by the communitarian writers' rhetoric of ushering in a "new age of responsibility." Since the 1960s, in fact, New York's public housing activists had invoked collective rights over individual freedoms in their demands that NYCHA use its institutional power to curb neighborhood disorder—insisting, for example, on more stringent enforcement of housing rules, on stricter eligibility requirements, for swifter and more certain evictions of wrongdoers, and for greater police coverage. This seasoned and homegrown political heritage within public housing got lost, unmentioned and unrecognized in the explosion of communitarian writings in the 1990s that emphasized the school's "new approach."[118]

The Authority did prevail in court, however. On April 19, 1996—almost nine years after NYCHA's first forfeiture evictions—Judge Loretta A. Preska issued a fifty-five-page opinion deciding that on balance it was permissible for the Authority to use the city's Housing Court for speedier evictions of unruly tenants, modifying the quarter-century-old *Escalera*.[119] The month before Preska's decision, President Bill Clinton made his famous "one-strike" announcement: "This policy today is a clear signal to drug dealers and to gangs: If you break the law, you no longer have a home in public housing, 'one strike and you're out.' That should be the law everywhere in America."[120] The president's strongly worded challenge echoed NYCHA's efforts to modify *Escalera*, but did not actually create new policy. As one housing authority director commented, "We really haven't changed anything. It just has a catchy little ring to it."[121] Clinton's announcement, in fact, merely solidified the eviction practices of many housing authorities dating back to 1988, the year Congress codified NYCHA's innovative use of federal forfeiture laws. Nonetheless, in the span of a decade, tenant pressure on NYCHA's management to "do something" about soaring drug-related crime had led impressively to a White House policy announcement.

Scholars and activists have pointed to "one-strike" and other strict tenancy regulations as examples of the penalizing excesses inherent to America's "carceral state." Public housing, in these arguments, is one of the key places where we can see the extent to which the government has rolled up the public safety net and replaced it with a newly punitive dragnet. According to this line of thought, the new eviction policies originated not with tenant activism but rather in a moral panic over crime, stoked and exploited by politicians. For example, political scientist Marie Fritz has argued that when Congress passed the 1988 law that first allowed narcotics-related evictions from public housing (building upon NYCHA's leasehold seizures the previous year), it was simply "capitalizing on the anti-drug sentiments and hostility directed toward recipients of cash assistance and public housing." Journalist Christian Parenti likewise argues in his widely read *Lockdown America* that the new eviction policies represent the "state's subordination of social service functions to policing functions."[122] Such analyses, although not entirely inaccurate, overlook the new eviction policies' deep roots within three decades of public housing activism. Conservative politicians may have eventually co-opted public housing activists' efforts, but the impetus for the policy changes emerged from residents' political demands and reflected the experiences of many tenant leaders. Without the cooperation of these tenant leaders, NYCHA and Congress would have faced much stiffer resistance in passing and implementing the new policies.

Recognizing the role of tenant activists in bringing about these policy changes, however, is not the same thing as holding them responsible for their current form or how they have been subsequently interpreted. And it is in the interpretation that real abuses have occurred. While HUD's policy circulars on eviction are straightforward, the underlying laws are so vague that they nearly constitute a legal Rorschach test. The Anti-Drug Abuse Act of 1988, as amended in 1998, gives public housing officials authority to include a new lease provision specifying that

> any criminal activity that threatens the health, safety, or right to peaceful enjoyment of the premises by other tenants or any drug-related criminal activity on or off such premises, engaged in by a public housing tenant, any member of the tenant's household, or any guest or other person under the tenant's control, shall be cause for termination of tenancy.[123]

The statute was silent, however, on what degree of culpability is required before triggering an eviction. Must the tenant know of the illegal activity? What if the offense occurred well off the grounds of the resident's complex? Courts split on these and other issues. It took a Supreme Court decision, *HUD v. Rucker* (2002), to resolve these uncertainties.

Pearlie Rucker was a sixty-three-year-old African American who lived in an Oakland (California) Housing Authority (OHA) unit with her mentally disabled daughter, two grandchildren, and one great-granddaughter. When police arrested Rucker's daughter three blocks from the apartment for cocaine possession, OHA moved to evict the family. Rucker protested, claiming her regular searches of her daughter's room for drugs always came up empty-handed. Having made reasonable efforts, she argued, she should not be held liable for behavior that was successfully concealed from her. The Ninth Circuit Court of Appeals agreed, noting that the law specified evictions only for the wrongdoing of those "under the tenant's control." But in a unanimous decision, the U.S. Supreme Court backed Rucker's ouster and that of any resident with a lawbreaking relative, regardless of what efforts a tenant might have made to stop the behavior or where the offense might have taken place. Rucker's misfortune before the court, it appears, sprang not from drugs but grammar. As Chief Justice William Rehnquist explained in his parsing of the law's text:

> [T]he *en banc* Court of Appeals also thought it possible that "under the tenant's control" modifies not just "other person," but also "member of the tenant's household" and "guest." The court ultimately adopted this reading, concluding that the statute prohibits eviction where the tenant "for a lack of knowledge or other reason, could not realistically exercise control over the conduct of a household member or guest." But this interpretation runs counter to basic rules of grammar. The disjunctive "or" means that the qualification applies only to "other person."

And if, concluded the justices, the phrase "under the tenant's control" modifies only "other person," then the fact that Rucker's daughter was not under her control offered her no reprieve from eviction.[124] Rucker found herself ejected from her home of more than two decades, while the courts were handed a new standard for deciding such cases—"strict liability"—that makes no exceptions for a tenant's lack of knowledge of the wrongdoing or allowances for preventive measures they might have taken.[125]

As can be gathered from Rehnquist's grammatical exegesis, the current draconian potential of one-strike eviction policies stems more from legal interpretation than anything inherent to the concept of using evictions to rid public housing of unruly tenants. Although NYCHA's tenant activists fought hard for swifter and more certain evictions, they never called for a policy as sweeping the one that emerged as a consequence of *Rucker*. But the Supreme Court's decision also does not *require* evictions; it leaves the decision to the public housing authorities' discretion. For its part, NYCHA has chosen a middle route: rather than evict an entire family when confronted with unruly behavior, the Housing Authority generally has made the tenant of record's lease conditional on the offending resident's permanent exclusion from its grounds—and a list of those thus barred appears in NYCHA's monthly newspaper, *The Journal*. In 2008, a little more than 0.20 percent of all of the Authority's households had a member barred in this fashion—suggesting NYCHA has exercised a judicious hand in selecting which bad apples to oust. Even this compromise, however, has provoked outcry from Legal Aid, which argues the costs of splintering individual families exceed the benefits to the community of ejecting troublemakers.[126]

Conclusion

Residents' anticrime activism in these years underscores just how distorted the popular image of public housing had become. Outsiders often assumed that NYCHA tenants were the living confirmation of a sociological theory winning cachet at the time among journalists, policy makers, and the broader public: the cultural pathology of an unprecedented "underclass" inhabiting America's cities. In this view, the projects warehoused a population so enfeebled by family breakdown and so hobbled by government handouts that its members could no longer be saved through either personal gumption or state action. In fact, the political mobilization and legal moxie of tenant associations in this period belies such stereotypes. Invoking both their rights as citizens and their roles as mothers, the largely female tenant leadership successfully prodded NYCHA into wielding its institutional power against disorder in "the PJs."

In demanding change, however, tenant leaders frequently privileged neighborhood welfare over individual freedoms, so these activists took aim at policies ushered in by the rights revolution that many blamed for the deterioration in their communities. Residents looked to their own past for inspiration in these struggles. Against the violent backdrop of project life in the dispiriting decade between 1985 and 1995, the memory of safe courtyards and stable neighbors watched over by "our cops" offered a powerful vision of what public housing communities could again achieve. Residents were not alone in casting a glance backward for guidance. The Housing Police, too, looked to their department's past as the "last neighborhood cops." In the wake of both growing resentments against HAPD officers and soaring crime in NYCHA developments, the Authority's police force struggled to rekindle effective community-based law enforcement—a story told in the next chapter.

FIGURE 5.1 Children outside Brooklyn's Red Hook Development, 1980. Photograph © Jamel Shabazz.

5

A Return to Origins and the Merger, 1990–1995

Losing, Saving–and Losing the Housing Police Again

At the same time that tenant leaders were pushing NYCHA) to return to the days of sure and speedy evictions, the Housing Authority Police Department (HAPD) and the Authority were seeking to restore the effective community policing practices that had prevailed in the 1960s and 1970s. A gale of public outrage over crime had helped make government resources for such efforts available through two new public policy initiatives: New York's Safe Streets, Safe City plan and HUD's Drug Elimination Program. For NYCHA's managers and HAPD's brass, the resulting infusion of manpower and cash made possible one last effort to save the Authority's distinctive police force. This was ultimately a doomed attempt, however.

Despite early signs that these various efforts were bearing fruit and reducing disorder, they soon were cut short. Rudolph Giuliani—now mayor—merged New York's three police departments (NYPD, Transit, and Housing) into a single, more compliant force in April of 1995. How Giuliani triumphed where his City Hall predecessors dating back to the 1970s had failed is a live question in policing circles. The changed demographics and orientations of the HAPD, however, go a long way toward explaining Giuliani's success. In comparison to previous mayors, he faced less resistance from Housing's Patrolmen's Benevolent Association (HPBA), whose dues-paying members now had fewer loyalties to public housing and more ambitions to be city rather than Housing cops. Many long-term officers opposed the destruction of their independent department, and the HPBA did attempt to use civil services laws to preserve their own union. But the HAPD's divided ranks often spoke with a divided voice, and opposition to the plan folded with the failure of the HPBA's court case. By this time, tenants too had fewer reasons to fight for the preservation of a separate force. In the 1960s and even 1970s, tenants had identified with "their" police, but by the 1990s the HAPD had changed. While critics condemned the loss of community policing, which they believed accompanied Giuliani's annexing of the HAPD, in reality the department had already abandoned many aspects of that strategy by the time of the merger.

Attempts to Restore Community Policing

In the summer of 1990, the city experienced one of its episodic spasms of street violence, and Mayor David Dinkins, in office for barely six months, faced a barrage of lurid tabloid crime coverage. A *New York Post* headline screamed in memorable two-inch-high block letters, "DAVE, DO SOMETHING!"—a plea the mayor himself would quote often. Dinkins, in fact, knew he was politically vulnerable on the issue of crime: his first official act as mayor had been to cancel a Police Academy class, hoping to relieve a budget crunch. (As mayor, Giuliani would later do the same.) Expending substantial political capital, Dinkins persuaded the New York's state legislature in early 1991 to raise $1.8 billion in statewide taxes to hire five thousand new officers for the city's three departments in the vaunted Safe Streets, Safe City plan. This plan, however, aimed to do more than merely add more cops to the payroll. Reflecting NYPD Commissioner Lee Brown's commitment to theories of community policing, Safe Streets also mandated assigning more than 60 percent of the three forces' combined manpower of 31,310 to patrol duties. The plan further envisioned a host of neighborhood-based social programs. For the HAPD, Safe Streets meant both 160 new officers and greater moral and fiscal support for community policing strategies.[1]

In 1990, NYCHA also began to tap a rich new vein of federal dollars: HUD funds from the Drug Elimination Program (DEP). Authorized by the Anti-Drug Abuse Act of 1988, the DEP dispensed between $250 million and $300 million annually in competitive grants to housing authorities across the country—but with a catch. DEP monies had to be spent on battling drug-related problems. Between 1990 and 1997, NYCHA secured and spent over $165 million of such funds. In a nod to criminologists' new thinking about "informal social control," NYCHA's DEP program coupled traditional enforcement strategies with community policing programs. To foster tenant participation, NYCHA earmarked resources to empower residents to identify and solve community problems through the organization of Drug Elimination Committees, Tenant Patrols, and Community Center Programs. Another allocation was to pay for physical improvements of NYCHA's buildings and grounds, redesigning public spaces to limit access and adding increased lighting to public areas and intercom systems to entrances.[2]

While NYCHA never funded these community-based programs at anything like the level it devoted to traditional police enforcement, the Authority nevertheless did spend significant sums on efforts to build the "collective efficacy" of New York's public housing residents. Between 1991 and 1995, for example, NYCHA's DEP expenditures on tenant patrol expanded eighteen-fold, from $59,000 to $1.1 million—largely because tenant patrol volunteers demanded support. Domestic violence programs similarly received close to $3 million of DEP funds between 1991 and 1996, or nearly $1 million more than NYCHA spent on its Anti-Narcotic Strike Force, which focused on evicting drug-dealing tenants. Likewise, for the years 1994 and 1995, $7.6 million went to a Seasonal Jobs Program for residents, or sixty-four times what NYCHA used to purchase police equipment over the eight years of DEP funding. In perhaps the most impressive measure, by 1994, $5.7 million, or 15 percent of NYCHA's total DEP budget, went to a Basic Skills Employment Training Program that trained residents in construction work in collaboration with local unions. But traditional uniformed patrol still consumed the bulk of NCYHA's DEP budget: nearly $130 million between 1991 and 1997.[3]

NYCHA, however, aimed to give the residents a large say in how the social program money was spent and what initiatives were developed at each complex. Under the program model, NYCHA's tenant advisory council would recommend residents of a particular development to serve as that complex's DEP administrators, responsible for designing and implementing programs as well as motivating other residents to participate. But the outcomes of this turn-of-the-millennium version of the 1960s enthusiasm for local control suggest that NYCHA's public housing communities had lost much of the leadership that had made them so resilient four decades earlier. By 1991, the tenant-run Drug Elimination Committees were struggling to design and implement their own programs, so NYCHA made available the option of using predesigned programs. By 1994, NYCHA reported that "many of the groups simply lacked the wherewithal to produce effective programs," a finding consistent with HUD evaluations of DEP programs nationwide. Some tenant leaders blamed NYCHA for sidelining their proposals. But as one community center director explained, most resident requests for DEP money were for "one-shot-deals," such as a picnic or talent show, rather than the ongoing or long-lasting programs that were fundable under DEP guidelines.[4]

One finding by the outside evaluators of NYCHA's DEP-funded efforts echoes the Authority's experience in the 1970s. Residents, the analysts discovered, were reluctant to participate in social and community programs for fear of attracting attention to themselves and thus becoming vulnerable to eviction "due to exposure of drugs, domestic violence, or other situation."[5] As the researchers observed, tenants' inventive—and sometimes illicit—strategies for both making ends meet and managing their own political marginalization could throw cold water on the Authority's efforts to expand community policing. The cash on the side coming in from, say, an off-the-books enterprise (legal or not) or an off-the-lease paramour (mild-mannered or not) provided ample incentives for tenants not to help grow community programs that might also invite greater scrutiny on their world. One resident, recalling her fears of eviction in the 1990s, summed up the paradox succinctly: "You don't want no one official knowing about your man or what you gotta do to make do. No way!"[6]

HAPD Officers and the New Community Policing

Housing officers, too, proved reluctant to embrace NYCHA's efforts to revive community policing. Central to the Authority's new strategy was a push to get more officers walking beats within the developments. NYCHA moved to civilianize administrative positions on the force in order to free more uniforms for "vertical patrols." The Authority designated 230 officers as Project Community Officers (PCO) and celebrated them as "old-fashioned 'beat cops.'" In an effort, as Assistant Chief of Department Joseph Keeney described it, "to at least get cops out of their RMPs every now and then," the department also instituted a Park and Walk program that required officers on motorized patrol to park their cruiser at least once during their shift and dedicate an hour to walking foot patrol. As NYCHA acknowledged, these policies would require "a major change" in the HAPD's "orientation and use of resources." Housing's rank and file, for whom more fixed beats on foot held little attraction, balked. As outside consultants found, many took to calling Operation Safe Home—the Authority's principal DEP-funded community policing program—"Operation Stand Here."[7] As former Housing officer Harold Massey recalled, "Standing around saying 'hello' to grandmothers just didn't feel like real policing to most of the new kids."[8] This attitude is summed up in Edward Conlon's *Blue Blood*, an acclaimed memoir in which the NYPD detective compares his experiences in public housing as a beat officer on foot patrol with his later appointment to a special narcotics enforcement detail. Although Conlon became an officer shortly after the 1995 merger of the city's three police forces, he worked as a DEP-funded Project Community Officer in NYCHA complexes as part of the NYPD's continuation of the program. Eventually, however, Conlon got himself transferred to the "more elite" Street Narcotics Enforcement Unit (SNEU). Contrasting his postings, he reflected:

> The change from a beat to SNEU was exhilarating. For one thing, you only dealt with criminals. There were no domestic disputes, EDPs [emotionally disturbed person], or DOAs, the morass of negotiable and non-negotiable difficulties people had with their neighbors or boyfriends or stepchildren. . . . People who had the cops called on them weren't happy to see you; people who called the cops didn't call when they were having a good time. In SNEU, all I did was catch sellers of crack and heroin, and

> catch their customers to show they sold it. Patrol was politics, but narcotics was pure technique.[9]

Much more than a disdain for walking a beat complicated NYCHA's efforts to expand community policing. A 1991 law had changed the relationship between the city's three police departments and obliged Housing—in a desperate bid to preserve morale—to siphon resources away from foot patrol to specialized details that often had little to do with the needs of the residents.

Advocated by the heads of the Transit and Housing PBAs, the new law ended the lottery system of assigning new officers to the three forces. The law's most disruptive provision, however, permitted a large number of those who had been assigned to Transit and Housing against their will to make a "lateral transfer" to NYPD, taking with them their seniority and benefits. NYCHA's management had opposed the law, accurately foreseeing it would unleash a recruiting and retention battle among the three forces. But the rank and file of Housing and Transit saw the legislation as a major victory, briefly filing suit when it appeared their departments might not implement it. Once the policy was in place, Housing officers—not surprisingly—publicly questioned why they should "not take advantage of lateral transfers to the NYPD" and the opportunities that department provided.[10] As Housing officers reported to organizational psychologists studying the force in the 1990s, the men and women in the department fiercely resented the "more numerous and multifaceted career paths" available to the city police.[11]

Just to keep the officers it had, Housing now had to create special details that would provide the same opportunities for advancement that were on offer at the NYPD. The Housing Police thus established twelve new task forces or special details in 1992 and 1993, including an Emergency Rescue Services Unit and a Disorder Control Unit. Chief DeForrest Taylor acknowledged to a reporter in 1991 the natural limits of his efforts to raise morale by creating opportunities beyond foot patrol, joking that when some of his officers had asked for a horse-mounted unit, he had replied, "'We can't get horses on the elevators.'" (This joke became funnier the next year when a number of the department's executive corps inexplicably took a course called "Mounted Unit: History and Practice" with colleagues from Transit and NYPD.) Each new special detail created lowered the status of walking a beat, so, as Officer Massey recalled, the rank and file often viewed being placed on foot patrol as a form of punishment meted out by supervisors. By 1994, NYCHA data revealed that one-third of its officers worked in specialized units outside the precinct-like Public Safety Areas (PSAs) and less than 12 percent devoted every tour to foot patrol—down from 90 percent in 1967.[12]

Some criminologists have labeled NYCHA's DEP-funded efforts at restoring community policing a "missed opportunity," faulting Housing for not using the federal money to fashion new techniques beyond "everyday command-and-control policing."[13] This critique overlooks, however, the situation the department found itself in after 1991. Given the larger history of the relationship between the city's three police forces, it is difficult to imagine how Housing—confronted with restless officers and competing with "Big Blue" for fresh recruits—might have pioneered and implemented a radically new vision of crime prevention. The tangled realities and often-thankless encounters of beat policing already held little appeal for the force's line officers. Trapped by the consequences of a law pushed for and defended in court by its own rank and file, Housing's brass understandably ended up replicating rather than revolutionizing familiar approaches to law enforcement.

"The Merge"

Just as community policing in New York's public housing had largely faded away, it made a larger-than-life (if brief) appearance in the nation's movie theaters. In what is likely the only mass culture representation of the HAPD, Spike Lee's 1995 film *Clockers*—adapted from Richard Price's novel of the same title—contrasts a black Housing officer, "André the Giant," with a variety of mostly white NYPD patrolmen and detectives. In writing the 1992 novel, Price drew extensively upon his experiences growing up in an NYCHA development in the Bronx during the 1950s and early 1960s, but he set the narrative in neighboring Jersey City. The screenplay, coauthored with Lee, placed the story in Brooklyn, a location more familiar to both. Price's childhood years in New York's public housing may help to explain why the film's André personifies so many of the qualities that the Authority's residents had once appreciated about the Housing Police.[14] Like thousands of real HAPD officers over the years, the fictional André lives in the development (Brooklyn's Gowanus Houses playing the role of the film's Nelson Mandela complex). Like the real HAPD officers whom residents still remember, he knows the tenants personally. And like the real Housing officers whose activities are recorded in the archival documents and oral histories used for this study, André collaborates with the project's mothers to enforce community norms. In comparison to André, the film's more two-dimensional NYPD officers are alien and predatory dragoons who descend by squad car upon the housing complex to impose laws the residents find senseless.

By the time of its release, however, the film's comparison of the separate forces had become an anachronism: Giuliani had already merged the city's three police departments that April. Such a merger had eluded New York City mayors dating back to Robert Wagner in the early 1960s.[15] Rarely shy, Giuliani and his biographers have celebrated his success where others have failed as proof of both his managerial competence and the need for governance with a firm hand.[16]

Changing demographics and technology, however, probably mattered more than executive decisiveness. For a quarter century, three phenomena had blocked previous attempts to merge the forces. First, as a careful 1980 study revealed, the costs of integrating the various radio systems of the three departments would have exceeded $30 million, overwhelming the savings that might be achieved by merging their administrations. Second, departmental brass and union chieftains—whose jobs depended on the city having one police force for its streets, one for its subways, and another for its housing developments—had long resisted consolidation.[17] Third, as many analysts had concluded, merging Housing with the NYPD might threaten HUD's sizable security subsidy ($18 million in 1978) to NYCHA, thus saddling the city with additional costs.[18] The first two of these three barriers, however, had largely fallen over the years.

By 1990, new microwave technology had made possible the integration of the three departments' communication and dispatch systems.[19] Similarly, new demographics had softened union resistance. Housing's post–fiscal crisis recruits, having arrived at the department through a lottery and often not captivated by public housing's social mission, often had limited commitment to a separate Housing police force. These younger hires soon outnumbered the older hands, and they pushed their union leadership toward a merger. An early sign of the importance of this demographic shift came in 1990 when the HPBA surveyed its membership and discovered "the sentiment for a merger is overwhelming." Although the HPBA president at the time, Jack Jordan, had previously opposed a merger, he now acknowledged the electoral realities of meeting the "members' demands." The Transit PBA president faced similar pressure and announced shortly after Jordan that his union, too, backed a merger. At both Transit and Housing, however, the department's brass opposed folding their force (and jobs) into the NYPD. Transit Police officials, in fact, took extreme measures to block the merger of the three forces. In the fall of 1990, for example, they tried to disrupt plans for the integration of all police dispatch systems by blocking the contractors working on the project from entering a communications center building. Only the contractor's lawsuit against the city forced the Transit Police officials to stand down and end their gambit of claiming the company lacked the proper permits.[20]

Union support for the merger, however, would waver somewhat the next year. The 1991 law permitting "lateral transfers" mellowed the HPBA membership's demand for a merger as individual officers could now switch forces at will. Equally importantly, though, scandal soon brought down Jordan as the union's president. Investigators picking over the HPBA's books found $60,000 worth of mysterious payments from Jordan to Richard Hartman, a lawyer for the PBAs of all three police forces. On its own, such greasing of palms might easily have been overlooked within the occasionally murky world of police union politics, but Hartman had recently been exposed for blowing away hundreds of thousands of dollars in union dues shooting craps at Trump's Castle during a 1987 Atlantic City excursion. Housing officer Timothy Nickels, running a reform slate, decisively beat Jordan in 1991 and dropped Hartman's firm (which reportedly cut the union's legal expenses in half).[21] The newly installed Nickels also opposed merging the forces—and losing his new union position.

By the time Giuliani formally proposed the merger in 1994, he faced a curious mix of support from former opponents and opposition from former supporters. Joseph Leake, then chief of the Housing Police, supported the merger; the recently booted chief, DeForrest Taylor, came out of retirement to oppose it. Giuliani's newly appointed NYPD commissioner, William Bratton, who, as chief of the Transit Police, had opposed merging the forces, now supported it. Although a long line of NYCHA chairman had opposed the merger on the grounds that the Authority might lose part of its HUD subsidy, Giuliani's new appointee—Chairman Ruben Franco—supported the merger, having been convinced by the mayor that he could wrangle HUD into continuing the funding. The union leadership of Transit and Housing, backing away from their 1990 support, now opposed the merger. Indeed, both PBAs filed lawsuits against the city to block the move. NYCHA resident leaders testifying at a congressional hearing also strongly opposed the merger. At the last minute, the Metropolitan Transportation Authority did an about-face and announced its support—but only after Giuliani strong-armed the agency by threatening to withhold $320 million in city cash.[22]

Giuliani—with a memorandum of understanding from HUD that preserved NYCHA's $70 million in federal security dollars in one hand and a court victory over the Housing and Transit PBAs in the other—consolidated the three departments just before midnight on April 30, 1995. Housing officers in some housing developments wrapped their shields in black bands. "We're mourning the death of Housing," explained one. And for many, Giuliani's annexation did seem the end of community policing in the projects. Former Housing Police chaplain Father Lawrence Lucas, for example, described the merger as representing "the end of respectful policing" by "cops who understood the people." But in many ways "the merge," as Housing officer refer to it, was less the death of community policing within NYCHA than a long-delayed funeral. The Housing Police as a department had for some time ceased to provide residents with something that properly could be called community policing.[23]

The slow dismantling of community policing within NYCHA seems more striking than ever today, because the conditions that gave rise to it have endured, even as much else about public housing has changed. The Authority's original rationale for its distinctive style of policing—vertical foot patrols by officers who knew the residents—had been grounded in public housing's high-rise architecture and superblock settings. But at the end of the 1970s, when community policing began to disintegrate, these distinguishing features remained as they had been in the 1950s when NYCHA inaugurated the approach. No harsh new reality of the urban landscape rendered community policing impractical. Rather, community policing failed in New York's public housing when the veins of popular and institutional support that had fed its success ran dry. The strategy could not withstand beleaguered tenants seeking to protect their stakes in a burgeoning informal economy and striving officers working to imitate the NYPD and escape foot patrol. At the same time, NYCHA hastened the collapse of community policing by adopting policies that seemed to answer the immediate demands of tenants for more cops who responded more quickly, but that ultimately eroded the arrangement of regular "vertical beats" for officers and enforcement of regulations for residents—a system that had long been central to community-based crime fighting in public housing.

It can be sobering to consider that many of the changes that fatally undermined community policing within the Housing Authority arrived not under duress but rather beneath the banner of reform. The "innovation" described in NYCHA's grant to underwrite the Bronx Model Precinct, for example, resulted in discarding as obsolete what police reformers would herald three decades later as the essential feature of "ground-breaking" community policing: foot patrolmen freed from excessive precinct oversight. As one currently popular police science textbook argues in that genre's characteristic phrasing, "there is an absolute necessity to empower line officers so that initiative can be exercised when operating within the philosophy of community policing."[24]

The unintended consequences of legal reform also oblige us to reconsider, in the light of history, aspects of the War on Poverty's legacy. The experience of New York's public housing residents highlights the asymmetrical impact of the OEO's efforts. Legal Services received enough resources to recruit an army of gifted and idealistic young lawyers who were committed to winning new rights for the poor at a time when the courts tended to be friendly to this cause. But funding for the War on Poverty's other and more complex and controversial efforts, such as creating jobs for the poor or remaking the inner city, was rarely adequate to the task. It is not surprising, then, that the results were imbalanced. Fair-hearing rights expanded rapidly to include welfare recipients, students, prisoners, and public housing residents. Wealth and power, however, seldom trickled down. In public housing, the disparity between increasingly robust individual legal rights and increasingly dismal day-to-day circumstances had the effect of making life for the majority of law-abiding tenants worse, not better. Having experienced this lopsidedness firsthand, NYCHA residents learned to draw on the strengths of their community in order to insist on rights for those communities. As they saw—and lived through—the consequences of progressive individual-rights litigation on the one hand, and of conservative penny-pinching on the other, they came to value claims grounded in the cohesiveness of their own neighborhoods over demands for personal freedoms.

Shaped by forces as local as police department hiring policies and as wide reaching as the federal government's War on Poverty, the rise and fall of the Housing Police offers an unexpected case study in the history of urban law enforcement in the post–World War II era. During the 1950s and 1960s, the largely African American and Latino public housing residents in New York City took an active role in local policing. The HAPD's "vertical patrols," enforcement of housing authority regulations, and open communication with residents constituted a form of community policing long before public policy analysts and politicians ever embraced it. Amid sensationalist media reports that can seem to present the "don't snitch" movement as having deep roots and a broad claim on African American culture, there is value in highlighting the homegrown anticrime activism of New York's public housing communities.[25] But community policing in New York's public housing, forged by happenstance and galvanized by the interlocking interests of both the residents and the officers, proved fragile as those interests diverged. The strategy was vulnerable from many directions: from the economic and political forces within the HAPD and within the policed communities, as well as from larger forces in the city, state, and nation.

For New York's public housing residents, the unraveling of community policing in the late 1970s and early 1980s could hardly have come at a worse time. In those same years, America's criminal justice system took what numerous scholars have characterized as a punitive turn. Since the early twentieth century, the corrections system—except in the South—had been made up of government agencies and private organizations that aimed to prepare offenders to return to society. Americans took for granted that crime was to be managed by such specialized institutions, which claimed to have the technical expertise to find the right balance between law enforcement and correctional treatment. But as the 1970s closed, the criminal justice system—wracked from within by fears that "nothing work[ed]" and assaulted from without by populist demands to stop coddling wrongdoers—rapidly shifted gears from rehabilitation to punishment.[26]

With the dawn of the Reagan administration in 1981, declining social service funding starved into near extinction the kinds of institutions—clinics, employment centers, and community organizations—that had once provided a buffer between law enforcement and vulnerable citizens in poor neighborhoods. Shifting national budget priorities also led to new policing techniques, including mass arrests and covert surveillance, that disrupted traditional uses of public space in the inner city, alienating many whose frayed budgets and cramped quarters led them to mingle in playgrounds, street corners, and hallways. Without their neighborhood cops to temper the new policies, New York's public housing residents now had to face alone the small indignities, outright abuse, and community devastation that occur when law enforcement relies almost entirely on arrest and incarceration to maintain order in a city's poorest districts.[27] Assessing the change in the policing of New York's public housing over four decades, Fredrich "Butch" Curtis, a former NYCHA resident and retired Department of Corrections employee, recalled his relationship with a Housing officer in the early 1960s:

> When I talked with him, I wouldn't see a uniform because . . . he would say: "I'm a man and you might be one too. . . . I'm trying to help you." So, he was like our big brother that pointed me away from those bad elements that were starting to enter the projects. . . . Tell me who is gonna do that now?[28]

Curtis's experience as an adolescent—and question as an adult—poignantly encapsulate how much was lost when community policing as a regular practice, and later, the HAPD as a distinct department, vanished from New York's housing projects and the longest experiment with neighborhood cops in postwar urban America came to an end. Meditating on the forty-year arc of the Housing Police, former NYCHA resident and HAPD officer Arthur Brown observed, "Community policing? We invented that! And I guess we were the first to have it fail on us."

Epilogue

"The merge," as former HAPD officers call it, did not mean the end of cops being assigned to the Authority's developments. The Housing Bureau, a new division within the New York Police Department, absorbed the HAPD's duties. The roughly 1,800 uniformed officers detailed to the Bureau are now entrusted with the task of providing for the security of the city's sprawling public housing. Although much of the community ethos of the Housing Authority Police Department's best years continues to thrive in the Bureau, there are more troubling signs of rupture between tenants and police as well.

Getting a handle on the HAPD's institutional successor presents a bit of challenge to the outside researcher. The merge cut off the flow of documents from the police in NYCHA's complexes to its managers in the central office and, ultimately, to the holdings of the La Guardia and Wagner Archives at La Guardia Community College. But that archival trove—uniquely deep for a modern police department—grows increasingly shallow after 1990 and stops abruptly in 1995 with the merge. Analyzing the Housing Bureau's current workings, then, differs little from grasping those of any other police force, and police departments are, for good reasons and bad, famously stingy with their information.

No surprise, then, that the story of policing and crime in NYCHA, since the merge, frequently depends on who gets to do the telling. As some former HAPD officers who continued to work with the Housing Bureau describe it, the Bureau suffers from an organizational culture obsessed with making arrests at the expense of community policing and NYCHA residents. Researchers assessing the Authority's DEP program between 2000 and 2003 reported that every one of the Housing Bureau officers they interviewed "referred to a push from police command to effect a minimum number of summons and arrests." As one cop described it to the researchers:

> There is always a push for numbers. Some officers will do anything to get their summons and some of it is petty. That makes the community not like us. [As a community-policing officer] I am supposed to be a buffer with the community. But at the same time [the police department] wants a certain level of production from me.[1]

Another officer pointed to the mismatch between the community-policing mission of the Housing Bureau and the dispensing of everyday rewards to cops: "If you expect me . . . to go to my project and make friends with everybody, that is fine. But at the end of the month, when I don't have an arrest, explain to me why I can't get a day off if my kid has a game or birthday." One former HAPD officer who worked with the Bureau until her recent retirement concurred, arguing that the Bureau "won't admit there's a quota, but there is."[2] If the Housing Bureau has hit upon a way to avoid the HAPD's long struggle to align institutional incentives with community policing's goals, no one has told the rank-and-file officers working NYCHA's complexes.

The Housing Bureau's brass, not surprisingly, see it differently. They point to the declining crime statistics in the city's public housing as proof of their continuing success. And at first glance, the Bureau's numbers are hard to argue with. In the first decade after the merge, violent crimes in public housing plunged 44 percent. Violent crime rates, however, also fell by 48 percent in the city at large in those same years. To the Bureau's credit, crime on NYCHA grounds no longer increases even as the rest of New York becomes safer, as it did during the late 1980s and early 1990s. But it is that growing citywide safety, ironically, that can make NYCHA's crime rates stick out. With New York's homicide rate at a low not seen by city residents since John F. Kennedy was president, public housing's very real crime drop can seem less meaningful.[3]

NYCHA's slice of New York's index crimes is now, again, lower than its slice of the city's total population, but the Authority continues to suffer from more than its share of three distinct types of violent crimes. NYPD statistics reveal that criminals disproportionately target public housing when trafficking drugs, engaging in gun violence, or committing sexual offenses. In 2003, although NYCHA tenants represented only 5 percent of New York's population, 11 percent of the city's murders and rapes, as well as 16 percent of its shootings, took place on NYCHA property. In addition, police believed roughly 65 percent of the shootings on the grounds of the Authority's complexes stemmed in some way from drugs—underscoring the role of the illicit economy in public housing violence.[4]

Tellingly, the Housing Bureau has sought to battle such crimes by trying to recapture aspects of the policing strategies that prevailed in NYCHA's complexes before the mid-1970s. But the Bureau now often turns to new tools to accomplish long-standing goals. Hoping, for example, to reduce NYCHA's criminal population without relying on the Authority's screening of tenants (which covers only formal tenants rather than "ghost" residents and guests), the Bureau implemented a policy called Operation Safe Housing (OSH) in 2004. OSH employs a new trespass policy—worked out with NYCHA—that takes aim at drug offenders. Under OSH, those arrested for felony narcotics charges on Authority property are legally barred from NYCHA grounds even as their names enter a database made available to the police. If discovered stepping foot back on any Housing Authority complex for any reason, they are subject to rearrest and prosecution. As New York's Criminal Justice Coordinator, John Feinblatt, argued, OSH aims to "deprive drug dealers of the places where they like to do business."[5]

Whatever the intentions of OSH's architects, this anticrime policy may have had unintended consequence out in the field. As several former HAPD officers subsequently detailed to the Housing Bureau confessed off the record, OSH provides a powerful incentive for cops patrolling the city's public housing to do a "stop-and-frisk." Known as a *Terry* stop, after the 1968 Supreme Court case *Terry v. Ohio*, this police action requires only that the officer have a "reasonable suspicion" of wrongdoing rather than the much higher threshold of "probable cause" demanded by either an arrest or a personal search. In fact, it doesn't take much for a cop to justify a *Terry* stop and do a brisk pat down in search of drugs or weapons. And when, on NYCHA property, a *Terry* detainee—even one carrying no contraband—shows up in the OSH database, an easy, career-boosting "collar" can fall into an officer's hands. As activists argue, *Terry* stops already provide an enticement for cops hoping to get lucky while still playing it safe; in 2008, for example, NYPD officers stopped 531,159 people citywide—more than five times the number in 2002—and found a weapon or other illegal items in only 2.6 percent of the stops.[6] OSH raises those stakes. It seems plausible that OSH's puffed-up rewards for stop-and-frisks has spurred a more heavy-handed surveillance of minority males in public housing—and a souring of relations with the police.

For their part, tenants generally don't wonder whether the cops are stopping residents more frequently or if many NYCHA teens bristle with barely contained resentment. Residents simply recount such seeming neighborhood truths matter-of-factly. A 2008 report by the Community Oversight of Policing Project of the New York Lawyers for the Public Interest tries to capture such community sentiments. Thirty percent of the tenants surveyed at Harlem's Thomas Jefferson Houses (1,487 units), for example, reported being charged with trespassing despite the fact they lived in the complex; 70 percent reported being repeatedly stopped by police "when simply coming and going around their homes." Similarly, more than four out of five of the complex's residents with children reported being "very dissatisfied with the relationship between

NYPD officers and their children." The researchers uncovered similar accounts from Brooklyn's Walt Whitman Houses (1,636 units). The study may end up packing some legal punch. As this book was being prepared for publication, a district court agreed to hear *Davis et al. v. City of New York*, a federal class-action suit challenging the NYPD over stops and trespass arrests on NYCHA grounds. Even the threat of this legal action may have recently prodded NYPD's brass into rethinking their strategies. After meeting with tenant groups in late 2009 and early 2010, NYPD Commissioner Ray Kelly reportedly instructed his staff to revise the department's handbook for Housing Bureau officers in ways that placed policy limits on trespass arrests.[7]

With less controversy, OSH also created a Special Hearing Part in the Authority's administrative hearing system that deals exclusively—and thus in theory faster and more efficiently—with NYCHA's most unruly residents: those who commit gun felonies, serious sex crimes, and the highest-level drug offenses. This fast-track evictions system attempts to rid public housing communities of those who pose the greatest risk to their neighbors and permits NYCHA to better target its increasingly scarce resources. The new procedures, despite the Housing Bureau's claims to the contrary, aren't a particularly novel solution—they hearken back, in fact, to the Authority's more intrusive practices before the *Escalera* consent decree. The approach has, a number of tenant leaders told me, reduced residents' angry perceptions that NYCHA no longer meets its obligations to the law-abiding.[8]

The Housing Bureau's proudest recent innovation may be the Juvenile Robbery Intervention Program (JRIP), which tracks juvenile offenders and then, unusually for law enforcement, takes a crack at steering them straight. Revealingly, JRIP replicates and institutionalizes the type of informal community guidance and knowledge that once represented the best of the HAPD's policing practices before the mid-1970s. First piloted in Brownsville, Brooklyn, in 2007, JRIP is the brainchild of the Bureau's impressive chief, Joanne Jaffe. With a master's in forensic psychology and three decades of police work under her belt, the Bureau's chief is no one's idea of a social worker masquerading as a cop. ("She's the real deal," a number of Bureau members assured me). But JRIP is precisely the sort of grassroots, community-based law enforcement that even police critics can get behind.

JRIP corrals the knowledge and resources of various city agencies—schools, law enforcement, and social services—in order to present teens arrested for robbery with a series of what are hoped will be life-changing carrots and sticks. To help such kids ("at-risk juveniles" in official parlance) avoid straying deeper into criminality, Housing Bureau officers conduct home visits, allowing the cops—Smith & Wessons riding their hips—to connect the teens and their families to a variety of social services and employment possibilities. But JRIP also relies on the efforts of district attorneys, probation and truant officers, and family court to ensure that JRIP youths know that if they are arrested again, they will face strict punishment. According to the Bureau, its Brooklyn JRIP pilot yielded real results. The 154 kids who ended up in the program had racked up over 180 robbery arrests among them in 2006. After a year of JRIP's tough love, however, the same group appeared only 29 times in NYPD's robbery arrest statistics. Impressed, Commissioner Kelly expanded the project into the Rockaways in 2008 and East Harlem the next year. Innovative police programs have a history of celebrated early successes followed by bureaucratic inertia and culminating in quietly shelved evaluations apt to use words like *disappointing* and *inconclusive.* It is fair, then, to wonder just how well JRIP will fare over the long haul. But it is also clear that more than a glimmer of what tenants and officers had forged together during the HAPD's four decades of operation continues to shape and inspire the policing of New York's public housing.

NOTES

INTRODUCTION

1. Mary and Tricia Alfson, interview by author and Nicholas Alfson, 15 December 2006, tape of interview in author's possession.
2. References to HAPD officers frequently appear in the informal literature produced for "Old Timer's Day" reunions at NYCHA developments. See, for example, the fond memories of the Amsterdam Houses' police officers "Bruzie, Kelly, and Luigi" in Spence Mayfield, "The Way We Were," *Reunion '87 Journal* (New York: Amsterdam Reunion Committee, 1987), and *Reflections: Celebrating 60 Years of Shared Love and Still Going Strong* (New York: Best Graphics, 2007), both in the author's possession.
3. For the broad support for community policing, see David Garland, *The Culture of Control: Crime and Social Order in Contemporary Society* (Chicago: University of Chicago Press, 2001), 125–127, and Michael Massing, "The Blue Revolution," *New York Review of Books*, 19 November 1988, 32–36; for Harris Polling data documenting the breadth of public awareness of community policing, see Stephen Mastrofski, "Community Policing: A Skeptical View," in *Police Innovation: Contrasting Perspectives*, ed. David Weisburd and Anthony Braga (New York: Cambridge University Press, 2006), 69.
4. Confident assertions of the effectiveness of community policing as a strategy include Malcolm Sparrow, Mark Moore, and David Kennedy, *Beyond 911: A New Era for Policing* (New York: Basic Books, 1990); David Bayley, *What Works in Policing* (New York: Oxford University Press, 1997); David Weisburd, Anthony Braga, Elin Waring, William Spelman, Lorraine Mazerolle, and Frank Gajewski, "Problem-Oriented Policing in Violent Crime Places: A Randomized Controlled Experiment," *Criminology* 37, no. 4 (1999): 89, and W. G. Skogan, ed., *Community Policing: Can It Work?* (Belmont, CA: Wadsworth, 2004); community policing's more aggressive cousin, broken-windows policing, is extolled in George Kelling and Catherine Coles, *Fixing Broken Windows: Restoring Order and Reducing Crime in Our Communities* (New York: Simon & Schuster, 1996).
5. Wendell E. Pritchett, *Brownsville, Brooklyn: Blacks, Jews, and the Changing Face of the Ghetto* (Chicago: University of Chicago Press, 2002), 89.
6. A sophisticated recent study of one department's experiment with community policing can be found in Peter Manning's ethnography of "Western" (his pseudonym for the midwestern city where he did his fieldwork) in *Policing Contingencies* (Chicago: University of Chicago Press, 2003). But as with other studies of other departments, the recentness of the adoption of community policing in "Western" meant Manning's analysis addressed what was a rather brief experience—three years—in both the department and the city's histories. A longer and more quantitative study can be found in W. G. Skogan, *Community Policing in Chicago, Year Ten: An Evaluation of*

Chicago's Alternative Policing Strategy (Springfield: Illinois Criminal Justice Information Authority, 2004).

7. For the term's rise in popular media, see Regina G. Lawrence, *The Politics of Force: Media and the Construction of Police Brutality* (Berkeley: University of California Press, 2000), 158–159.
8. For operating definitions of community policing as the phrase is understood within police departments, see Harry W. More, W. Fred Wegener, and Larry S. Miller, "Community Policing: Serving the Neighborhoods," *Effective Police Supervision* (Cincinnati: Anderson Publishing, 2003). See also Bernard E. Harcourt, *Illusion of Order: The False Promise of Broken Windows Policing* (Cambridge, MA: Harvard University Press, 2001).
9. "Elements of the Security Strategy for the New York City Housing Authority," 15 January 1992, folder 1, box 100B3, New York City Housing Authority Papers, La Guardia and Wagner Archives, La Guardia Community College (hereafter NYCHA), 4.
10. For an argument fusing faith in community gardens and community policing, see Walter Thabit, *How East New York Became a Ghetto* (New York: New York University Press, 2003), 225–227, 50–51. A number of pedestrian malls, including the Granville Mall in Vancouver, British Columbia, Canada, emerged out of early police-community conferences; see Harvey M. Rubenstein, *Pedestrian Malls, Streetscapes, and Urban Spaces* (New York: Wiley, 1992), 215–216; for a facile skewering of liberal sensibilities and pedestrian malls, see David Brooks, *Bobos in Paradise: The New Upper Class and How They Got There* (New York: Simon & Schuster, 2000), 104–105; for federal grants and the number of departments that claim to practice community policing, see John L. Worrall and Tomislav V. Kovandzic, "Cops, Grants and Crime Revisited," *Criminology* 45, no. 1 (2007): 159–190; for community policing and terrorism, see David Rieff, "Policing Terrorism," *New York Times Sunday Magazine*, 22 July 2007.
11. Jerome G. Miller, *Search and Destroy: African-American Males in the Criminal Justice System* (New York: Cambridge University Press, 1996), 110; W. H. Matthews, "Policing Distressed Public Housing Developments," *Public Management* 75, no. 7 (1993): 2–8.
12. See, for example, Jack Greene Alex Piquero, James Fyfe, Robert J. Kane, and Patricia Collins, "Implementing Community Policing in Public Housing Developments in Philadelphia: Some Early Results," in *Community Policing: Contemporary Readings*, ed. Geoffrey P. Alpert and Alex R. Piquero (Long Grove, IL: Waveland, 2000), 95–112.
13. For recent critiques of community policing's advocates use of "community," see Peter K. Manning, *Police Work: The Social Organization of Policing* (Cambridge, MA: MIT Press, 1977), 13; Michael Berger, "A Tale of Two Targets: Limitations of Community Anticrime Actions," in *Community Justice: An Emerging Field*, ed. David R. Karp (Lanham, MD: Rowman & Littlefield, 1998), 137–166; and Mark E. Correia, *Citizen Involvement: How Community Factors Affect Progressive Policing* (Washington, DC: Police Executive Research Forum [PERF], 2000), chapter 2; the argument, however, predates community police, see Albert J. Reiss, *The Police and the Public* (New Haven, CT: Yale University Press, 1971), 209–210. A summary of nearly a century of sociological thinking regarding the inapplicability of "community" to modern American neighborhoods, particularly urban ones, can be found in Nicole P. Marwell, *Bargaining for Brooklyn: Community Organizations in the Entrepreneurial City* (Chicago: University of Chicago Press, 2007), 13–19. For a critique of "Mayberry" nostalgia, see William Lyons, *The Politics of Community Policing: Rearranging the Power to Punish, Law, Meaning, and Violence* (Ann Arbor: University of Michigan Press, 1999), chapter 8.

14. For the dynamic quality and surprising power of tenant organizations, see Terry Williams and William Kornblum, "Public Housing Projects as Successful Environments for Adolescent Development," in *The Anthropology of Lower Income Urban Enclaves: The Case of East Harlem*, ed. Judith Freidenberg (New York: New York Academy of Sciences, 1995), 137–152.

15. Wesley Skogan, *Police and Community in Chicago: A Tale of Three Cities* (New York: Oxford University Press, 2006), 141.

16. Dorothy Shields, interview by Edward Paulino, John Jay College, 16 August 2008, tape of interview in author's possession.

17. For the New Deal, see Lizabeth Cohen, *Making a New Deal: Industrial Workers in Chicago, 1919–1939* (New York: Cambridge University Press, 1990). For the War on Poverty, see Annelise Orleck, *Storming Caesar's Palace: How Black Mothers Fought Their Own Poverty* (Boston: Beacon Press, 2005); Premilla Nadasen, *Welfare Warriors the Welfare Rights Movement in the United States* (New York: Routledge, 2005); Felicia Kornbluh, *The Battle for Welfare Rights Politics and Poverty in Modern America* (Philadelphia: University of Pennsylvania Press, 2007).

18. For both the emergence of the idea of a "culture of poverty" and its intellectual trajectory, see Alice O'Connor, *Poverty Knowledge: Social Science, Social Policy, and the Poor in Twentieth-Century U.S. History* (Princeton, NJ: Princeton University Press, 2001), chapter 4. Even in its crudest early formulations—such as Oscar Lewis, *La Vida: A Puerto Rican Family in the Culture of Poverty—San Juan and New York* (New York: Random House, 1966)—this notion was broadly understood at the time as an argument for reform, not inaction. Despite the firestorm that famously greeted the most controversial of these arguments, Daniel Moynihan's 1965 *The Negro Family: The Case for National Action*, Moynihan merely distilled the consensus among social scientists. Subsequent scholarship, even from the political left, echoed aspects of these earlier interpretations. William J. Wilson, for example, has written: "Lower-income blacks had little involvement in civil rights politics up to the mid-1960s"; see William J. Wilson, *The Declining Significance of Race: Blacks and Changing American Institutions* (Chicago: University of Chicago Press, 1978), 735. The pathologies of black communities after the Great Migration to the North play prominent roles in Nicholas Lemann, *The Promised Land: The Great Black Migration and How It Changed America* (New York: Alfred A. Knopf, 1991), 120–121, 55.

19. Daryl Michael Scott, *Contempt and Pity: Social Policy and the Image of the Damaged Black Psyche, 1880–1996* (Chapel Hill: University of North Carolina Press, 1997). The best-known argument that public assistance exacerbated rather than ameliorated poverty is Charles A. Murray, *Losing Ground: American Social Policy, 1950–1980* (New York: Basic Books, 1984), although an early instance can be found in Edward C. Banfield, *The Unheavenly City: The Nature and Future of Our Urban Crisis* (Boston: Little, Brown, 1970). A good taste of this logic as it was applied to public housing can be found in the televised debate on CNN between Melissa Pardue of the Heritage Foundation and Judith Goldiner of the Legal Aid Society, aired 22 August 2003. The perceived need to restore public housing residents' lost sense of personal responsibility can best be seen in the Title V requirements of the Quality Housing and Work Responsibility Act of 1998 specifying, "Every adult resident of public housing will be required to perform eight hours of community service each month." As others have noted, proponents calling for public housing residents to work in return for their subsidy rarely insist recipients of mortgage deductions on private housing do the same, see Thomas W. Hanchett, "The

Other 'Subsidized Housing': Federal Aid to Suburbanization, 1940s–1960s," in *From Tenements to the Taylor Homes: In Search of an Urban Housing Policy in Twentieth-Century America*, ed. John F. Bauman, Roger Biles, and Kristin M. Szylvian (University Park: Pennsylvania State University Press, 2000), 163–205.

20. Robert O. Self, *American Babylon: Race and the Struggle for Postwar Oakland: Politics and Society in Twentieth-Century America* (Princeton, NJ: Princeton University Press, 2003), 178.

21. Jeanne Theoharis and Komozi Woodward, eds., *Groundwork: Local Black Freedom Movements in America* (New York: New York University Press, 2005), 5; John Dittmer, *Local People: The Struggle for Civil Rights in Mississippi* (Urbana: University of Illinois Press, 1994). Scholars have recently documented the ways in which Black Power embraced local organizing as well as media spectacle; see Peniel E. Joseph, *The Black Power Movement: Rethinking the Civil Rights–Black Power Era* (New York: Routledge, 2006), and his "The Black Power Movement: A State of the Field," *Journal of American History* 96, no. 3 (December 2009): 751–776.

22. Rhonda Y. Williams, *The Politics of Public Housing: Black Women's Struggles against Urban Inequality* (New York: Oxford University Press, 2004); Roberta M. Feldman and Susan Stall, *The Dignity of Resistance: Women Residents' Activism in Chicago Public Housing* (New York: Cambridge University Press, 2004); Lisa Levenstein, *A Movement without Marches: African American Women and the Politics of Poverty in Postwar Philadelphia* (Chapel Hill: University of North Carolina Press, 2009).

23. See, for example, "Press Release," 12 December 1992, folder 5, box 1100B5, NYCHA.

24. This notion has been most influentially encapsulated and pushed by Allen J. Matusow, *The Unraveling of America: A History of Liberalism in the 1960s* (New York: Harper & Row, 1984); Jonathan Rieder, *Canarsie: The Jews and Italians of Brooklyn against Liberalism* (Cambridge, MA: Harvard University Press, 1985); and Thomas Byrne Edsall and Mary D. Edsall, *Chain Reaction: The Impact of Race, Rights, and Taxes on American Politics* (New York: Norton, 1992).

25. Tom Wolfe, *Radical Chic & Mau-Mauing the Flak Catchers* (New York: Farrar, Straus, & Giroux, 1970).

26. Arnold R. Hirsch, *Making the Second Ghetto: Race and Housing in Chicago, 1940–1960* (Chicago: University of Chicago Press, 1998); Thomas J. Sugrue, *The Origins of the Urban Crisis: Race and Inequality in Postwar Detroit* (Princeton, NJ: Princeton University Press, 1996). See also Matthew D. Lassiter, *The Silent Majority: Suburban Politics in the Sunbelt South* (Princeton, NJ: Princeton University Press, 2006), introduction.

27. Lassiter, *The Silent Majority*; Kevin Michael Kruse, *White Flight: Atlanta and the Making of Modern Conservatism: Politics and Society in Twentieth-Century America* (Princeton, NJ: Princeton University Press, 2005).

28. Alex S. Vitale, *City of Disorder: How the Quality of Life Campaign Transformed New York Politics* (New York: New York University Press, 2008), 54; for local versus national liberal agendas, see Guian A. McKee, *The Problem of Jobs: Liberalism, Race, and Deindustrialization in Philadelphia* (Chicago: University of Chicago Press, 2008); for the persisting importance of community uplift, see Clarence Taylor, *Black Religious Intellectuals: The Fight for Equality from Jim Crow to the Twenty-First Century* (New York: Routledge, 2002), 40–42, and Thomas J. Sugrue, *Sweet Land of Liberty: The Forgotten Struggle for Civil Rights in the North* (New York: Random House, 2008), 368–369; for liberalism and the valorizing of personal autonomy, see Mark V. Tushnet, *The Rights Revolution in the Twentieth Century* (Washington, DC: American Historical Association, 2009). Relying on a federally funded

legal infrastructure, liberal activists nationwide contested public schools' authority to impose discipline on students, bringing at least 1,204 court challenges between 1965 and 1975; see Richard Arum, *Judging School Discipline: The Crisis of Moral Authority* (Cambridge, MA: Harvard University Press, 2003).

29. *Escalera v. New York City Housing Authority*, 67 Civ. 4307 (S.D.N.Y, 1971).

30. Michael Massing, *The Fix* (New York: Simon & Schuster, 1998), 40–41; Roger Starr, "Which of the Poor Shall Live in Public Housing," *Public Interest* 23 (Spring 1971): 116–125; Valerie D. White, "Modifying the Escalera Consent Decree: A Case Study on the Application of the *Rufo* Test," *Fordham Urban Law Journal* 23 (1996).

31. Massing, *The Fix*, 40–41; Starr, "Which of the Poor Shall Live in Public Housing"; White, "Modifying the Escalera Consent Decree: A Case Study on the Application of the *Rufo* Test"; Ross Sandler and David Schoenbrod, *Democracy by Decree: What Happens When Courts Run Government* (New Haven, CT: Yale University Press, 2003), 128–129.

32. For an example, see Sophie Body-Gendrot, *The Social Control of Cities?: A Comparative Perspective* (Oxford: Blackwell Publishers, 2000), 35.

33. For NYCLU's objection to video surveillance in public housing, see David M. Halbfinger, "As Surveillance Cameras Peer, Some Wonder If They Also Pry," *New York Times*, 22 February 1998; see also American Civil Liberties Union [ACLU], "NYCLU Urges New York City Council to Support Civilian Complaint Review Board and to Reject Increased Surveillance" (ACLU press release, 2006).

34. Quoted in Joan Shepard, "TV Screening Crime at City Housing Project," *New York Daily News*, n.d., in collected press clippings, folder 4, box 90A5, NYCHA; see also "Vote Vote Vote," 1979, folder 3, box 90A5, NYCHA. For the name change of Mae Miller's organization to the African Liberation Center, see Pauline Dortch to Blanca Cedeno, 12 May 1977, folder 4, box 90 A5, NYCHA, and accompanying membership card.

35. Marie Gottschalk, *The Prison and the Gallows: The Politics of Mass Incarceration in America* (New York: Cambridge University Press, 2006), 8–10, 13, chapter 5.

36. Samuel Walker, "'Broken Windows' and Fractured History: The Use and Misuse of History in Recent Police Patrol Analysis," *Justice Quarterly* 1 (1984): 53.

37. The classic expression of this tripartite division is Malcom K. Sparrow, Mark H. Moore, and David M. Kennedy, *Beyond 911: A New Era for Policing* (New York: Basic Books, 1990), chapter 2. Historians of policing generally concur with this chronology but question the accuracy of its assessments of law enforcement for both the political and reform eras.

38. Robert M. Fogelson, *Big-City Police* (Cambridge, MA: Harvard University Press, 1977), 17.

39. Sparrow, Moore, and Kennedy, *Beyond 911*, 34; Fogelson, *Big-City Police*, 16.

40. Samuel Walker, *The Police in America: An Introduction* (New York: McGraw-Hill, 1999), 26–27.

41. See for example, Michael Palmiotto, *Community Policing: A Policing Strategy for the 21st Century* (Gaithersburg, MD: Aspen, 2000), chapter 1. The same notion has also recently been invoked to justify more recent "intelligence-driven" policing strategies; see Heather Mac Donald, "The N.Y.P.D. Diaspora," *City Journal* 18, no. 3 (2008): 3–5.

42. Historians of policing generally distinguish between two waves of reform: an earlier, elite-driven effort originating with civic, religious, and commercial groups and a second wave, starting in the early twentieth century, embraced by the police themselves. The second wave is generally believed to have produced deeper and more durable change. See Fogelson, *Big-City Police*, 166–182; Eric H. Monkkonen, *Police in Urban*

America, 1860–1920 (New York: Cambridge University Press, 1981), 148–150. The phrase "reform era" is broadly used to describe both waves.

43. Walker, *The Police in America*, 31–32.

44. Sparrow, Moore, and Kennedy, *Beyond 911*, 38.

45. Manning, *Police Work*; see also Walker, "'Broken Windows' and Fractured History," 60; the various studies of police routine are reviewed in Victor E. Kappeler, Mark Blumberg, and Gary W. Potter, *The Mythology of Crime and Criminal Justice* (Prospect Heights, IL: Waveland Press, 1993), 212.

46. Police reformer August Vollmer developed the uniform system of crime classification and today known as the Uniform Crime Reports, see Walker, *The Police in America*, 18.

47. For a discussion of the role of arrests in measuring the value of individual officers at the high-point of "reform" policing, see Arthur Niederhoffer, *Behind the Shield: The Police in Urban Society* (Garden City, NY: Doubleday, 1967), 74–75.

48. Initially, even President Johnson was among those who believed the riots to be a product of conspiracy. See Thomas J. Bray, "Reading America the Riot Act: The Kerner Report and Its Culture of Violence," *Policy Review* (Winter 1988): 32–36. The 1967 riots, the public response, and the Kerner Commission are discussed in Michael W. Flamm, *Law and Order: Street Crime, Civil Unrest, and the Crisis of Liberalism in the 1960s* (New York: Columbia University Press, 2005), chapters 5 and 6; National Advisory Commission on Civil Disorders, *Report* (New York: Bantam Books, 1968), 157–159.

49. President's Commission on Law Enforcement and Administration of Justice, *The Challenge of Crime in a Free Society: Report: The Police* (Washington, DC: Government Printing Office, 1967), 99–100.

50. The Kansas City (Missouri) Patrol Experiment's conclusions faced significant academic criticism in later years. See, most recently, David Weisburd and Lawrence Sherman, "General Deterrent Effects of Police Patrol in Crime 'Hot Spots': A Randomized Trial Experiment," *Justice Quarterly* 12, no. 4 (1995): 541–571; George Kelling, T. Pate, D. Dieckman, and C. Brown, "The Kansas City Preventive Patrol Experiment: A Technical Report" (Washington, DC: Police Foundation, 1974); William Spelman, Dale K. Brown, and National Institute of Justice (U.S.), *Calling the Police: Citizen Reporting of Serious Crime*, National Institute of Justice Research Report (Washington, DC: U.S. Dept. of Justice, National Institute of Justice, 1984), 74; the various studies of police response time are reviewed in Walker, *The Police in America*, 82–83. Carl B. Klockars, "The Rhetoric of Community Policing," in *Community Policing: Rhetoric or Reality*, ed. Jack R. Greene and Stephen D. Mastrofski (New York: Praeger, 1988), 131.

51. Peter W. Greenwood and Joan R. Petersilia, "The Criminal Investigation Process Volume I: Summary and Policy Implications" (RAND Corporation, 1975); Larry J. Siegel, *Criminology* (New York: Thomson Wadsworth, 2005), 523.

52. Samuel Walker, "The Origins of the Police-Community Relations Movement: The 1940s," *Criminal Justice History* 1 (1980): 225–246.

53. Egon Bittner, "The Impact of Police-Community Relations on the Police System," in *Community Relations and the Administration of Justice*, ed. David Patrick Geary (New York: John Wiley and Son, 1972), 371. See also George L. Kelling and Mark H. Moore, "The Evolving Strategy of Policing" (Washington, DC: U.S. Dept. of Justice, National Institute of Justice, 1988), chapter 3.

54. Police departments in New York, Cincinnati, Detroit, and Kansas City (Missouri) all briefly embraced team policing—also known as "community sector policing," "beat

commander project," and "basic car plan"—partly as the result of Police Foundation. See Lawrence Sherman, Catherine H. Milton, and Thomas V. Kelly, "Team Policing: Seven Case Studies" (Washington, DC: Police Foundation, 1973); for a discussion of the longest of such experiments, in St. Paul, see Kelling and Moore, "The Evolving Strategy of Policing," chapter 3, and Marilyn D. McShane and Franklin P. Williams, *Law Enforcement Operations and Management* (New York: Garland, 1997), 37.

55. National Research Council Committee to Review Research on Police Policy and Practices, "Fairness and Effectiveness in Policing: The Evidence" (Washington, DC: National Research Council Committee to Review Research on Police Policy and Practices, 2004).
56. Herman Goldstein, *Problem-Oriented Policing* (Philadelphia: Temple University Press, 1990), 14; see also Herman Goldstein, "Improving Policing: A Problem-Oriented Approach," *Crime & Delinquency* 25 (1979).
57. Mark Harrison Moore, "Problem-Solving and Community Policing," in *Modern Policing*, ed. Michael Tonry and Norval Morris (Chicago: University of Chicago Press, 1992), 123, 26.
58. Kelling and Moore, "The Evolving Strategy of Policing," 19.
59. George L. Kelling and Mary A. Wycoff, "Evolving Strategy of Policing: Case Studies of Strategic Change" (Washington, DC: National Criminal Justice Reference Service, 2001), 14–19. At times, the borrowings from the corporate world were explicit. For example, police supervisors in Madison, Wisconsin, received training in "Total Quality Management." Ibid., 15.
60. George Kelling, "Newark Foot Patrol Experiment" (Washington, DC: Police Foundation, 1981), 122–124.
61. James Q. Wilson and George L. Kelling, "Broken Windows," *Atlantic Monthly*, March 1982, 31.
62. Ibid., 31, 33.
63. Researchers, using not the impressions of select residents but videotapes of Chicago streets and observers trained at the National Opinion Research Center, found no significant correlation between visible signs of disorder and rates of neighborhood crime, although disorder and poverty were closely linked. See Stephen W. Raudenbush and Robert J. Sampson, "Seeing Disorder: Neighborhood Stigma and the Social Construction of 'Broken Windows,'" *Social Psychology Quarterly* 67, no. 4 (2004): 319–342. Likewise, a study of Moving to Opportunity—a federal program that provides vouchers for families living in public housing communities characterized by high rates of crime and social disorder to move to less disadvantaged and disorderly communities—documented that living in such communities did not, on balance, lead to reductions in criminal behavior for young males but did partially reduce such behavior in females. See Bernard E. Harcourt and Jens Ludwig, "Broken Windows: New Evidence from New York City and a Five City Social Experiment," *University of Chicago Law Review* 73 (2006): 271–320. See also Jeffrey R. Kling, Jens Ludwig, and Lawrence F. Katz, "Neighborhood Effects on Crime for Female and Male Youth: Evidence from a Randomized Housing Voucher Experiment," *Quarterly Journal of Economics* 120, no. 1 (2005): 87–130. The literature that sees a loss of civil liberties with the implementation of "broken windows" is now vast. A good example of the more popular accounts can be found in Christian Parenti, *Lockdown America: Police and Prisons in the Age of Crisis* (London and New York: Verso, 2001), chapter 4. For a scholarly take on the issue, see Harcourt, *Illusion of Order*, chapter 5.

64. Kelling and Moore, "The Evolving Strategy of Policing," 9–17.

65. See for example, Skogan, *Police and Community in Chicago*, 10; see also David Weisburd and John E. Eck, "What Can Police Do to Reduce Crime, Disorder, and Fear?" *Annals of the American Academy of Political and Social Science* 593, no. 42 (2004): 42–65.

66. Patricia Collins, Jack R. Greene, Robert Kane, Robert Stokes, and Alex Piquero, "Implementing Community Policing in Public Housing: Philadelphia's 11th Street Corridor Program. Final Report" (Washington, DC: U.S. Dept. of Justice, National Institute of Justice, 1998), iv, v.

67. Wesley Skogan and Lynne Steiner, "Crime, Disorder and Decay in Chicago's Latino Community," *Journal of Ethnicity in Criminal Justice* 2 (2004): 26.

68. Dorothy Guyot has described changing police departments in order to implement community policing as "bending granite"; see Dorothy Guyot, *Policing as Though People Matter* (Philadelphia: Temple University Press, 1991), 5.

69. Transcript of "A Roof Over Our Heads: How Will New York Save Its Public Housing?" (round table discussion, Milano School for Management and Urban Policy, 23 October 2007), transcript in author's possession.

70. Richard Wisniewski and J. Amos Hatch, *Life History and Narrative* (London: Taylor & Francis, 1995).

CHAPTER 1 "OUR BUILDINGS MUST BE PATROLLED BY FOOT"

1. Weather data from National Severe Storms Laboratory Historical Weather Data Archives, Norman, Oklahoma, at http://data.nssl.noaa.gov; for the history of San Juan Hill see Marcy Sacks, *Before Harlem: The Black Experience in New York City before World War I* (Philadelphia: University of Pennsylvania Press, 2006), 72–73; City Wide Tenants Council Press Release, 16 October 1941, folder, box 54D5, New York City Housing Authority Papers, La Guardia and Wagner Archives, La Guardia Community College (hereafter NYCHA); Carr, president of the New York Metropolitan Montford Point Marine Association, interview by author, 19 June 2008. The larger history of this unit is told in Melton Alonza McLaurin, *The Marines of Montford Point: America's First Black Marines* (Chapel Hill: University of North Carolina Press, 2007); Grosvenor Atterbury (1869–1956), Harvey Wiley Corbett (1873–1954), and Arthur Holden (1890–1994) served as the Amsterdam Houses' architects. Atterbury designed the American Wing of the Metropolitan Museum of Art (1936) and the Blue Room in New York's City Hall (1915); Corbet worked on many New York's best-loved buildings, including the Bush Building (1916), the Metropolitan Life North Building (1933), the Criminal Courts Building (1939), and Rockefeller Center. See Robert A. M. Stern, Thomas Mellins, and David Fishman, *New York 1960: Architecture and Urbanism between the Second World War and the Bicentennial* (New York: Monacelli Press, 1995), 675; Mayor's Comments, 11 October 1941, folder 2, box 54D5, NYCHA; " Farewell to the Slums," *New York Times*, 6 October 1941, 19; "Threat to Housing Minimized by Mayor," *New York Times*, 11 October 1941; for reformers emphasis on light and air, see Karen A. Franck and Micheal Mostellor, "From Courts to Open Space to Streets: Changes in the Site Design of U.S. Public Housing," *Journal of Architectural and Planning Research* 12 (1995): 186–220, and Alexander von Hoffman, "High Ambitions: The Past and Future of American Low-Income Housing Policy," *Housing Policy Debate* 7, no. 3 (1996): 423–446; for the origins of NYCHA's building designs, see Nicholas Dagen Bloom, *Public Housing That Worked: New York in the Twentieth Century* (Philadelphia: University of Pennsylvania Press, 2008), chapter 3.

2. "58% of Manhattan Crime Is Traced to Slum Areas," *New York Times*, 5 April 1934; Irving W. Halpern, John Norman Stanislaus, and Bernard Botein, *A Statistical Study of the Distribution of Adult and Juvenile Delinquents in the Boroughs of Manhattan and Brooklyn, New York City* (New York: Published for the New York City Housing Authority, 1934), 21, iii, 2; the faith in modern architecture is insightfully reviewed in Nathan Glazer, *From Cause to a Style: Modernist Architecture's Encounter with the American City* (Princeton, NJ: Princeton University Press, 2007); Bloom, *Public Housing That Worked*, chapter 1; Ellen Lurie, "Community Action in East Harlem: Draft of a Paper for Presentation to the 39th Annual Meeting of the Ortho-psychiatric Association," n.d., folder 2, box 18, Union Settlement Records, Rare Book and Manuscript Library, Columbia University. See also her essay "Community Action in East Harlem," in *The Urban Condition: People and Policy in the Metropolis*, ed. Leonard J. Duhl (New York: Basic Books, 1963), 246–258.
3. For the growth of NYCHA in the immediate postwar years see Bloom, *Public Housing That Worked*, 112–117.
4. Gerald E. Markowitz and David Rosner, *Children, Race, and Power: Kenneth and Mamie Clark's Northside Center* (Charlottesville: University Press of Virginia, 1996), 7–12; Eric Schneider, *Vampires, Dragons, and Egyptian Kings: Youth Gangs in Postwar New York* (Princeton, NJ: Princeton University Press, 1999), chapter 1. For an increase in gang violence and juvenile arrests in Brooklyn in the early 1950s, see Wendell E. Pritchett, *Brownsville, Brooklyn: Blacks, Jews, and the Changing Face of the Ghetto* (Chicago: University of Chicago Press, 2002), 114. For the housers' vision of tightly managed community, see Bloom, *Public Housing That Worked*, chapter 5.
5. Schneider, *Vampires, Dragons, and Egyptian Kings*, 29–30.
6. Ibid., 32–33; Emily Rosenbaum and Samantha R. Friedman, *The Housing Divide: How Generations of Immigrants Fare in New York's Housing Market* (New York: New York University Press, 2007), 93.
7. Schneider, *Vampires, Dragons, and Egyptian Kings*, 42–47.
8. Press Release, 8 October 1958, folder 6, box 69D5, NYCHA; Bloom, *Public Housing That Worked*, 144–148.
9. Police Department, 14 January 1944, folder 5, box 63D6, NYCHA.
10. For the dates of construction of NYCHA's developments, see Bloom, *Public Housing That Worked*, appendix A; Albert Mayer, "So Far, So Good in Public Housing," *New York Times*, 15 September 1940; for the history of the deputized patrolmen in NYCHA, the 1948 and 1950 surveys, as well as NYCHA's rejections of the proposals for a separate police force, see "Strengthening of Project Protection," 1951, folder 1, box 70D5, NYCHA; for vandalism in private tenements see Woody Klein, *Let in the Sun* (New York: Macmillan, 1964), chapter 6.
11. For opposition to the program, see D. Bradford Hunt, "How Did Public Housing Survive the 1950s?" *Journal of Policy History* 17, no. 2 (2005): 193–216.
12. "The Rise of Senator Legend," *Time*, 24 March 1952; Marie Gottschalk, *The Prison and the Gallows: The Politics of Mass Incarceration in America* (New York: Cambridge University Press, 2006), 73–74, David Halberstam, *The Fifties*, 1st ed. (New York: Villard Books, 1993), 188–191; William Howard Moore, *The Kefauver Committee and the Politics of Crime, 1950–1952* (Columbia: University of Missouri Press, 1974), 55.
13. "Who's a Liar?" *Life*, 2 April 1951, 19–25.
14. George Walsh, *Public Enemies: The Mayor, the Mob, and the Crime That Was*, 1st ed. (New York: Norton, 1980), part 5.

15. Michael Woodiwiss, *Crime, Crusades and Corruption: Prohibitions in the United States, 1900–1987* (Totowa, NJ: Barnes & Noble, 1988), 122–123.
16. "Who's a Liar?"; Moore, *The Kefauver Committee*, 172, 183–185; Estes Kefauver, *Crime in America* (Garden City, NY: Doubleday, 1951), 325–326; see also the introduction Kefauver wrote to Dale Kramer and Madeline Karr, *Teen-Age Gangs* (New York,: Holt, 1953); "Senators Ask 20 Years for Narcotics Peddlers," *New York Times*, 19 June 1951. Kefauver would also assume the chair of the Senate Subcommittee to Investigate Juvenile Delinquency in 1955. See James Burkhart Gilbert, *A Cycle of Outrage: America's Reaction to the Juvenile Delinquent in the 1950s* (New York: Oxford University Press, 1986), chapter 9.
17. "Halley Is Named for Council Head," *New York Times*, 1 June 1951; Moore, *The Kefauver Committee*, 235.
18. William Reilly, "Survey of New York City Housing Protection Methods," 25 July 1951, folder 1, box 70D5, NYCHA; routing slip attached to report.
19. "Police Inspector William J. Reilly Dies; Headed a Division of Uniformed Forces," *New York Times*, 15 January 1958.
20. Pearl Lufrod to William Poulson, 21 June 1951, folder 1, box 70D5, NYCHA; D. Allen to Roger Flood, 22 June 1951, folder 1, box 70D5, NYCHA. See the collection of other such "Vandalism and Delinquency" reports in the same folder.
21. Reilly, "Survey of New York City Housing Protection Methods."
22. "Strengthening of Project Protection," 1951, folder 1, box 70D5, NYCHA,
23. "New Force Will Patrol City Housing Projects," *New York Times*, 14 November 1952; "Nineteenth Annual Report," 1952, page 29, folder 13, box 98D1, NYCHA; "Dear Tenant," n.d., folder 1, box 70D5, NYCHA.
24. "Department of Investigation Reports MR 11285E/Mr11285F New York City Housing Authority Property Protection and Security Division," 28 March 1957, folder 6, box 65C8, NYCHA.
25. J. Lennox, "General Instructions for Housing Officers," January 1953, folder 1, box 70D5, NYCHA; "Department of Investigation Reports MR 11285E/Mr11285F New York City Housing Authority Property Protection and Security Division" 28 March 1957, folder 6, box 65C8, NYCHA.
26. "Instructions and Procedures for Housing Officers in the New York City Housing Authority," 12 December 1952, folder 1, box 70D5, NYCHA; J. Lennox to "Manager," January 1953, folder 1, box 70D5, NYCHA. Note instructions to "Please Post on Housing Officers' Bulletin Board," folder 1, box 70D5, NYCHA.
27. J. Lennox, "General Instructions for Housing Officers CP–5," 5 May 1953, folder 1, box 70D5, NYCHA.
28. Vic Romano, interview by author, 19 April 2008, tape of interview in author's possession.
29. "Investigation," 23 January 1958, folder 8, box 65C8, NYCHA; Charles F. Preusse, "Police Protection in the New York City Housing Authority," 17 May 1957, 3, Special Collections, John Jay College, City University of New York. Note that Preusse issued two reports: the interim report on security cited here, and a broader survey of NYCHA's operations, released later that year. See folder 3, box 61B3, NYCHA.
30. David Garland, *The Culture of Control* (Chicago: University of Chicago Press, 2001), 42–44. Historian Alice O'Connor notes that these theories often explained delinquency as a "reflection of the personality disorders wrought by the matriarchal

household, in which children, and boys especially, had no one to meet their developmental and disciplinary needs." Alice O'Connor, *Poverty Knowledge: Social Science, Social Policy, and the Poor in Twentieth-Century U.S. History* (Princeton, NJ: Princeton University Press, 2001), 109.

31. J. Lennox, "CP–30," 3 May 1954, folder 1, box 70D5, NYCHA.
32. Sal Barzino, interview by author, 3 July 2007; Vic Romano interview; tapes of interviews in author's possession.
33. "What's a Policeman?" *New York Times*, 21 April 1955.
34. J. Lennox, "CP–7," 7 May 1954; "CP–78," J. Lennox, 19 June 1956, folder 1, box 70D5, NYCHA.
35. "Investigation," 23 January 1958.
36. As quoted in Preusse, "Police Protection in the New York City Housing Authority," chapter 3. The Lincoln and Weldon houses were among the twelve troubled houses to which NYCHA had assigned Housing Police officers in 1952. See "State Program—Schedule C," 27 November 1951, folder 1, box 70D5, NYCHA.
37. The status change came with an amendment to Section 154 of the Code of Criminal Procedure of New York State (1. 1956, Ch 562). See "CP–73," 30 April 1956, folder 1, box 70D5, NYCHA; for the carrying of weapons before 1956, see J. Lennox to Managers, 1953, folder 1, box 70D5, NYCHA; for the size of the Housing Police, see Joseph Garber, "The History, Organization and Structure of the Hew York City Housing Authority Police Department" (honors thesis, City University of New York, 1970), 87. J. Lennox to "Managers of Projects Having Housing Officers," 24 September 1956, folder 1, box 70D5, NYCHA.
38. Martha Biondi, *To Stand and Fight: The Struggle for Civil Rights in Postwar New York* (Cambridge, MA: Harvard University Press, 2003), chapter 1, 87.
39. Robert A. Caro, *The Power Broker: Robert Moses and the Fall of New York* (New York: Vintage Books, 1975), 722–726.
40. For the limited political patronage in NYCHA, see Bloom, *Public Housing That Worked*, 93; as quoted in Caro, *The Power Broker*, 724.
41. Caro, *The Power Broker*, 725.
42. Ian Fisher, "Warren Moscow, 84, a Reporter and Top Aide to Mayor Wagner," *New York Times*, 21 September 1992.
43. For Shanahan's boycott see, "7 Groups Protest New Housing Job," *New York Times*, 26 June 1957.
44. For the board's fear see Caro, *The Power Broker*, 726; curiously, Caro omits any discussion of the *Daily News* articles that followed Wilson's threat. In contrast, Bloom briefly addresses the series and some of its consequences, but omits its origin in both NYCHA's corruption and Wilson's threat. See Bloom, *Public Housing That Worked*, 120. For the history of cold war politics in New York more broadly see Joshua B. Freeman, *Working Class New York: Life and Labor since World War Two* (New York: New Press, 2000), chapter 5.
45. Dominic Peluso, Joseph Martin, and Sydney Mirkin, "Reveal Red Plot to Turn City Projects into Slums," *Daily News*, 18 February, 1957; "The Housing That Your Jack Built Is Now Tobacco Road," *Daily News*, 19 February 1957; "Housing Bungle Piped Afar, Even to Kitchen Sink," *Daily News*, 20 February 1957; "Housing Execs Admit Red Role," *Daily News*, 21 February 1957; "Bronx Housing a Sick Baby, All Run Down," *Daily News*, 22 February 1957; "Slums Built into City's Housing," *Daily News*, 23 February 1957; "Repair Charges Harass Tenants," *Daily News*, 25 February 1957; "Tag 5 Project Mgrs. As Red,"

Daily News, 26 February 1957; "The Project Tenants Sound Off," *Daily News*, 27 February 1957; "Project Half Built-and Shot," *Daily News*, 29 February 1957; "Red Hook—Pearl of a Project," *Daily News*, 1 March 1957; "Thick on Brass, Thin on Project Coppers," *Daily News*, 4 March 1957.

46. For the board's vote, see "7 Groups Protest New Housing Job."

47. Charles Grutzner, "New Housing Job Draws More Fire," *New York Times*, 2 May 1957; Bloom, an otherwise meticulous researcher, inaccurately concludes that Shanahan's request for an assistant had been "blocked at the state level but helped fuel suspicions" of Communism at the Authority. In fact, not only did Shanahan get his aide, but that hire, Hartnett, wouldn't be forced to resign by Wagner until February 1958. See Charles Bennett, "3 in Housing Office Resign Amid Strife," *New York Times*, 21 February 1958, and Bloom, *Public Housing That Worked*, 120.

48. Bloom, *Public Housing That Worked*, 121. For Wallander and O'Dwyer, see Walsh, *Public Enemies*, 109; Peluso et al., Joseph Martin, "The Housing That Your Jack Built Is Now Tobacco Road"; "Thick on Brass, Thin on Project Coppers."

49. See, for example, Donald Craig Parson, *Making a Better World: Public Housing, the Red Scare, and the Direction of Modern Los Angeles* (Minneapolis: University of Minnesota Press, 2005).

50. Bloom, *Public Housing That Worked*, 120–122.

51. "Investigation," 23 January 1958.

52. "Bias Inquiry Set for Housing Unit," *New York Times*, 16 January 1958; "Officer Suicide Has Odd Sequel," *New York Times*, 29 May 1958.

53. Richard D. Lyons, "George Gregory Jr., 88, Athlete and a Civic Leader in Harlem," *New York Times*, 21 May 1994.

54. White Council of Housing Officers to "Nigger," n.d., folder 6, box 65C8, NYCHA.

55. "Unbelievable!: Jimmy Hicks' Inside Story of Lynch Trial," *Afro-American*, 8 October 1955; "Missing 3rd Witness in Till Case Located," *Afro-American*, 29 October 1955.

56. James Hicks, "Suicide Cop Asked Amsterdam News Aid," *New York Amsterdam News*, 18 January 1958.

57. For Wallander and police brutality see Marilynn S. Johnson, *Street Justice: A History of Police Violence in New York City* (Boston: Beacon Press, 2003), 210–213, and Biondi, *To Stand and Fight*, 72–73; for Lennox's work history, see John Mitchell to Gerald Carey, 29 January 1958, folder 8, box 65C8, NYCHA.

58. Foundational works in the extensive scholarship on the postwar suburban migration and attendant exclusion of African Americans include Kenneth Jackson, *Crabgrass Frontier: The Suburbanization of the United States* (New York: Oxford University Press, 1985); Douglas S. Massey and Nancy A. Denton, *American Apartheid: Segregation and the Making of the Underclass* (Cambridge, MA: Harvard University Press, 1993); and Thomas J. Sugrue, *The Origins of the Urban Crisis: Race and Inequality in Postwar Detroit* (Princeton, NJ: Princeton University Press, 1996). More recent and fine-grained case studies of these patterns can be found in David M. Freund, *Colored Property: State Policy and White Racial Politics in Suburban America* (Chicago: University of Chicago Press, 2007); and Howard Gillette, *Camden after the Fall: Decline and Renewal in a Post-Industrial City* (Philadelphia: University of Pennsylvania Press, 2005). For a discussion of these forces at work in Brooklyn, see Pritchett, *Brownsville, Brooklyn: Blacks, Jews, and the Changing Face of the Ghetto*, 119; publicly assisted private developments—such as Stuyvesant Town, Peter Cooper Village, and Parkchester—became subject to

antidiscrimination with the passage of the 1951 Brown-Isaacs Ordinance, but these developments largely managed to evade the law. At Stuyvesant Town in 1960, for example, black tenants represented less than two-tenths of one percent of the total. New York State would outlaw discrimination in all private housing in 1963. For this history as well as a survey of the larger fight for fair housing in New York City in these years, see Biondi, *To Stand and Fight*, 113–116, 32–35; Rosenbaum and Friedman, *The Housing Divide*, 105; Hilary Ballon and Kenneth T. Jackson, eds., *Robert Moses and the Modern City: The Transformation of New York* (New York: Norton, 2007), 255–256; "Racial Distribution in Operating Project at Initial Occupancy and On December 31, 1960 All Programs," 18 January 1961, manuscript box IVB, NYCHA; for NYCHA's estimate of residents leaving the program to purchase private homes, see NYCHA, "1951 Annual Report," December 1951, folder 12, box 98D1, NYCHA. Note that at the time of this writing (2008), the La Guardia Archives were in the process of moving the annual reports from box 59D6 to box 98D1.

59. "City Housing Aide Is a Suicide Here," *New York Times*, 11 January 1958.

60. "Bias Inquiry Set for Housing Unit"; "Officer Suicide Has Odd Sequel"; Hicks, "Suicide Cop Asked Amsterdam News Aid."

61. Arthur Wallander to Members of the New York City Housing Authority, February 1958, folder 3, box 64E7, NYCHA.

62. Arthur Wallander to Members of the New York City Housing Authority, 1 October 1957, folder 3, box 64E7, NYCHA.

63. Arthur Wallander, "Reorganization of Housing Authority Police, Progress Report," 4 December 1957, folder 3, box 64E7, NYCHA.

64. Association of Public Housing Managers, "A Look at New York City's Public Housing Today," January 1958, folder 8, box 65C8, NYCHA.

65. See, for example, Stephanie Greenberg and WIlliam Rohe, "Informal Social Control and Crime Prevention in Modern Neighborhoods," in *Urban Neighborhoods: Research and Policy*, ed. R. Taylor (New York: Praeger, 1986), 79–122.

66. Elizabeth Wood, "The Small Hard Core: The Housing of Problem Families in New York City. A Study and Recommendations" (New York: Citizens' Housing and Planning Council [CHPC] of New York, 1957), 19. General Research and Humanities Collection, New York Public Library. Note that the CHPC released several versions of this pamphlet with inconsistent pagination; Association of Public Housing Managers, "A Look at New York City's Public Housing Today," January 1958, folder 8, box 65C8, NYCHA.

67. See, for example, California Attorney General's Office, "Community-Oriented Policing and Problems Solving (Copps) Definition and Principles" (Sacramento, CA: Crime Prevention Center, 1992); for a discussion of a contemporary effort to implement this principle, see Wesley Skogan, *Police and Community in Chicago: A Tale of Three Cities* (New York: Oxford University Press, 2006), 76–81, 97.

68. Association of Public Housing Managers, "A Look at New York City's Public Housing Today," January 1958.

69. "Low Morale Noted in City Housing Unit," *New York Times*, 12 January 1958.

70. "Agenda of Pending Matters Requiring the Attention of the New Authority," 1 May 1958, folder 8, box 65C8, NCHA.

71. "City Centralizes Police of Housing," *New York Times*, 14 July 1958.

72. Albert Morgan to Supt. John Mitchell, 13 November 1958, folder 4, box 64C3, NCHA; Lewis Butler to John Mitchell 18 November 1958, folder 4, box 64c3, NCHA.

73. Vic Romano interview, 19 April 2008.
74. As quoted in John Mitchell to "All Members of the Force," 29 August 1958, folder 4, box 64c3, NYCHA.
75. John Mitchell to "All Members of the Force," 29 August 1958.
76. John Mitchell, "Report on Pct. #13—Fort Greene," 30 September 1958, folder 4, box 64C3, NYCHA.
77. William Reid to Commissioner Game Gaynor, 5 May 1959, folder 3, box 64C1, NYCHA; Gerald Carey to Herman Hillman, 29 June 1959, folder 3, box 64C1, NYCHA.

CHAPTER 2 "A PARADOX IN URBAN LAW ENFORCEMENT"

1. "New Force Will Patrol City Housing Projects," *New York Times*, 14 November 1952; for the start date of the patrols, see "Dear Tenant," January 1953, folder 1, box 70D5, New York City Housing Authority Papers, La Guardia and Wagner Archives, La Guardia Community College (hereafter NYCHA); for the numbers of officers on that first patrol, see George Genung to Division Heads, 5 January 1953, folder 2, box 70D5, NYCHA. As noted in chapter 1, NYCHA's police officers were designated "special patrolmen" until 11 April 1956 when, by virtue of an amendment to Section 154 of the Code of Criminal Procedure of New York State, they became "peace officers." See "CP–73," 30 April 1956, folder 1, box 70D5, NYCHA.
2. United States Commission on Civil Rights, *1961 Report, Book 5: Justice* (Washington, DC: 1961), 5–28; see also Marilynn S. Johnson, *Street Justice: A History of Police Violence in New York City* (Boston: Beacon Press, 2003), 229–234. Victor Gonzalez, interview by author, 17 September 2008, tape of interview in author's possession.
3. For NYCHA's changing architecture, see Nicholas Dagen Bloom, *Public Housing That Worked: New York in the Twentieth Century* (Philadelphia: University of Pennsylvania Press, 2008), chapter 3.
4. Gerald Carey to Herman Hillman, 22 May 1957, folder 3, box 64E7, NYCHA.
5. Lawrence Friedman, *Crime and Punishment in American History* (New York: Basic Books, 1993), 151, 358–359, 361. See also Samuel Walker, *A Critical History of Police Reform* (Lexington, MA: Lexington Books, 1977); and Eric H. Monkkonen, *Police in Urban America, 1860–1920* (Cambridge, UK: Cambridge University Press, 1981).
6. Carey to Hillman, 22 May 1957.
7. Morton Bard, "Police Management of Conflicts Among People," 8 August 1970, folder 10, box 60E7, NYCHA; Prepared remarks by Joseph Christian, 19 November 1973, folder 7, box 65B1, NYCHA.
8. For the percentage of black officers in 1965, see John J. Truta, "A Comprehensive Study of Recruitment of Negroes by the New York City Police Department with Other Law Enforcement Agencies" (master's thesis, Bernard M. Baruch College, 1969), 70. For the ethnicity of HAPD officers in the 1970s, see "Ethnic Survey, Housing Authority Police Department," 15 August 1974, folder 1, box 88B5, NYCHA. Black and Hispanic patrol officers represented 60.6 percent of the patrol force in 1974. For the size of the HAPD relative to other departments, see Joseph Weldon and Robert Ledee, "High Rise Policing Techniques," publication unclear, circa 1966, folder 4, box 60E7, NYCHA.
9. Ira Rosenwaike, *Population History of New York City* (Syracuse, NY: Syracuse University Press, 1972), 121, 134, 139, 188–190; Stephen Leinen, *Black Police, White Society* (New York: New York University Press, 1984). Breslin quoted in Vincent Cannato, *The Ungovernable City: John Lindsay and His Struggle to Save New York* (New York: Basic Books, 2001), 163.

10. "Felony Conviction Will Not Automatically Bar Men," *New York Times*, 28 May 1968; Friedman, *Crime and Punishment in American History*, 377–378; Robert M. Fogelson, *Big-City Police* (Cambridge, MA: Harvard University Press, 1977), 250–252. For the impact of police height requirements on minority police recruitment, see Leinen, *Black Police, White Society*, 23; for height differentials, see Ricardo Godoy, Elizabeth Goodman, Richard Levins, Mariana Caram, and Craig Seyfried, "Adult Male Height in an American Colony: Puerto Rico and the USA Mainland Compared, 1886–1955," *Economics & Human Biology* 5, no. 1 (March 2007): 82–99; see also Truta, "A Comprehensive Study of Recruitment of Negroes," 67.
11. See, for example, Roger L. Abel, *The Black Shields* (Bloomington, IN: AuthorHouse, 2006); Kennan Bolton and Joe Feagin, *Black in Blue: African-American Police Officers and Racism* (New York: Routledge, 2004); W. Marvin Dulaney, *Black Police in America* (Bloomington: Indiana University Press, 1996), Leinen, *Black Police, White Society*; and James N. Reaves, *Black Cops* (Philadelphia: Quantum Leap, 1991).
12. For comparative number of minority officers, see Dulaney, *Black Police in America*, appendix B. The NYCHA population figures include what the Authority estimated to be the 100,000 unregistered residents who double up in the same unit with the tenant(s) of record. For racial composition, see NYCHA, "Racial Distribution in Operating Project at Initial Occupancy and on December 31, 1960 All Programs," 18 January 1961, manuscript box IVB, NYCHA. For the size of the HAPD in 1975, see Joseph Christian to Hon. Matthew J. Troy Jr., Chairman Finance Committee New York City Council, 17 June 1975, folder 1, box 88B5, NYCHA.
13. Gonzalez interview.
14. Joseph Keeney, interview by author, February 2007 and July 2008, tape of interviews in author's possession.
15. The literature documenting racial exclusion in postwar suburbs is vast; early works on the topic include Kenneth Jackson, *Crabgrass Frontier: The Suburbanization of the United States* (New York: Oxford University Press, 1985), and Thomas J. Sugrue, *The Origins of the Urban Crisis: Race and Inequality in Postwar Detroit* (Princeton, NJ: Princeton University Press, 1996); for a summary of the New York City context, see Martha Biondi, *To Stand and Fight: The Struggle for Civil Rights in Postwar New York* (Cambridge, MA: Harvard University Press, 2003), chapter 6. For press coverage at the time see, Joel Mandelbaum, "Race Discrimination in Home Buying Resists Tough Laws " *New York Times*, 3 December 1972; Lena Williams, "After the Job Hunt, Minorities Tackle Housing," *New York Times*, 30 April 1978. Former HAPD officer Richard Luke recalled it was impossible as an African American in the 1960s to purchase a home in the suburban neighborhood he and his wife had chosen (Richard Luke, interview by author, 1 February 2008, tape of interview in author's possession).
16. A Depression-stricken New York City had enacted the Lyons Law (named after the Bronx borough president) in 1937 to protect established New Yorkers from job competition. The law "required three years of city residency for appointment to most municipal jobs and continued residency to maintain them." Under heavy lobbying from the Patrolmen's Benevolent Association, a loophole for police officers was created in 1960. Mayor Robert Wagner engineered the removal of the law altogether in 1962; see Joshua B. Freeman, *Working-Class New York: Life and Labor since World War II* (New York: New York Press, 2000), 182; United States Commission on Civil Rights, *1961 Report, Book 5: Justice;* Fogelson, *Big-City Police*, 248–250.
17. Mary and Tricia Alfson, interview by author and Nicholas Alfson, 15 December 2006; Maria Vasquez, interview by author and Christian Nunez and Maria Figueroa, 29

November 2006; Rachael Ryans, interview by author, 3 December 2006; tapes of all interviews in author's possession.

18. Judith Cummings, "230 Inducted as Housing Police; One Is the First Woman Recruit," *New York Times*, 20 November 1973. In 1965, NYCHA centralized both time records and check payments, and record rooms continued ceased to play this function; see "Centralization of Time Records in Security Headquarters," 10 November 1965, folder 3, box 64C3, NYCHA.

19. Allen Jones and Mark Naison, *The Rat That Got Away: A Bronx Memoir*, 1st ed. (New York: Fordham University Press, 2009), 4.

20. Raymond Henson, interview by author, 28 November 2007,. tape of interview in author's possession.

21. Richard Schauss, interview by author, 1 February 2008, tape of interview in author's possession.

22. Terri Sheeps, interview by author, 7 February 2007, tape of interview author's possession.

23. For Gottehrer's role in Lindsay's administration see Vincent Cannato, *The Ungovernable City: John Lindsay and His Struggle to Save New York* (New York: Basic Books, 2001), 129. For Chicago in 1968, see James T. Patterson, *Grand Expectations: The United States, 1945–1974* (New York: Oxford University Press, 1996), 694–697. For UFT's Jewish percentage, see Freeman, *Working-Class New York*, 223. The school strike has attracted much scholarly labor. To Freeman, the UFT "self-consciously followed a policy of overkill" that reflected a "reemergence of the tough Jew in New York civic life" ushered in by the 1967 Six Day War and captured famously in Woody Allen's 1973 film, *Sleeper*, which portrayed UFT president Albert Shanker as the destroyer of civilization. More recently, Richard Kahlenberg has reappraised Shanker, arguing that he was no racist and there were legitimate motivations behind the union's actions. See Richard D. Kahlenberg, *Tough Liberal: Albert Shanker and the Battles over Schools, Unions, Race, and Democracy* (New York: Columbia University Press, 2007). See also Jerald E. Podair, *The Strike That Changed New York: Blacks, Whites, and the Ocean Hill–Brownsville Crisis* (New Haven, CT: Yale University, 2004). For a more nuanced understanding of the Ocean Hill-Brownsville activists and their goals, see Thomas J. Sugrue, *Sweet Land of Liberty: The Forgotten Struggle for Civil Rights in the North* (New York: Random House, 2008), 472–477.

24. Barry Gottehrer to Albert Walsh, 23 September 1968, folder 3, box 64C3, NYCHA. The second of the three strikes would be resolved the next, after Lindsay reentered talks. See Cannato, *The Ungovernable City*, 321.

25. Housing Police, "HPS #284," 10 December 1969, folder 3, box 62c1, NYCHA; Housing Police, "HPS#264," 17 November 1969, folder 3, box 62c1, NYCHA; Housing Police, "HPS #143," 20 January 1970, folder 3, box 62c1, NYCHA; Housing Police, "HPS#264," 17 November 1969, folder 3, box 62C1, NYCHA; Housing Police, "HPS#284," 10 December 1969, folder 3, box 62C1, NYCHA; Sarah Martin, interview by author, 14 April 2009, tape of interview in author's possession; "Tenants Fete Police," *New York Amsterdam News*, 20 November 1971.

26. For the persistent journalistic trope of public housing's "demeaning, impersonal" architecture, see A. Scott Henderson, "'Tarred with the Exceptional Image': Public Housing and Popular Discourse, 1950–1990," *American Studies* 36, no. 1 (1995): 31–52.

27. Peter Grymes, interview by author, 10 February 2008, tape of interview in author's possession.

28. Harold Berger to Irving Wise, 14 October 1966, folder 10, box 66E8, NYCHA.
29. Malcolm K. Sparrow, Mark H. Moore, and David M. Kennedy, *Beyond 911*: A New Era for Policing (New York: Basic Books, 1990), 123; Robert R. Friedmann, *Community Policing: Comparative Perspectives and Prospects* (New York: St. Martin's Press, 1992), 19–21.
30. Albert Walsh to Ralep Romero, 25 March 1969, folder 1, box 65A6, NYCHA.
31. Preston David to William Reid, 24 April 1964, folder 2, box 70D3, NYCHA.
32. Joseph Rothblatt to Donald Schatz, "Special Police Force—Albany Houses," 27 January 1969, folder 1, box 65A6, NYCHA; and Joseph Weldon to Donald Schatz, 20 May 1968, folder 1, box 65A6, NYCHA.
33. K. Volner to Mr. Genung, 11 June 1945, folder 3, box 71B7, NYCHA.
34. Mrs. Lumsden to Mr. Volner, n.d., folder 3, box 71B7, NYCHA; May Lumsden to Mr. Volner, 2 July 1945, folder 3, box 71B7, NYCHA.
35. NYCHA lease quoted in "Fines in Public Housing," *Columbia Law Review* 68, no. 8 (1968): 1540.
36. William Reid to Hon. James Gaynor, 5 May 1959, folder 3, box 71B7, NYCHA. Average violations reported extrapolated from state-funded projects data for both complaints and Juvenile Record Cards. Using population totals for state funded projects with HAPD coverage as of 1959, the rate of violations reported to managers was roughly 0.8 per 1,000 project residents. For population totals, see Property Protection and Security Division, "Present Assignments and Additional Personnel Requested," n.d., folder 3, box 71B7, NYCHA. For a list of finable offenses, "Red Hook Houses," 11 June 1945, folder 2, box 71B7, NYCHA.
37. Arthur Wallander to the Members of the New York City Housing Authority, 1 October 1957, folder 3, box 64E7, NYCHA.
38. Ellen Lurie, "Rough Draft of a Study of the George Washington Houses," 1956, II-32, folder 13, box 11, Union Settlement Records, Rare Book and Manuscript Library, Columbia University.
39. Martin interview.
40. Occupancy was not complete at Castle Hill until December 1960, but residents started moving in by 1959. For completion dates on NYCHA developments, see Bloom, *Public Housing That Worked*, appendix A; Grymes interview.
41. Terri Sheeps, interview by author, 10 February 2007, tape of interview in author's possession; Victor Gonzalez, interview by author, 17 September 2008, tape of interview in author's possession.
42. J. S. Fuerst and D. Bradford Hunt, *When Public Housing Was Paradise: Building Community in Chicago* (Urbana: University of Illinois Press, 2005), 180, 82; John Hope Franklin, foreword to Fuerst and Hunt, *When Public Housing Was Paradise*, xiii.
43. Manpower Demonstration Research Corporation, *Tenant Management: Findings from a Three-Year Experiment in Public Housing* (Cambridge, MA: Ballinger Publishing, 1981), 14, 62, 87, 198–205; Gregg G. Van Rysin, "The Impact of Resident Management on Residents' Satisfaction with Public Housing: A Process Analysis of Quasi-Experimental Data," *Evaluation Review* 20, no. 4 (1996): 499.
44. For the assumptions of poverty experts in these years, see Alice O'Connor, *Poverty Knowledge: Social Science, Social Policy, and the Poor in Twentieth-Century U.S. History* (Princeton, NJ: Princeton University Press, 2001), 124–135.
45. Lawrence Grossman, "Organizing Tenants in Low-Income Public Housing," in *Community Organizers and Social Planners; a Volume of Case and Illustrative Materials*, ed. Joan Levin Ecklein and Armand Lauffer (New York: John Wiley, 1972), 175, 80.

46. Gonzalez interview.
47. Before 1980s, the most significant public housing police force outside of NYCHA's was the Chicago Housing Authority (CHA). Although the CHA employed only private guards until 1966, that year it supplemented its forty-man security force by securing federal funds for seventy-six police officers. A fifty-five-man police detail from the Chicago Police Department supplemented this force in 1971, but it soon faltered. The CHA had its own police force between 1989 and 1999 but now pays the Chicago Police Department for extra police services. In 2004, these payments totaled twelve million dollars. San Francisco and Boston both established police forces before 1980, but with fewer than seventy officers in both cases. Los Angeles and Washington, DC, established larger forces in the 1980s, but by 2006 all of these cities had moved away from dedicated police forces. New York City, by contrast, had 1,435 housing police by 1970. See D. Bradford Hunt, "What Went Wrong with Public Housing in Chicago? A History of the Robert Taylor Homes," *Journal of the Illinois State Historical Society* 94, no. 1 (2001): 96–123; D. Bradford Hunt, *Blueprint for Disaster: The Unravelling of Chicago Public Housing* (Chicago: University of Chicago Press, 2009); Mary C. Johns and Brian J. Rogal, "Lack of Force," *Chicago Reporter*, July 2004; Terence Dunworth and Kevin Roland, "Public Housing Police," in *The Encyclopedia of Police Science*, ed. Jack R. Greene (New York: Routledge, 2006), 1078–1081.
48. Grymes interview.
49. Mercer L. Sullivan, *"Getting Paid": Youth Crime and Work in the Inner City* (Ithaca, NY: Cornell University Press, 1989), 149–152.
50. The youth Sullivan studied for *Getting Paid* did eventually turn to selling crack cocaine. See Mercer Sullivan, "Crime and the Social Fabric," in *Dual City: Restructuring New York*, ed. John H. Mollenkopf and Manuel Castells (New York: Russell Sage Foundation, 1991), 225–244.
51. Sullivan, *"Getting Paid,"* 150.
52. For a discussion of police discretion at it existed in the early 1960s, see Wayne R. LaFave, *Arrest: The Decision to Take a Suspect into Custody* (Boston: Little, Brown, 1965), chapter 3; for the legal challenges to police discretion in this period, see Debra Livingston, "Police Discretion and the Quality of Life in Public Places: Courts, Communities, and the New Policing," *Columbia Law Review* 108, no. 5 (1997): 551–672.
53. President's Commission on Law Enforcement and Administration of Justice, *The Challenge of Crime in a Free Society; Task Force Report: The Courts* (Washington, DC: Government Printing Office, 1967), 399.
54. For an example of police use such statutes against civil rights demonstrators, see *Cox v. Louisiana*, 379 U.S. 536 (1965), where police in Baton Rouge, Louisiana, used a "breach of peace" statute to arrest students picketing stores maintaining segregated lunch counters.
55. For restricted discretion's impact on policing, see Livingston, "Police Discretion and the Quality of Life in Public Places"; for the impact of the Warren Court on policing, see Lawrence Friedman, *Crime and Punishment in American History* (New York: Basic Books, 1993), 299–304.
56. Robert C. Ellickson, "Controlling Chronic Misconduct in City Spaces: Of Panhandlers, Skid Rows, and Public-Space Zoning," *Yale Law Journal* 105 (1996): 1165–1248; Livingston, "Police Discretion and the Quality of Life in Public Places: Courts, Communities, and the New Policing"; Katherine Beckett and Steve Herbert, " Dealing with Disorder: Social Control in the Post-Industrial City," *Theoretical Criminology* 12, no. 1 (2008): 5–28.

57. *Papachristou v. City of Jacksonville*, 405 US 156 (1972).
58. Jennie McIntyre, "Public Attitudes toward Crime and Law Enforcement," *Annals of the American Academy of Political and Social Science* 374, no. 1 (1967).
59. J. Anthony Lukas, "City Revising Its Prostitution Controls," *New York Times*, 14 August 1967.
60. For a discussion of the deemphasizing of victimless crime in general and prostitution in particular, see Alex S. Vitale, *City of Disorder: How the Quality of Life Campaign Transformed New York Politics* (New York: New York University Press, 2008), 119–121.
61. New York City Police Department, *Statistical Report: Complaints and Arrests, Crime Analysis Section* (New York: Office of Management, 1960–1982). Until 1968, the lowest grade for arrests was "offenses" but the 1968 revision of the New York State penal code replaced that term with "violation." In 1964, 86,319 of the 190,289 total arrests were for "offenses" but by 1970, of the 250,902 total arrests, only 44,243 were for violations.
62. "Fines in Public Housing," 1542; Roger Starr, "Which of the Poor Shall Live in Public Housing," *Public Interest* 23 (Spring 1971): 116–125; Martha F. Davis, *Brutal Need: Lawyers and the Welfare Rights Movement, 1960–1973* (New Haven, CT: Yale University Press, 1993), chapter 4; Patterson, *Grand Expectations*, chapter 21.
63. See *Lockman v. New York City Housing Authority, Civ. Act. No. 4414/67* (S.D.N.Y., Oct. 31, 1968), which a lower court had dismissed—but that on appeal (consolidated with related cases) was decided in favor of the plaintiffs, see *Escalera v. NYCHA*, 425 F2d 853 (2d Cir 1970). See also chapter 3 of this book for a sustained discussion of *Escalera*.
64. "Fines in Public Housing"; Starr, "Which of the Poor Shall Live in Public Housing."
65. Annual Report, 1968, folder 3, box 64C3, NYCHA; Annual Report, 1971, folder 3, box 64C3, NYCHA.
66. Annual Statistical Report—1976, 30 March 1977, folder 3, box 89A3, NYCHA.
67. Sugrue, *Sweet Land of Liberty*, 327–328.
68. "Seminar Finds Wide Gulf Separates Police and Minority-Group Relations," *New York Times*, 8 March 1973.
69. For a discussion of Harlem's 1964 riot and the less well known 1963 "fruit riot," see Janet L. Abu-Lughod, *Race, Space, and Riots in Chicago, New York, and Los Angeles* (New York: Oxford University Press, 2007), chapter 5; for Harlem's other antipolice riot in 1963, see "Negroes Fight Police in Harlem; Several Injured and 27 Arrested," *New York Times*, 18 June 1963; Baldwin quoted in Randal Kennedy, *Race, Crime, and the Law* (New York: Random House, 1997), 26; the riots of 1967 and their origins were extensively analyzed in the *Kerner Commission Report: The 1968 Report of the National Advisory Commission on Civil Disorders* (Washington, DC: 1968; repr., 1988); "PARADE: Salute to Progress," 22 April 1967, folder 5, box 164B7, NYCHA.
70. "Riot Flares in Brooklyn Project; 8 Persons Injured, 5 Arrested," *New York Times*, 16 August 1962; "2 Housing Officers Pelted with Bottles by a Harlem Crowd," *New York Times*, 31 August 1974.
71. Max Siegel, "S.I. Broker and 3 Indicated in Damaging Black's Home," *New York Times*, 15 October 1975; George Todd, "Former Cops Guilty of Vandalizing Black Home," *New York Amsterdam News*, 2 October 1976.
72. Cummings, "230 Inducted as Housing Police; One Is the First Woman Recruit."
73. Haile Selassie, interview by author, 1 February, 2008, tape of interview in author's possession.

74. John T. McQuiston, "Murphy, in Test, Assigns Patrolman to Home Precinct," *New York Times*, 20 January 1972; Peter Kihss, "24th Designated the First 'Model Precinct,'" *New York Times*, 3 February 1972; Arthur Niederhoffer and Alexander B. Smith, *New Directions in Police Community Relations* (Corte Madera, CA: RineHart Press, 1974), 22–23.
75. "Police Department, HPS # 284," 10 December 1969, and "Police Department, HPS #3," 2 February 1970, both in folder 3, box 62C1, NYCHA.
76. Rhonda Y. Williams, *The Politics of Public Housing: Black Women's Struggles against Urban Inequality* (New York: Oxford University Press, 2004), 6, 8; for the role of tenant patrols as "viable community spokespersons" within NYCHA, see "Tenant Organizations in Public Housing—The Need for Professional Mediation," 6 December, 1976, folder 13, box 90B4, NYCHA.
77. Bonnie Bucqueroux, "Community Policing is Alive and Well," *Community Policing Exchange* (May-June 1995), http://www.ncjrs.gov/txtfiles/cpe0595.txt.
78. So certain, for example, was Howard Husock, director of public policy case studies at Harvard, that "everyone knows how quickly . . . housing projects . . . in big cities turn into dangerous, demoralized slums," that he neglected even to provide a citation for this sweeping generalization in his *America's Trillion-Dollar Housing Mistake: The Failure of American Housing Policy* (New York: Ivan R. Dee, 2003), 1.
79. An important recent exception can be found in Tamar Carroll, "Grassroots Feminism: Direct Action Organizing and Coalition Building in New York City, 1955–1995" (Ph.D. diss., University of Michigan, 2007).
80. Joel Schwartz, "Tenant Unions in New York City's Low-Rent Housing, 1934–1949," *Journal of Urban History* 12 (August 1986): 436.
81. Ibid., 438.
82. Although, as José Ramón Sánchez has observed, not until the 1970s would Puerto Rican residency in public housing reflect their share of the city low-income population, this pattern was much less true in East Harlem. The Johnson Houses, for example, were 25.4 percent Puerto Rican at their initial occupancy in 1949. See José Ramón Sánchez, "Housing Puerto Ricans in New York City, 1945 to 1984: A Study in Class Powerlessness" (Ph.D. diss., New York University, 1990), 563.
83. Ellen Lurie would eventually acquire fame as an activist defending community control in the Ocean Hill–Brownsville strike. See Podair, *The Strike That Changed New York*, 175.
84. Ellen Lurie, "Las Vigilantes," September 1959, folder 1, box 17, Union Settlement Records, Rare Books and Manuscript Library, Columbia University; Leonard J. Duhl, *The Urban Condition: People and Policy in the Metropolis* (New York: Basic Books, 1963), 249.
85. Patricia Hill Collins, *Black Feminist Thought: Knowledge, Consciousness, and the Politics of Empowerment: Perspectives on Gender* (Boston: Unwin Hyman, 1990); Nancy Naples, "Activist Mothering: Cross-Generational Continuity in the Community Work of Women from Low-Income Urban Neighborhoods," *Gender & Society* 6, no. 3 (1992): 441–463.
86. Lurie, "Las Vigilantes"; Duhl, *The Urban Condition*, 255.
87. Bloom, *Public Housing That Worked*, 192–196; for the number of tenant associations, see William Reid, "Towards a Slumless City: 1954–1965," November 1965, folder 5, box 59D5, NYCHA.
88. Val Coleman, "Tenant Organization in Public Housing—The Need for Professional Mediation," 6 December 1976, folder 13, box 90B4, NYCHA; see also Blanca Cedeno,

"Human Relations Committee Meeting from Millbrook House," 19 October 1972, folder2, box 88B4, NYCHA; Blanca Cedeno to Albert Walsh, 30 November 1967, folder 1, box 70D5, NYCHA.

89. Randall Bennett Woods, *LBJ: Architect of American Ambition* (New York: Free Press, 2006), 710–711.

90. Sugrue, *Sweet Land of Liberty*, 369–374.

91. David Preston, "New Expectations for Public Housing: Paper Presented at the 1965 annual meeting of the American Orthopsychiatric Association, New York, New York," *American Journal of Orthopsychiatry* 36, no. 4 (1966): 678; David Preston, "Department of Social and Community Services," 1966, 1, box 59D5, NYCHA. Bloom, *Public Housing That Worked*, 236–237, Nancy Naples, *Grassroots Warriors: Activist Mothering, Community Work, and the War on Poverty* (New York: Routledge, 1998), 76–77, 210–211.

92. Les Mathews, "Greenpoint Slaying Laid to Race Strife," *New York Amsterdam News*, 17 December 1960. Tudy's activism, however, long predated the 1960 events described by the *Amsterdam News*; as Tudy recounted, her grandmother took her to protests on 125th Street organized by Adam Clayton Powell Jr. It is likely that Tudy was recalling Powell's "Don't Buy Where You Can't Work" Harlem campaign. See Colin Campbell, "A Lifetime of Leadership: An Interview with Mildred Tudy," *Greenline*, 10 October 1986, folder 23, box 97, National Congress of Neighborhood Women Records, Sophia Smith Collection, Women's History Manuscripts, Smith College.

93. Harold Berger to Irving Wise, 14 October 1966, folder 10, box 66E8, NYCHA; Harold Berger to Irving Wise, "Follow-up to Cooper Park Houses Community Meeting," 17 October 1966, folder 10, box 66E8, NYCHA.

94. Richard A. Cloward and Frances Fox Piven, *The Politics of Turmoil; Essays on Poverty, Race, and the Urban Crisis* (New York: Pantheon Books, 1974), 24, 21–22, 7–9.

95. For Tudy's record of activism, see Mathews, "Greenpoint Slaying Laid to Race Strife"; Rhea Callaway, "Hi There!" *New York Amsterdam News*, 28 November 1970; "Locals Demand Jobs on Hospital Site," *New York Amsterdam News*, 24 July 1971; "Residents Demand Jobs on Williamsburgh Site," *New York Amsterdam News*, 18 December, 1971; "Charge Racism on District 14 School Board," *New York Amsterdam News*, 11 December 1971; "Blacks Fear Exclusion in Williamsburg Housing," *New York Amsterdam News*, 22 January 1972; "Black Principal Ouster May End School Peace," *New York Amsterdam News*, 9 June 1973; "Court Hears Arguments in Woodhull Suit," *New York Amsterdam News*, 19 July 1980; "A Call to Convene the Black Population of New York," *New York Amsterdam News*, 15 May 1982; "Community Service—Mildred Tudy," *New York Amsterdam News*, 28 December 1991. For Tudy's conception of "basic needs" community activism, see Campbell, "A Lifetime of Leadership."

96. Jim Fuerst and Roy Petty, "Public Housing in the Courts, Pyrrhic Victories for the Poor," *The Urban Lawyer* (Summer 1977): 503.

97. For evictions, see relevant tables, folder 13, box 64A4, NYCHA; for population totals, see NYCHA, "Racial Distribution in Operating Project at Initial Occupancy and on December 31, 1960 All Programs," 18 January 1961, manuscript box IVB, NYCHA; Martin interview; for telegrams, see Tompkins Tenants Association to Walter Washington, 1 June 1967, folder 10, box 66E8, NYCHA.

98. See, for example, the failure of New York City's "Sunshine Project" discussed in Michael Massing, *The Fix* (New York: Simon & Schuster, 1998), 247–249. A more systematic evaluation of community policing projects in eight cities conducted by the Vera Institute for Justice concluded that of all of the implementation problems, "the

most perplexing . . . was the inability of the police department to organize and maintain active community involvement in their projects." See Randolph Grinc, "'Angels in Marble': Problems in Stimulating Community Involvement in Community Policing," *Crime & Delinquency* 40, no. 3 (1994): 437.

99. For participation rates at NYCHA meetings, see Alan Rudolph, "Tenant Reaction to Public Housing" (M.A. thesis, Pratt Institute, 16 January 1970), 68, Citizens Housing and Planning Council Archive, New York City; for Chicago, Wesley G. Skogan and Susan M. Hartnett, *Community Policing, Chicago Style* (New York: Oxford University Press, 1997), 117.

100. For the ethnic breakdown of the George Washington Houses at the time, see the demographic tabulations in manuscript box 15, NYCHA. Alice Suzuku, "NYCHA Social and Community Services Report," November 1962–May 1965, folder 3, box 12, Union Settlement Records, Rare Book and Manuscript Library, Columbia University; for the Washington Houses population of 5,940 in 1964, see the oversized crime sheets tabulated by development that year, Manhattan Division #2, folder 12, box 65D7; compare with data regarding CAPS from Skogan and Hartnett, *Community Policing, Chicago Style.*

101. "Meeting Held at Pioneer Civic Action Org. Center," n.d., folder 3, box 64C3, NYCHA; "Tension Report—Marcy Houses," n.d., folder 3, box 64C3, NYCHA. For Johnson's background, see Les Mathews, "Bronxite with 'Harem,' Convicted in Coke Killing," *New York Amsterdam News*, 24 April 1982.

102. "Mayor Consoles Mom of Slain Boro Youth," *New York Amsterdam News*, 13 July 1968.

103. "Mayor Calms Brooklyn Group, Upset by Fatal Police Shooting," *New York Times*, 27 June 1968.

104. Ibid.; "Mayor Consoles Mom of Slain Boro Youth."

105. "Meeting Held at Pioneer Civic Action Org. Center," n.d., folder 3, box 64C3, NYCHA.

106. Barry Gottehrer, *The Mayor's Man* (Garden City, NY: Doubleday, 1975), 79–82.

107. For the new Black Power historiography, see Peniel E. Joseph, *The Black Power Movement: Rethinking the Civil Rights–Black Power Era* (New York: Routledge, 2006), and Peniel E. Joseph, "The Black Power Movement: A State of the Field," *Journal of American History* 96, no. 3 (December 2009): 751–776. For the symbiotic relationship between the press and Black Power militants, see Sugrue, *Sweet Land of Liberty*, 351–355; Jane Rhodes, *Framing the Black Panthers: The Spectacular Rise of a Black Power Icon* (New York: New Press, 2007); Jeffrey Ogbonna Green Ogbar, *Black Power: Radical Politics and African American Identity* (Baltimore: Johns Hopkins University Press, 2004), 87; Earl Caldwell, "Booth Gives View of I.S.201 Dispute," *New York Times*, 11 March 1968.

108. "Report on Pioneer Civic Action Org. Center," n.d., folder 3, box 64C3, NYCHA.

109. "Meeting Held at Pioneer Civic Action Org. Center," n.d., folder 3, box 64C3, NYCHA; "Tension Report—Marcy Houses," n.d., folder 3, box 64C3, NYCHA.

110. Joseph Keeney, interview by author, 18 November 2008, tape of interview in author's possession.

111. Edward Rogowsky, Louis H. Gold, and David W. Abbott, "Police: The Civilian Review Board Controversy," in *Race and Politics in New York City*, ed. Jewel Bellush and Stephen M. David (New York: Praeger Publishers, 1971), 59–97, 61–62; Cassese quoted in James P. Gifford, "Dissent in Municipal Employee Organizations," *Proceedings of the Academy of Political Science* 30, no. 2 (December 1970): 166.

112. Shooting of Officer Defended by Police," *New York Times*, 15 April 1982; Mathews, "Bronxite with 'Harem,' Convicted in Coke Killing."

113. For the first of these, a three-week vigil in 1963, see the discussion of past protests in Manhattanville Improvement Association, "Press Release," 15 April 1968, folder 1, box 64D3, NYCHA; Les Mathews, "New Locks, More Policemen Promised St. Nicholas Houses," *New York Amsterdam News*, 2 April 1966; notice posted in the lobbies at Marble Hill Houses, "Project Families Demand Our Own Lock," 10 March 1967, folder 5, box 65D8, NYCHA; Edith Paris to Sidney Schackman, 8 August 1967, folder 10, box 65E3, NYCHA; Metropolitan Council on Housing, "Press Release: Rutgers Project Stands Firm to Continue Vigil Until Guards Are Place [sic] in Lobby," 11 August 1967, folder 4, box 64B7, NYCHA; Alfredo Graham to Mr. Roberts, 13 November 1967, folder 4, box 65E4, NYCHA; Simon Anekwe, "Mugged as Others Picket," *New York Amsterdam News*, 18 November 1967; Manhattanville Improvement Association, "Press Release"; Ben Gould to Stanley Roberts, 1 May 1968, folder 4, box 60D8, NYCHA; "City School Budget Assailed; Housing Police Funds Allotted," *New York Times*, 24 May 1968; Stanley Roberts to Joseph Christian, "Patterson Houses Delegation at Mayor's Officer," 6 August 1968, folder 7, box 65E1, NYCHA; "Threaten Rent Strike," *New York Amsterdam News*, 8 August 1970; "Potential Tension Situations," 20 November 1970, folder 4, box 70D2, NYCHA; "Potential Tension Situations," 4 December 1970, folder 4, box 70D2, NYCHA; "Potential Tension Situations," 12 December 1970, folder 4, box 70D2, NYCHA; "Potential Tension Situations," 29 January 1971, folder 4, box 70D2, NYCHA; Les Mathews, "Lincoln Project Crime Wave 'Unfounded,'" *New York Amsterdam News*, 20 March 1971; "Tenants Protest Cutbacks," *The Chief*, 12 May 1971; "Project Tenants Threaten Rent Strike," *Long Island Press*, 30 May 1971; "Redfern Tenants Patrol Plans Protest," *Long Island Press*, 30 May 1971; "Project Groups Hits Golar on V-Gals," *Daily News*, 11 November 1971; "Baruch Tenants in a Protest," *New York Post*, 30 November 1971; Arthur Mulligan, "Lindsay Won't Hike Force: Housing Cops," *Daily News*, 11 December 1971; George Todd, "Angry Tenants Group Launches Drive for More Housing Cops," *New York Amsterdam News*, 25 December 1971; "Potential Tension Situations," 14 January 1972, folder 7, box 70D2, NYCHA; "Public Housing Tenants Demand 2,500 More Cops," *New York Amsterdam News*, 5 February 1972; "Bronx Tenants Demand Security," *New York Voice*, 11 August 1972; "Vladeck Tenants Hold Rally," *Daily News*, 21 July 1972; "Tension Report," n.d., but shortly after 3 August 1972, folder 7, box 65C5, NYCHA. See reference to demonstration at Millbrook Houses: "Tenants Demonstrate at Lehman Village Housing," *New York Amsterdam News*, 8 December 1973; "Law Makers Support the Rent Strike," *New York Amsterdam News*, 3 August 1974; Ad Hoc Committee Against the New York City Housing Policy to Mayor Beame, 8 November 1974, folder 5, box 88B2, NYCHA, "New York City Housing Authority Police—Federal Program," 12 December 1976, folder 5, box 90B4, NYCHA; Les Mathews, "Manhattanville Tenants Demand Protection," *New York Amsterdam News*, 24 July 1976; Department of Housing and Urban Development, "Dear Friend," 11 May 1977, page 4, folder 4, box 89E7, NYCHA; "Williamsburg Houses—Security Demonstration," 3 June 1980, folder 1, box 90A4 NYCHA.

114. Sugrue, *Sweet Land of Liberty*, 402–410.

115. See, for example, Jeanne Theoharis and Komozi Woodward, eds., *Groundwork: Local Black Freedom Movements in America* (New York: New York University Press, 2005); Felicia Kornbluh, *The Battle for Welfare Rights Politics and Poverty in Modern America* (Philadelphia: University of Pennsylvania Press, 2007); Van Gosse and Richard R. Moser, *The World the Sixties Made: Politics and Culture in Recent America* (Philadelphia: Temple University Press, 2003); Williams, *The Politics of Public Housing*; Sugrue, *Sweet Land of Liberty*.

116. For Gray's alliance with MFY, see Roberta S. Gold, "City of Tenants: New York's Housing Struggles and the Challenge of Postwar America" (Ph.D diss., University of Washington, 2004), 158–159; Cloward and Piven, *The Politics of Turmoil*, 154. In e-mail communications with the author, Piven was uncertain that Gray had collaborated with MFY, but Gold's sources are numerous and detailed and thus persuasive on the point (France Fox Piven to author, 6 January 2009).

117. Charles M. Payne, *I've Got the Light of Freedom: The Organizing Tradition and the Mississippi Freedom Struggle* (Berkeley: University of California Press, 1995), 426.

118. In a recent dissertation, for example, historian Tamar Carrol addresses MFY's 1964 rent strike and lovingly details the activism of a number of women in NYCHA developments from the 1970s onward, but skips over the 1968 rent strikes for more police officers. See Carroll, "Grassroots Feminism."

119. For the history of "section 755" that provided legal protection for striking tenants under certain conditions, see Joel Schwartz, "Tenant Power in the Liberal City 1943–1971," in *The Tenant Movement in New York City, 1904–1984*, ed. Ronald Lawson and Mark Naison (New Brunswick, NJ: Rutgers University Press, 1986), 134–208; see also Junius Griffin, "'Guerrilla War' Urged in Harlem; Rent Strike Chief Calls for '100 Revolutionaries,'" *New York Times*, 20 July 1964.

120. For rent strikers getting priority for admission to NYCHA, see Michael Lipsky and Margaret Levi, "Community Organization as a Political Resource," in *People and Politics in Urban Society*, ed. Harlan Hahn (Beverly Hills, CA: Sage, 1972), 195–196; Michael Lipsky, *Street-Level Bureaucracy: Dilemmas of the Individual in Public Services*, Publications of Russell Sage Foundation (New York: Russell Sage Foundation, 1980), 63–64; Simone Anekwe, "Call Tenants Vigil a 'Beautiful Thing,'" *New York Amsterdam News*, 20 April 1968; for Anekwe's career, J. Zamgba Browne, "Simon Anekwe: A True Journalist," *New York Amsterdam News*, 7 December 2000.

121. For MFY's internal decisions, see Schwartz, "Tenant Power in the Liberal City 1943–1971"; Roberta Gold argues that the Harlem rent strikes were more effective than Schwartz believes them to have been, but she doesn't take issue with his analysis of MFY at the time. See Gold, "City of Tenants," chapter 4.

122. Noel A. Cazenave, *Impossible Democracy: The Unlikely Success of the War on Poverty Community Action Programs* (Albany: State University of New York Press, 2007), 120–121; Griffin, "'Guerrilla War' Urged in Harlem"; Harold H. Weissman and Mobilization for Youth, *Individual and Group Services in the Mobilization for Youth Experience* (New York: Association Press, 1969), 120.

123. For Rangel see Simon Anekwe, "Tenants' 'Lobby Vigil' Shows Union," *New York Amsterdam News*, 15 May 1968.

124. *New York City Housing Authority v. Medlin*, 57 Misc. 2d 145, 291 N.Y.S. 2d 672 (New York County, 1968); "Tenants of East Side Projects Vow to Continue Rent Strike," *New York Times*, 14 April 1968; "Harlem Tenants Open Vigil to Press Protection Drive," *New York Times*, 5 May 1968; "Tenant Protection Held Outside Scope of Housing Board," *New York Times*, 28 June 1968; David K. Shipler, "City Is Evicting Rent Protesters," *New York Times*, 7 January 1969.

125. Pablo "Yorúba" Guzman quoted in Young Lords Party and Michael Abramson, *Palante: Young Lords Party*, 1st ed. (New York: McGraw-Hill, 1971), 75.

126. For the Young Lord Organization's origins and a discussion of its activities in New York 1969–1970, see Matthew Gandy, *Concrete and Clay: Reworking Nature in New York City* (Cambridge, MA: MIT Press, 2002), 162–175. See also Johanna Fernandez, "The Young

Lords and the Postwar City: Notes on the Geographical and Structural Reconfigurations of Contemporary Urban Life," in *African American Urban History since World War II*, ed. Kenneth L. Kusmer and Joe William Trotter (Chicago: University of Chicago Press, 2009).

127. For the Young Lords' thirteen-point program, see Lois Palken Rudnick, Judith E. Smith, and Rachel Rubin, *American Identities* (Malden, MA: Blackwell, 2006), 170–173.

128. "Tension Report—Carver Houses," December 1970, folder 4, box 70D2, NYCH; Sánchez, "Housing Puerto Ricans in New York City, 1945 to 1984," 565.

129. For Red Hook, see NYCHA, "Potential Tension Situation," 4 December 1970, and "Potential Tension Situation," 11 December 1970, folder 4, box 70D2, NYCHA; for the Lincoln Houses, see "Want Police Protection," *New York Amsterdam News*, 10 April 1971; "Lincoln Project Crime Wave Unfounded," *New York Amsterdam News*, 20 March 1971. For Ingersoll Houses, see "Promising End to a Rent Strike," *Daily News*, 21 September 1971. For Queensbridge Houses, see "Project Tenants Threaten Rent Strike," *Long Island Press*, 30 May 1971. For Resident Advisory Council, see Mulligan, "Lindsay Won't Hike Force," and Todd, "Angry Tenants Group Launches Drive for More Housing Cops."

130. "Threaten Rent Strike."

131. For the funding history of the HAPD, see "Comprehensive HUD Review," September 1983, folder 1, box 91C4, NYCHA; for HAPD's size, see New York City Council Resolution, 13 April, folder 4, box 62 C2, NYCHA; and Joseph Garber, "The History, Organization and Structure of the Hew York City Housing Authority Police Department" (honors thesis, John Jay College of Criminal Justice, City University of New York, 1970), For the population of NYCHA, see "Project Data Statistics (Blue Book)," 1965–1975, box 72A1 and box 72A2, NYCHA. For the size of the NYPD, see New York Police Department, "Annual Reports," 1965–1971, Special Collection, John Jay College of Criminal Justice, City University of New York. For the hiring freeze, see Murray Schumach, "City Ends Freeze on Police, Fire, Sanitation Jobs," *New York Times*, 3 November 1972; Martin Tolchin, "City Puts Freeze on Jobs of Police and Garbage Men," *New York Times*, 27 April 1970.

132. "Minutes of Project Security Problems Meeting," 18 October 1968, folder 5, box 64B7, NYCHA.

133. Walter Washington to Mayor John V. Lindsay, 22 September 1968, folder 5, box 64B7, NYCHA.

134. Joseph Christian to James Cavanagh, Deputy Mayor, 2 July 1974, folder 5, box 88B2, NYCHA.

CHAPTER 3 A CONFLUENCE OF CRISES

1. Helen L. Alfred and National Public Housing Conference, *Municipal Housing* (New York: National Public Housing Conference, 1935), 14.
2. Martha F. Davis, *Brutal Need: Lawyers and the Welfare Rights Movement, 1960–1973* (New Haven, CT: Yale University Press, 1993), 10–11.
3. Mark H. Maier, *City Unions: Managing Discontent in New York City* (New Brunswick, NJ: Rutgers University Press, 1987), 98–100.
4. For the narrowing gap in pay, see "Fire, Police Pay Is Raised by City," *New York Times*, 19 December 1963.
5. "Welfare Guards Strike for Raise," *New York Times*, 20 June 1961. See also "Welfare Policemen Picket and 40 Sit In," *New York Times*, 1 October 1968; and "Metropolitan Briefs," *New York Times*, 24 April 1973.

6. "City Will Add 100 to Housing Police," *New York Times*, 24 August 1962.
7. Studs Terkel, *Working: People Talk About What They Do All Day and How They Feel About What They Do* (New York: Pantheon Books, 1974), 582; A. H. Raskin, "A Rash of 'Me-Tooism' Raises Havoc in the Uniformed Services," *New York Times*, 27 October 1968. See also Christopher Wren, "Rivalry in Blue: Housing Police vs. City Police," *New York Times*, 15 February 1973.
8. Haile Selassie, interview by author, 1 February 2008, and Peter Grymes, interview by author, 10 February 2008; tapes of interviews in author's possession.
9. Chapter 734 of the Laws of New York State, 1967.
10. For the history of the Transit Police, see Robert Jackall, *Street Stories: The World of Police Detectives* (Cambridge, MA: Harvard University Press, 2005), 27–28.
11. Maier, *City Unions*, 77–83; Jean T. McKelvey "Fact Finding in Public Employment Disputes: Promise of Illusion?" *Industrial and Labor Relations Review* 22, no. 4. (July 1969): 528–543; Raymond D. Horton, "Public Employee Labor Relations under the Taylor Law," *Proceedings of the Academy of Political Science* 31, no. 3, *Governing New York State: The Rockefeller Years* (May 1974): 161–174; "Upsetting the Balance," *New York Times*, 16 October 1968.
12. Francis Madigan to Walter Washington, "Conference with the Housing Patrolman's Benevolent Association Officers and Trustees at the Niagara Falls on May 15, 1967 and at this office on May 23, 1967," 25 May 1967, folder 5, box 64B7, New York City Housing Authority Papers, La Guardia and Wagner Archives, La Guardia Community College (hereafter NYCHA).
13. Chief Weldon to Vice-Chairman Madigan, "Comments on your memorandum to Mr. Washington relative to discussions with the P.B.A.," 6 June 1967, folder 5, box 64B7, NYCHA.
14. Michael Luchuf, "An Analysis of the Administration of Policing of Public and Private Housing Developments" (master's thesis, Bernard M. Baruch College, 1967), 29–30.
15. Memorandum, eight-page analysis of the "crisis in the New York City Housing Authority Police Department," n.d. folder 4, box 62C1, NYCHA; Daniel Daley to Simeon Golar, "Job Action [report]," 21 January 1971; and Joseph Balzano to Simeon Golar, 8 February 1971, folder 4, box 62C1, NYCHA.
16. Balzano to Golar, 8 February 1971.
17. Daniel Daley to Simeon Golar, 8 April 1971, folder 5, box 62C1, NYCHA.
18. "Grant Pre-Application," n.d. [likely September 1971], folder 4, box 62C1, NYCHA. Nixon believed strongly that crime control was a states' rights issue and so provided money to individual states to regrant as they saw fit. NYCHA's grant, accordingly, was to New York's Office of Crime Control Planning, which funneled LEAA money to grantees in the state. For a history of such funding under Nixon and the ideological shifts in the LEAA in these years, see Nancy E. Marion, *A History of Federal Crime Control Initiatives, 1960–1993*, Praeger Series in Criminology and Crime Control Policy (Westport, CT: Praeger, 1994), chapter 4.
19. Joseph Christian to Joseph Balzano, 7 May 1975, folder 1, box 88B5, NYCHA; Edward Yarosz, "Synopsis of Interim Evaluation Report: Model Precinct, South Bronx," n.d., folder 2, box 65B2, NYCHA; and Daniel Daley to Joseph Christian, "Evaluation—South Bronx Model Precinct," 29 April 1975, folder 1, box 88B5, NYCHA.
20. Daniel Daley to Joseph Christian, "Evaluation—South Bronx Model Precinct," 29 April 1975, folder 1, box 88B5, NYCHA.

21. Joseph Christian to Honorable Louis de Salvio, 23 May 1975, folder 1, box 88B5, NYCHA.
22. Herman Hillman to Albert Walsh, 31 December 1968, folder 1, box 65A6, NYCHA; see also the same sentiment expressed by the Division of Housing and Community Renewal in William Meyers to Joseph Christian, 16 December 1968, folder 1, box 65A6, NYCHA.
23. For the hiring freeze, see Murray Schumach, "City Ends Freeze on Police, Fire, Sanitation Jobs," *New York Times*, 3 November 1972, and Martin Tolchin, "City Puts Freeze on Jobs of Police and Garbage Men," *New York Times*, 27 April 1970.
24. Bruce J. Schulman, *The Seventies: The Great Shift in American Culture, Society, and Politics* (New York: Free Press, 2001), 25–28; Edwin Sprenger to Marcus Levy, 14 July 1972, folder 1, box 62C2, and I. Margaret White to Marcus Levy, 8 August 1972, folder 1, box 62C2, NYCHA.
25. Chief Joseph Weldon and Captain Robert Ledee, "High-Rise Policing Techniques," 1966, folder 4, box 60E7, NYCHA.
26. Gladys Sturns, interview by the author, 31 October 2006; tape of interview in author's possession.
27. Thomas McAndrews to Daniel Daley, "Supervisory Patrol—Around the Clock," 19 November 1970, folder 5, box 62C1, NYCHA; Daniel Daley to Marcus Levy, "Supervisory Patrol," April 1971, folder 5, box 62C1, NYCHA. That same year, new recruits to the HAPD complained to CUNY psychologist Morton Bard, who was studying the force, about "supervisors' plainclothes surveillance" of patrolmen's beats. See Morton Bard, "Police Management of Conflicts among People," 48, August 1970, folder 10, box 60E7, NYCHA.
28. Daniel Daley to Marcus Levy, "Activity—Internal Affairs Unit," 2 August 1972, folder 1, box 62C2, NYCHA.
29. The 1979 experiment was evaluated in Steven Edwards, *A Process Evaluation of the Urban Initiatives Anti-Crime Program* (John F. Kennedy School of Government at Harvard University and The Police Foundation, 1982), vol. 1, "Leveraging," 8, 12, and vol. 2, "Case Studies: Jersey City," 8, available at the Police Foundation, Washington, DC.
30. While the nature of the first two of these causes for New York's woes in the 1970s generates little debate, there is scant consensus as to who mismanaged what in the city's finances. On the political left, commentators note the city's welfare rolls and union contracts were not significantly out of line with other cities and so finger other causes. Charles Morris, assistant New York City budget director under Lindsay, blames the rapid expansion of hospitals and the City University of New York. See Charles R. Morris, *The Cost of Good Intentions: New York City and the Liberal Experiment, 1960–1975*, 1st ed. (New York: Norton, 1980), chapter 8. More recently, Kim Moody blames the city's politically influenced procurement process for equipment and supplies, where costs far outran inflation. See Kim Moody, *From Welfare State to Real Estate* (New York: The New Press, 2007), chapter 1. The political right frames the emergency as the inevitable consequence of financial drains caused by a bloated welfare system and unreasonable union demands. See Ken Auletta, *The Streets Were Paved with Gold* (New York: Random House, 1979).
31. John H. Mollenkopf and Manuel Castells, eds., *Dual City: Restructuring New York* (New York: Russell Sage Foundation, 1991), 56–57; for the shrinkage in the public sector, see E. Surpin, T. Bettridge, and D. Smith, "Economic Development: Problem Analysis and Policy Directions" (New York: Community Service Society, 1986). Public sector employment, however, given its rapid expansion between 1970 and 1975, ended the

decade up by 6.2 percent. For unemployment figures see "Annual Report," New York State Department of Social Services (Albany, 1976).

32. Michael B. Katz, *In the Shadow of the Poorhouse: A Social History of Welfare in America* (New York: Basic Books, 1986), 297–298.

33. Mark K. Levitan and Susan S. Wieler, "Poverty in New York City, 1969–99: The Influence of Demographic Change, Income Growth and Income Inequality," *Economic Policy Review* 14, no. 1 (2008): 15.

34. For the origins of the term and its broader cultural meanings, see Sudhir Alladi Venkatesh *American Project: The Rise and Fall of a Modern Ghetto* (Cambridge, MA: Harvard University Press, 2000), chapter 3.

35. For a study of the new informal economy in the 1970s on the Lower East Side of Manhattan, see Jagna Sharff, "The Underground Economy of a Poor Neighborhood," in *Cities of the United States: Studies in Urban Anthropology*, ed. Leith Mullings (New York: Columbia University Press, 1987), 19–50. See also Russell Leigh Sharman, *The Tenants of East Harlem* (Berkeley: University of California Press, 2006), 69; Phillippe Bourgois, *In Search of Respect: Selling Crack in El Barrio* (New York: Cambridge University Press, 1995). Also Carlos Rhonda, interview by author and Maria Jimenez, 23 October 2006; Jacqueline Hines, interview by author and Marie Figeroa, 11 October 2006; Rosa Cruz, interview by author and Cristian Nunez, 18 October 2006; Gladys Sturns interview; Maria Vasquez, interview by author and Christian Nunez and Maria Figueroa, 29 November 2006; Sarah Martin, interview by author, 14 April 2009; tapes of all interviews in author's possession.

36. Diana Perez, interview by Edward Paulino, 12 September 2008; tape of interview in author's possession.

37. Cyril Grossman, interview by Marcia Robertson, 1 August 1990, NYCHA Oral History Project, box 1, NYCHA; Anna Lou Dehavenon, "Superordinate Behavior in Urban Homes: A Video Analysis of Request-Compliance and Food Control Behavior in Two Black and Two White Families Living in New York City" (Ph.D. diss., Columbia University, 1978), 81; Anna Lou Dehavenon, telephone interview by author, 12 September, 2008. For public housing's portrayal in the popular press, see A. Scott Henderson, "'Tarred with the Exceptional Image': Public Housing and Popular Discourse, 1950–1990," *American Studies* 36, no. 1 (1995): 31–52.

38. "Synopsis of Interim Evaluation Report, Model Precinct, South Bronx," folder 2, box 65B2, NYCHA.

39. "Transcript of the Meeting of the Committee on Public Safety, City Hall," 20 September 1978, folder 3, box 91C4, NYCHA. At the time I consulted these papers, the La Guardia and Wagner Archives was planning to relocate them.

40. Jesus Morales, interview by author, 1 February 2008, and Artie Brown, interview by author, 15 June 2005; tapes of interviews in author's possession.

41. Chief Daley to Chairman Christian, "Integration of Housing Authority Police Department's Communications with that of the New York City Police Department," 2 July 1974, and Daniel Daley, "Meeting re: Crime South Bronx Area," 31 October 1974, folder 2, box 65B2, NYCHA; "Transcript of the Meeting of the Committee on Public Safety, 20 September 1978, 34, folder 3, box 91C4, NYCHA.

42. Sudhir Venkatesh, "American Project: An Historical-Ethnography of Chicago's Robert Taylor Homes" (Ph.D. diss., University of Chicago, 1997), 90, 93, 95, 75.

43. Sudhir Venkatesh, *Off the Books: The Underground Economy of the Urban Poor* (Cambridge, MA: Harvard University Press, 2006), 90.

44. Nicholas Lemann, *The Promised Land: The Great Black Migration and How It Changed America* (New York: Alfred A. Knopf, 1991), 198; James Patterson, *Grand Expectations: The United States, 1945–1974* (New York: Oxford University Press, 1996), 648–649. For the history of the changing academic assessment of Model Cities, see Robert Wood, "Model Cities: What Went Wrong—the Program or Its Critics?" in *Neighborhood Policy and Programmes: Past and Present*, ed. Naomi Carmon (New York: St. Martin's Press, 1990), 61–73.

45. Janet L. Abu-Lughod, *Race, Space, and Riots in Chicago, New York, and Los Angeles* (New York: Oxford University Press, 2007), chapter 4; Thomas J. Sugrue, *Sweet Land of Liberty: The Forgotten Struggle for Civil Rights in the North* (New York: Random House, 2008), 327.

46. "Central Brooklyn Model Cities—Overview," 23 January 1969, 10, folder 4, box 64B7, NYCHA.

47. "Central Brooklyn Model Cities—Problem Analysis," 23 January 1969, 2, folder 4, box 64B7, NYCHA.

48. "Central Brooklyn Model Cities—Goals Safety and Sanitation," 23 January 1969, 2–4, folder 4, box 64B7, NYCHA.

49. President's Commission on Law Enforcement and Administration of Justice, *The Challenge of Crime in a Free Society: Report: The Police* (Washington, DC: Government Printing Office, 1967), 123–124; James Vorenberg, "The War on Crime: The First Five Years," *The Atlantic*, May 1972.

50. "Central Brooklyn Model Cities—Program Approaches," 23 January 1969, 3, folder 4, box 64B7, NYCHA; Will Lissner, "City Plans to Hire Youths in Slums as Police Cadets," *New York Times*, 24 February 1969.

51. "Public Safety Task Force Meeting," 9 April 1968, folder 1, box 65A6, NYCHA; "Central Brooklyn Model Cities—Program Approaches," 23 January 1969, 8; Eugenia Flatow, telephone interview by author, 2 February 2009.

52. James Erickson, "Community Service Officer," *The Police Chief*, June 1973, 43, 42.

53. Deputy Chief Robert Ledee, "The Housing Authority Community Service Officer Program," 30 April 1975, folder 4, box 91D5, NYCHA.

54. William M. Rohe and Lauren B. Gates, *Planning with Neighborhoods*, Urban and Regional Policy and Development Studies (Chapel Hill: University of North Carolina Press, 1985), 36–50; Lemann, *The Promised Land*, 165.

55. "The Conversion of John Lindsay," *Time*, 23 August 1971; Martin Tolchin, "Lindsay Bids U.S. Quadruple Its Aid for Jobless Here," *New York Times*, 15 August 1971; Ledee, "The Housing Authority Community Service Officer Program."

56. As late as 1965, Irish and Italians constituted 42 and 25 percent respectively of the NYPD; see Arthur Niederhoffer, *Behind the Shield: The Police in Urban Society* (Garden City, NY: Doubleday, 1967), 143. For the sense of instability during the 1970s in one working-class white neighborhood, see Jonathan Rieder, *Canarsie: The Jews and Italians of Brooklyn against Liberalism* (Cambridge, MA: Harvard University Press, 1985), chapter 3. For the response to riots, see Edward Rogowsky, Louis H. Gold, and David W. Abbott, "Police: The Civilian Review Board Controversy," in *Race and Politics in New York City*, ed. Jewel Bellush and Stephen M. David (New York: Praeger Publishers, 1971), 59–67.

57. Emanuel Perlmutter, "State High Court Quashes Model Cities Job Project," *New York Times*, 4 July 1973; for the rehiring of laid-off HAPD officers using funds from the federal Comprehensive Employment and Training Act of 1973 (CETA), see "Suggested

Remarks for Mayor Beame," 5 April 1977, folder 26, box 89E6, NYCHA; for the nationwide pattern of CETA funds used to rehire laid-off city workers, see Helene Slessarev, *The Betrayal of the Urban Poor* (Philadelphia: Temple University Press, 1997), 54–59. Although nationwide most recipients of CETA jobs were white males until 1978, in major cities like New York CETA was an overwhelmingly minority program.

58. Robert Lane, "Fire, Police Aides Air Gripes," *New York Sunday News*, 25 June 1972; "Police, Fire Aide Filing Still Open," *New York Amsterdam News*, 18 September 1971.

59. Grymes interview.

60. For the origins of the Black Liberation Army (BLA), see Akinyele Omowale Umoja, "Repression Breeds Resistance: The Black Liberation Army and the Radical Legacy of the Black Panther Party," in *Liberation, Imagination and the Black Panther Party: A New Look at the Black Panthers and Their Legacy*, ed. K. Cleaver (New York: Routledge, 2001), 3–19; and Peniel E. Joseph, *Waiting 'Til the Midnight Hour: A Narrative History of Black Power in America* (New York: Henry Holt, 2006), 269; Robert Daley, *Target Blue: An Insider's View of the N.Y.P.D* (New York: Delacorte Press, 1971), 76. The story of the BLA's campaign against police officers in New York is told in Robert Tanenbaum and Philip Rosenberg, *Badge of the Assassin* (New York: E. P. Dutton, 1979).

61. William Frederici, "Seek Revenge Motive in Cop Killing," *New York Daily News*, 5 June 1971.

62. Michael Patterson, "Violence Bared in HA, City Police Feud," *New York Sunday News*, 27 August 1972; Edward Ranzal, "Study Is Ordered on Police Roles," *New York Times*, 5 June 1971; Wren, "Rivalry in Blue: Housing Police vs. City Police." For the relationship between police brutality and the rise of the Black Panthers, see Jeffrey Ogbonna Green Ogbar, *Black Power: Radical Politics and African American Identity* (Baltimore: Johns Hopkins University Press, 2004), 85–87.

63. "Balzano Urges Probe of HA Police Shortage," *The Chief*, 11 October 1973; for dates of the original court action, see "Slum-Job Tests Voided as Biased," *New York Times*, 3 March 1972.

64. "Block Plan to Train Minorities," *New York Amsterdam News*, 2 October 1971; Douglas Martin, "Robert Lowery, First Black Fire Commissioner, Dies at 85," *New York Times*, 27 July 2001. The case took a number of twists. That September, Justice Samuel Silverman placed a stay on the scheduled test until he could hear arguments; he later lifted the order, but refused to allow results from the test to be published until the legality of the CSO program could be determined, and in March 1972, he ruled against the recruitment program. Justice Harold Stevens of New York's Appellate Court overturned that decision in March 1973, finding in favor of the city. The uniformed services unions appealed Stevens's decision that July before the New York State Court of Appeals, which upheld Justice Silverman's original 1972 ruling. See "2000 Seek Cop, Fire Aide Jobs," *New York Post*, 17 September 1971; "Slum-Job Tests Voided as Biased"; "Model Cities Firemen, Police Must Come from Low-Income Area," *Civil Service Leader*, 13 March 1973; Perlmutter, "State High Court Quashes Model Cities Job Project."

65. Robert M. Fogelson, *Big-City Police* (Cambridge, MA: Harvard University Press, 1977), chapter 11; Detroit Police Department, "Community Service Officer First Year Report," 31 March 1973, MSU Planning Report Collection, Michigan State University, East Lansing; City of Newark Police Department, "Community Service Officer Program and Robbery Prevention Officer Program: An Evaluation Report Submitted to the Prevention Committee of the Governor's Commission on Criminal Justice," January 1978, National Criminal Justice Reference Service.

66. Randolph Taylor, interview by author, 15 December 2008, tape of interview in author's possession.

67. Edward Kirkman, "Link California Skyjacker to Harlem Cop Murders," *Daily News*, 11 January 1972; Umoja, "Repression Breeds Resistance"; Michael Kaufman, "9 in Black 'Army' Are Hunted in Police Assassinations," *New York Times*, 9 February 1972; Randy Jurgensen, *Circle of Six: The True Story of New York's Most Notorious Cop-Killer and the Cop Who Risked Everything to Catch Him*, 1st ed. (New York: Disinformation Co., 2006), xix; Umoja, "Repression Breeds Resistance."

68. Patterson, "Violence Bared in HA, City Police Feud"; "Black Cop Beaten by White Cop," *New York Amsterdam News*, 23 June 1973; "P.B.A. Is Opposing Recruiting Plan," *New York Times*, 20 August 1973. Demographics of the HAPD eligibles list calculated from Jack Marvin Weisel, "The Effect of Recruit Training on Authoritarian Attitudes of Housing Police" (master's thesis, John Jay College of Criminal Justice, City University of New York, 1973), 18–19. "Housing Police Call M'Kiernan's Stand on Recruits 'Racist,'" *New York Times*, 22 August 1973; "Three Police Groups Accuse McKiernan of Betrayal, Poor Tactics, Deception," *New York Times*, 25 August 1973.

69. The city heralded 230 newly hired HAPD officers in November of 1973, but in reality such appointments merely replaced the twenty-year-old department's first wave of retirees who, having served their two decades, had become eligible for pensions. See Judith Cummings, "230 Inducted as Housing Police; One Is the First Woman Recruit," *New York Times*, 20 November 1973; "How Poor Fight Crime in Projects," *New York Post*, 10 November 1971 (note that the reporter mistakenly identifies the complex as the "Lillian Smith" Houses); "Housing PBA Blasts Lindsay Budget Allocation," *Civil Service Leader*, 13 February 1973; "Housing Unit to Test Private Guards," *New York Times*, 1 October 1972; memorandum by Blanco Deneno to Marcus Levy, "Guard Services at Meltzer-Hernandez," 13 September 1972, folder 2, box 88B4, NYCHA; "Balzano Urges Probe of HA Shortage," *The Chief*, 11 October 1972; "HA Police Superiors, City Reach Impasse," *The Chief*, 14 March 1973.

70. Terry Ann Knopf and Lemberg Center for the Study of Violence, *Youth Patrols: An Experiment in Community Participation* (Waltham, MA: Brandeis University, Lemberg Center for the Study of Violence, 1969).

71. "Sentinel of the Streets," *New York Sunday News*, December 1972; see also Charlayne Hunter, "Fear Is Steady Companion of Many Harlem Residents," *New York Times*, 3 June 1971; "Residential Security Program, NAHRO Conference," 15 September, 1978, folder 13, box 92E1, NYCHA.

72. "Transcript of the Meeting of the Committee on Public Safety," 20 September 1978, 116.

73. Ibid., 127–128, 30, 52; "Transcript of the Meeting of the Committee on Public Safety," 31 October 1978, folder 3, box 91C4, NYCHA.

74. Alvin Rabushka and William G. Weissert, *Caseworkers or Police?: How Tenants See Public Housing* (Stanford, CA: Hoover Institution Press, 1977), xvi, xvii.

75. Ibid., 79.

76. Percy Sutton to Joseph Christian, 4 April 1974, and Joseph Christian to Percy Sutton, 7 May 1974, both in folder 1, box 65B2, NYCHA; Percy Sutton to Joseph Christian, 25 July 1974, folder 2, box 65B2, NYCHA; for conflict over assignments see handwritten notes of Joseph Christian, "Meeting with Praetorians/Hispanics," 23 August 1974, folder 2, box 65B2, NYCHA.

77. Geoffrey Alpert and Mark Moore, "Measuring Police Performance in the New Paradigm of Policing," in *Community Policing: Contemporary Readings*, ed. Geoffrey Alpert and Alex Piquero (Long Grove, IL: Waveland Press, 1998), 219.
78. Grymes interview.
79. Morton Bard, "Police Family Crisis Intervention and Conflict Management: An Action Research Analysis" (report prepared for the Department of Justice Law Enforcement Assistance Administration, John Jay College of Criminal Justice, City University of New York, 1972), 117–118.
80. The first such evaluative instruments were proposed in 1935 by a protégé of the Progressive-era reformer August Vollmer. See Arthur Bellman, "A Police Service Rating Scale," *Journal of Criminal Law and Criminology* 26 (1935), 74–114; George L. Kelling and Mary A. Wycoff, "Evolving Strategy of Policing: Case Studies of Strategic Change" (National Criminal Justice Reference Service, 2001), 3–4; Patrick O'Hara, *Why Law Enforcement Organizations Fail: Mapping the Organizational Fault Lines in Policing* (Durham, NC: Carolina Academic Press, 2005). For the use of the phrase in the corporate context, see Louis Lowenstein, *The Investor's Dilemma: How Mutual Funds Are Betraying Your Trust and What to Do About It* (Hoboken, NJ: John Wiley, 2008), 45.
81. Grymes interview.
82. "Transcript of the Meeting of the Committee on Public Safety," 20 September 1978, 80, folder 3, box 91C4, NYCHA; City of New York, "Driving Crime, Disorder and Fear from the Public Housing of New York" (New York, September 13, 1994), 6.
83. For a comparison of the impact of expanding civil rights upon different public housing authorities in the United States, see Nathan Glazer, *From Cause to a Style: Modernist Architecture's Encounter with the American City* (Princeton, NJ: Princeton University Press, 2007), 182.
84. Mary and Tricia Alfson, interview by author and Nicholas Alfson, 15 December 2006; Terri Sheeps, interview by author and Rasheda Denny, 10 February 2007; Sister Gibbs, interview by author, 7 July 2007; tapes of all interviews in the author's possession.
85. Grymes interview; Joseph Keeney, interview by author, 6 December 2007; tapes of interviews in author's possession.
86. David Steigerwald, *The Sixties and the End of Modern America* (New York: St. Martin's Press, 1995), 202–205.
87. John Knowles, "My Separate Peace," *Esquire*, March 1985, 106–109.
88. G. Calvin Mackenzie and Robert Weisbrot, *The Liberal Hour: Washington and the Politics of Change in the 1960s* (New York: Penguin Press, 2008).
89. Steigerwald, *The Sixties and the End of Modern America*, 203.
90. Michael Appleby and Hentry Heifetz, "Legal Challenges to Formal and Informal Denials of Welfare Rights," in *Justice and the Law, in the Mobilization for Youth Experience*, ed. Harold H. Weissman (New York: Associated Press, 1969), 104.
91. Steigerwald, *The Sixties and the End of Modern America*, 203.
92. Allen J. Matusow, *The Unraveling of America: A History of Liberalism in the 1960s* (New York: Harper & Row, 1984), 123.
93. H. P. Stumpf, "Law and Poverty: A Political Perspective," *Wisconsin Law Review* 13, no. 3 (1968): 711.
94. Herbert Mitgang, "The Storefront Lawyer Helps the Poor," *New York Times*, 10 November 1968; Joel F. Handler, Ellen Jane Hollingsworth, and Howard S. Erlanger,

Lawyers and the Pursuit of Legal Rights, Poverty Policy Analysis Series (New York: Academic Press, 1978), 73.

95. Handler, Hollingsworth, and Erlanger, *Lawyers and the Pursuit of Legal Rights*, 29.

96. Between 1967 and 1972, roughly eight hundred Reginald Heber Smith Fellowships helped subsidize and train poverty lawyers nationwide. Legal Aid was one of a number of "favored" jobs that provided deferment from the draft. See Kris Shepard, *Rationing Justice: Poverty Lawyers and Poor People in the Deep South* (Baton Rouge: Louisiana State University Press, 2007), 17–18.

97. See Harold Rothwax, "The Law as an Instrument of Social Change," in *Justice and the Law, in the Mobilization for Youth Experience*, ed. Harold H. Weissman, 137–144.

98. Susan E. Lawrence, *The Poor in Court : The Legal Services Program and Supreme Court Decision Making* (Princeton, NJ: Princeton University Press, 1990), 100; Davis, *Brutal Need*, chapter 2; Laura Kalman, *The Strange Career of Legal Liberalism* (New Haven, CT: Yale University Press, 1996), 43.

99. Davis, *Brutal Need*, 35.

100. George Brager, quoted in ibid., 29.

101. Ibid., 31–32.

102. Susan Youngblood Ashmore, *Carry It On: The War on Poverty and the Civil Rights Movement in Alabama, 1964–1972* (Athens: University of Georgia Press, 2008), 72–73.

103. For the history of NYCHA's tenant policies, see Nicholas Dagen Bloom, *Public Housing That Worked: New York in the Twentieth Century* (Philadelphia: University of Pennsylvania Press, 2008), chapter 9. For the origins of the "New Journalism" in 1950s New York, see Carol Polsgrove, *It Wasn't Pretty Folks but Didn't We Have Fun?: Surviving the '60s with Esquire's Harold Hayes* (Oakland, CA: RDR Books, 2001), 132–133, and Dan Wakefield, *New York in the Fifties* (Boston: Houghton Mifflin/Seymour Lawrence, 1992), 296–299. Underscoring the linkages in New York "poverty" journalism at the time, Salisbury offered Wakefield a job at the *New York Times*. See Wakefield, *New York in the Fifties*, 329.

104. Dan Wakefield, *Island in the City: The World of Spanish Harlem* (Boston: Houghton Mifflin, 1959), 242–243. Wakefield's writings on this topic originally appeared in *Harper's*, *Commentary*, and *The Nation*; Harrison E. Salisbury, "Lethargy of Public Found at Root of Youth Problem," *New York Times*, 30 March 1958; Harrison E. Salisbury, *The Shook-up Generation* (New York: Harper, 1958), 75.

105. "Urban Redevelopment Is Assailed Here; Housing Projects Called 'Bleak Towers,'" *New York Times*, 26 June 1958.

106. Patricia Cayo Sexton, *Spanish Harlem: An Anatomy of Poverty* (New York: Harper & Row, 1965), 42, 37. James Baldwin at much the same time famously wrote that "the projects in Harlem are hated. They are hated almost as much as policemen, and that is saying a great deal." Years later, however, Baldwin was forced to retreat somewhat from his argument and acknowledged that the residents of Harlem's projects were "much embittered by this description." See James Baldwin, *The Price of the Ticket: Collected Nonfiction, 1948–1985*, 1st ed. (New York: St. Martin's/Marek, 1985), 209–210; Bloom, *Public Housing That Worked*, 178.

107. Michael B. Rosen, "Tenants' Rights in Public Housing," in *Housing for the Poor: Rights and Remedies*, ed. Norman Dorsen (New York: New York University School of Law, 1967), 156. For MFY's role in the article, see Rosen's dedications. Rosen had actually written the article the previous year for a law class.

108. Michael Rosen, interview by author, 5 May 2009, tape of interview in author's possession.

109. Ibid.; Rosen, "Tenants' Rights in Public Housing," 156–157, 214.

110. Public Housing Administration, Consolidation Annual Contributions Contract, Part 1 § 206, Admission Policies, April 1966; for MFY's efforts to extract the rules, see Rosen, "Tenants' Rights in Public Housing"; "Proposed Revision of Tenant Selection Policies and Procedures," 14 December, folder 12, box 65C8, NYCHA.

111. Rosen, "Tenants' Rights in Public Housing," 225–227.

112. Steven Roberts, "Behavior at Issue in a Housing Case," *New York Times*, 10 April 1966.

113. *Manigo v. New York City Housing Authority*, 51 Misc.2d 829, 273 NYS2d 1003 (Sup. Ct. 1966), aff'd 27 AD2d 803, 279 NYS2d 1014 (1st Dept. 1967); Roberts, "Behavior at Issue in a Housing Case"; Edward C. Burks, "Housing Agency Upheld on Screening," *New York Times*, 11 August 1966; Roberts, "Behavior at Issue in a Housing Case," 236; Rosen, "Tenants' Rights in Public Housing."

114. *Holmes v. New York City Housing Authority* (398 F.2d 262 [2d Cir. 1968]); Justice Ryan quoted in Roger Starr, "Which of the Poor Shall Live in Public Housing," *The Public Interest* 23 (Spring 1971): 119.

115. Owen M. Fiss, *The Law as It Could Be* (New York: New York University Press, 2003), 207.

116. Davis, *Brutal Need*, 87–88, chapter 8; Starr, "Which of the Poor Shall Live in Public Housing," 120–122.

117. David Frum, *How We Got Here: The 70's, the Decade That Brought You Modern Life (for Better or Worse)* (New York: Basic Books, 2000), 228–235; Henry J. Friendly, "Some Kind of Hearing," *University of Pennsylvania Law Review* 123 (1975): 1279–1295.

118. Starr, "Which of the Poor Shall Live in Public Housing," 121.

119. *Escalera v. NYCHA*, 425. F. 2d 853 (2d Cir. 1970), cert. denied 500 IS 853 (1971).

120. For the ways in which New York was uniquely friendly to renters (and hostile to landlords), see Roberta S. Gold, "City of Tenants: New York's Housing Struggles and the Challenge of Postwar America" (Ph.D. diss., University of Washington, 2004).

121. Valerie D. White, "Modifying the Escalera Consent Decree: A Case Study on the Application of the *Rufo* Test," *Fordham Urban Law Journal* 23 (1996): 377–412.

122. Philip G. Schrag and Michael Meltsner, *Reflections on Clinical Legal Education* (Boston: Northeastern University Press, 1998), 43–44.

123. "NYCHA-Legal," Comprehensive Review, NYCHA, HUD, Region II, September 1983, folder 1, box 91C4 XXX–3–XXX–4, NYCHA; total number of households (138,706) calculated from the number of units in operation as of 1979, excluding developments for the elderly and minus an estimated 8 percent of all households in non-elderly complexes headed by a resident over sixty-five over the course of the decade. See the complete list of developments at http://www.nyc.gov/html/nycha/downloads/pdf/dev_data_book.pdf; Val Coleman, interview by author, 27 November 2007, tape of interview in author's possession.

124. For a discussion of the conflicts between the "not-so-old Left and the not-so-New," see Steigerwald, *The Sixties and the End of Modern America*, chapter 5.

125. Richard Arum, *Judging School Discipline: The Crisis of Moral Authority* (Cambridge, MA: Harvard University Press, 2003), 8.

126. "NYCHA chairman Joseph Christian discusses with Harold Pinkney . . . ," December 1973, photograph number 02.015.444, La Guardia Wagner Archive/NYCHA

Photograph Collection. NYCHA. For the symbolism of this hairstyle to African American culture in the period, see Angela Y. Davis and Joy James, *The Angela Y. Davis Reader*, Blackwell Readers (Malden, MA: Blackwell, 1998), chapter 18; Harold Pinkney to Joseph Christian, 22 March 1976, folder 2, box 88A6 NYCHA.

127. Lewis Ehrenshaft to Blanca Cadeno, 9 March 1977, folder 1, box 90A4, NYCHA; Mildred Rosenberg to H. Calcanes, 28 December 1979, folder 1, box 90A4, NYCHA; Elois Crenchaw to Edward McClendon, 31 October 1977, folder 5, box 90A4, NYCHA; Cyril Grossman, interview by Marcia Robertson, 1 August 1990, NYCHA Oral History Project, box 1, NYCHA, 29.

128. David K. Shipler, "The Case of a City Tenant and Guilt by Association," *New York Times*, 28 February 1972; "Meeting of the Committee on Public Safety, 31 October 1989," 123; Charles Rangel to Simeon Golar, 21 March 1973, and Golar to Rangel, 18 April 1973, both in folder 4, box 70D2, NYCHA.

129. "Minutes of Authority Meeting with Tenant Association Executive Board," 30 June 1980, folder 1, box 90A4, NYCHA.

130. Sheeps interview.

131. "Tenants Advisors Group Cites Major Victories," *New York Amsterdam News*, 29 May 1971; for MFY's position, see Nancy LeBlanc to "Secretary," 28 May 1971, folder 6, box 89E6, NYCHA.

132. Anonymous, but likely John Simon, n.d. but likely August 1973, "Dogs in Public Housing," folder 6, box 89E6, NYCHA. For likely author and date see Edward Norton to John Simon, 14 August 1973, folder 6, box 89E6, NYCHA.

133. I have drawn extensively here from Vanessa Barker, *The Politics of Imprisonment: How the Democratic Process Shapes the Way America Punishes Offenders* (Oxford: Oxford University Press, 2009), 148–153, Gerald Fraser, "Harlem Response Mixed," *New York Times*, 5 January 1973; Francis X. Clines, "Harlem Leaders Back Life Terms for Drug Sale," *New York Times*, 23 January 1973 "Governor Rockefeller Proposes New Laws," *New York Amsterdam News*, 13 January 1973; Paul Montgomery, "Parents Storm City Hall over Boy's Pill Death," *New York Times*, 18 February 1970; Richard Maddens, "Rangel Discovers His Campaign against Drugs Is Bearing Results," *New York Times*, 13 September 1971. As Barker argues, however, many Harlem residents expressed opposition to mandatory sentences for addicts who sold drugs to support their habit.

CHAPTER 4 THE END OF COMMUNITY POLICING

1. Wasserman Associates, Inc., "Providing a Secure Environment in NYCHA Housing Developments," 15 January 1992, folder 1, box 100B3, New York City Housing Authority Papers, La Guardia and Wagner Archives, La Guardia Community College (hereafter NYCHA).

2. Lawrence Meir Friedman, *Government and Slum Housing: American Federalism* (New York: Arno Press, 1978), 131.

3. The role of mother-only families in poverty has been highly contentious since Patrick Moynihan's 1965 "The Negro Family: The Case for National Action," but has experienced renewed scholarly and popular attention of late. As the authors of Economic Policy Institute's *The State of Working America* have detailed, although such households have significantly higher rates of poverty, the impact of such families on poverty rates nationally is secondary compared to other forces such as job growth and inequality. The formation of such families pushed the nation's poverty rate up by 3.3 percent since 1969,

although the relative role of such families in elevating poverty rates has declined over time. In short, although a great deal of data suggests that single parenthood imposes hardships on children, families, and often communities, marriage is hardly a cure for America's growing poverty. See Lawrence R. Mishel, Jared Bernstein, and Heidi Shierholz, *The State of Working America 2008/2009* (Ithaca, NY: Cornell University Press, 2009), 320–322, and Kathryn Edin and Maria Kefalas, *Promises I Can Keep: Why Poor Women Put Motherhood before Marriage* (Berkeley: University of California Press, 2005).

4. Nicholas Dagen Bloom, *Public Housing That Worked: New York in the Twentieth Century* (Philadelphia: University of Pennsylvania Press, 2008), chapter 11; David Dinkins, "A Shelter Is Not a Home: A Report of the Manhattan Borough President's Task Force on Housing for Homeless Families" (New York: Manhattan Borough President's Office, March 1987); Sheila Rule, "17,000 Families in Public Housing Doubling up Illegally, City Believes," *New York Times*, 21 April 1983; Langley C. Keyes, *Strategies and Saints: Fighting Drugs in Subsidized Housing* (Washington DC: Urban Institute, 1992), 93. For the relationship between "missing men" and underground economy, see Philippe I. Bourgois, *In Search of Respect: Selling Crack in El Barrio* (New York: Cambridge University Press, 1995), 4–6.
5. Keyes, *Strategies and Saints*, 95.
6. Greg Donaldson, *The Ville: Cops and Kids in Urban America* (New York: Ticknor & Fields, 1993), 39.
7. C. J. Vergara, "Hell in a Very Tall Place," *Atlantic Monthly*, September 1989; Bloom, *Public Housing That Worked*.
8. Christian Parenti, *Lockdown America: Police and Prisons in the Age of Crisis* (London and New York: Verso, 2001); Mike Gray, *Drug Crazy: How We Got into This Mess and How We Can Get Out*, 1st ed. (New York: Random House, 1998).
9. Giuliani's official biography on New York City's Web site emphasizes that he "spearheaded the effort to jail drug dealers." See http://www.nyc.gov/html/records/rwg/html/bio.html, accessed 9 July 2009. A largely uncritical biography can be found in Frederick F. Siegel and Harry Siegel, *The Prince of the City: Giuliani, New York, and the Genius of American Life*, 1st ed. (San Francisco: Encounter Books, 2005); more critical assessments include Parenti, *Lockdown America*, chapter 4. Peter Noel, *Why Blacks Fear "America's Mayor": Reporting Police Brutality and Black Activist Politics under Rudy Giuliani* (New York: iUniverse, 2007), while rarely substantiating its claims, succinctly captures sentiments in many poor neighborhoods.
10. Jonathan Simon, *Governing through Crime: How the War on Crime Transformed American Democracy and Created a Culture of Fear* (New York: Oxford University Press, 2007), 194–198.
11. For a history and definition of urban liberalism, see Alex S. Vitale, *City of Disorder: How the Quality of Life Campaign Transformed New York Politics* (New York: New York University Press, 2008), chapter 3.
12. Barry Gottehrer, "The Public Housing Problem. . . . ," *Herald Tribune*, 26 March 1965. For Ginsberg, see Martha F. Davis, *Brutal Need: Lawyers and the Welfare Rights Movement, 1960–1973* (New Haven, CT: Yale University Press, 1993), 42; Ginsberg's testimony quoted in Bloom, *Public Housing That Worked*, 209.
13. George Sternlieb and Bernard P. Indik, *The Ecology of Welfare: Housing and the Welfare Crisis in New York City* (New Brunswick, NJ: Transaction Books, 1973), chapter 1. McCandlish Phillips, "City Marks Birth of Public Housing," *New York Times*, 4 December 1960.

14. *Thomas v. Housing Authority of City of Little Rock*, 282 F. Supp. 575 (1967).
15. Albert Walsh, "Standards for Admission of Tenants," 1 May 1968, folder 5, box 60D8, NYCHA; Thomas Poster, "City Removes Morality Test for Its Housing," *New York Sunday News*, 12 May 1968.
16. Poster, "City Removes Morality Test for Its Housing."
17. Phillip Thompson, "Public Housing in New York City," in *Housing and Community Development in New York City: Facing the Future*, ed. Michael H. Schill (Albany: State University of New York Press, 1999), 130–131.
18. Harry Fialkin to Simeon Golar, 17 July 1973, folder 3, box 67B7, NYCHA; Bloom, *Public Housing That Worked*, 211; NYCHA, "Tenant Data, 1966–1974," folder 13, box 89E6, NYCHA.
19. Neil Smith, *The New Urban Frontier: Gentrification and the Revanchist City* (London: Routledge, 1996), chapter 3; Michael Pacione, *Urban Geography: A Global Perspective*, 3rd ed. (London: Routledge, 2009), 210.
20. David Shipler, "Welfare Housing," *New York Times*, 26 January 1971. For the coining of "limousine liberal" in the 1968 campaign, see Vincent Cannato, *The Ungovernable City: John Lindsay and His Struggle to Save New York* (New York: Basic Books, 2001), 428; press release, "Golar Announces Plan to House and Offer Employment to all Welfare Hotel Families," 9 March 1971, folder 14, box 60E3, NYCHA; Glenn Fowler, "Public Housing Helpless to Aid Most Who Apply," *New York Times*, 5 September 1971; Simeon Golar to John Lindsay, 4 January 1973, folder 3, box 66E, NYCHA; see also Emmanuel P. Popolizio, "What Housing Authority Does for the Homeless," *New York Times*, 15 March 1986.
21. Hofstra University sociologist Cynthia Bogard carefully traces how homelessness in New York and elsewhere emerged as a social concern (or in her phrase, was "talked into being") in the 1980s and who framed the issue. See Cynthia J. Bogard, *Seasons Such as These: How Homelessness Took Shape in America* (New York: Aldine De Gruyter, 2003).
22. Estimates of the homeless, it should be noted, are both notoriously unreliable and inescapably politicized. For a discussion of these issues, see Christopher Jencks, *The Homeless* (Cambridge, MA: Harvard University Press, 1994), chapter 1. For the unexpected growth of the homeless population, see chapter 10.
23. Ibid., 42–43. Sixty-six percent of single adults in general purpose shelters tested positive.
24. John Karaagac, *Between Promise and Policy: Ronald Reagan and Conservative Reformism* (Lanham, MD: Lexington Books, 2000), 140; Bloom, *Public Housing That Worked*, 214–219; Vitale, *City of Disorder*, chapter 4; "Good Riddance to the Welfare Hotels," *New York Times*, 5 January 1989; "A Halfhearted Homeless Policy," *New York Times*, 24 August 1992; Ellen Tumposky, "Homeless a Burden: Housing Authority," *New York Daily News*, 9 July 1992.
25. Center for Residential Security Design, "The Achievement of Crime Free, Stable Communities in Federally Assisted Housing," folder 4, box 89A3, NYCHA.
26. Morton Bard, "Police Family Crisis Intervention and Conflict Management: An Action Research Analysis" (New York City: Graduate Center of the City University of New York Prepared for the Department of Justice Law Enforcement Assistance Administration, 1972), 132, 48.
27. "Potential Tension Situations," 6 November 1970, folder 4, box 70D2, NYCHA; Hyman Resnick to S. Friedman 5 May 1972, folder 5, box 90A5, NYCHA; see the various reports

submitted by the manager of Van Dyke Houses, 1970–1973, in folder 13, box 66E8, NYCHA. See, for example, Lewis Ehrenshaft to Blanco Cadeno 3 November 1976, folder 1, box 90A4, NYCHA. "Project Survey Report," 11 September 1980, folder 1, box 90A4, NYCHA. Wendy Schuman, "Public Housing Revises Its Approach to 'Problem Families,'" *New York Times*, 29 June 1975.

28. "Linda Nichols to Your Honor," 21 January 1987, box 101, National Congress of Neighborhood Women Records, Sophia Smith Collection, Smith College. See discussion of Tenant Review and Orientation Committee in Keyes, *Strategies and Saints*, 102–103. NYCHA now implements this policy through its Applicant Review and Orientation Committee; see NYCHA, "Guide to Departments" at www.nyc.gov/html/nycha/downloads/pdf/nycha_guide_to_depts.pdf.

29. "Taft Houses Minutes of Meeting," 16 March 1983, folder 9, box 90A4, NYCHA; John Tierney, "Using Housing Projects for Welfare Angers Tenants," *New York Times*, 28 June 1990.

30. See, for example, Robert J. Sampson, Jeffrey Morenoff, and Stephen Raudenbush, "Neighborhood Inequality, Collective Efficacy, and the Spatial Dynamics of Urban Violence," *Criminology* 39 (2001): 517–560.

31. *In rem*, Latin for "against the thing," is the legal mechanism by which the city forecloses against such properties. These structures have since acquired the name *in rem* buildings. For the city's struggles managing such see Malcolm Gladwell, "Savior to Slumlord; City Doesn't Sell Bankrupt Buildings, It Manages Them—Not Very Successfully," *Washington Post*, 27 March 1994.

32. Susan Saegart, Gary Winkel, and Charles Swartz, "Social Capital and Crime in New York City's Low-Income Housing," *Housing Policy Debate* 13, no. 1 (2002): 209.

33. Peter K. B. St. Jean, *Pockets of Crime: Broken Windows, Collective Efficacy, and the Criminal Point of View* (Chicago: University of Chicago Press, 2007), 41.

34. Rhonda Y. Williams, *The Politics of Public Housing: Black Women's Struggles against Urban Inequality* (New York: Oxford University Press, 2004), 132.

35. Mary and Tricia Alfson, interview by author and Nicholas Alfson, 15 December 2006, tape of interview in author's possession.

36. Ibid.

37. Rule, "17,000 Families in Public Housing Doubling up Illegally, City Believes"; Alan Finder, "Apartment Doubling-up Hits the Working Class," *New York Times*, 25 September 1990; Alan Finder, "Doubling-up by Tenants Costing New York Millions," *New York Times*, 1 October 1988.

38. Harold Massey, interview by author, 9 March 2007, tape of interview in author's possession.

39. Mildred Rosenberg and Leo Marinconz to Mr. H Calcanes, 28 December 1979, folder 1, box 90A4, NYCHA; Lewis Ehrenshaft to Edward McClendon, 3 June 1980, folder 1, box 90A4, NYCHA.

40. Terri Sheeps, interview by author and Rasheda Denny, 10 February 2007, tape of interview in author's possession.

41. Jennifer Gonnerman, *Life on the Outside: The Prison Odyssey of Elaine Bartlett*, 1st ed. (New York: Farrar, Straus, and Giroux, 2004), 232–234; Massey interview.

42. For the percentage of white officers in 1965, see John J. Truta, "A Comprehensive Study of Recruitment of Negroes by the New York City Police Department with Other Law Enforcement Agencies" (master's thesis, Bernard M. Baruch College, 1969), 70. For

1973–1982, see Norman Parnass to Alton Maddox, 29 November 1983, folder 4, box 74C4, NYCHA.

43. Robert M. Fogelson, *Big-City Police* (Cambridge, MA: Harvard University Press, 1977), chapter 11.

44. Terry H. Anderson, *The Pursuit of Fairness: A History of Affirmative Action* (New York: Oxford University Press, 2004), 127–130. *Ward's Cove Packing Co. v. Atonio,* 490 U.S. 642 (1989) effectively overturned Griggs but was itself overturned by the Civil Rights Act of 1991, which shifted the burden of proof back to the employers. See N. Scott Arnold, *Imposing Values: An Essay on Liberalism and Regulation* (New York: Oxford University Press, 2009), chapter 12.

45. *Guardians Association of New York City Police Department Inc v. Civil Service Commission of City of New York* (490 F2d 40).

46. State Division of Human Rights, "Complaint," 13 April 1971; Daniel Daly to Marcus Levy, 20 April 1971; Robert Ledee to Marcus Levy, 11 August 1971; Carl Irish to Nathaniel Leventhal, "Housing Police Promotions," 14 September 1971; all in folder 4, box 62C1, NYCHA.

47. Bernard Cohen and Jan M. Chaiken, "Police Civil Service Selection Procedures in New York City" (RAND Corporation, 1973).

48. Richard Allen Epstein, *Forbidden Grounds: The Case against Employment Discrimination Laws* (Cambridge, MA: Harvard University Press, 1992), 218–222.

49. Deirdre Carmody, "Record Minority Percentage Foreseen for Police Recruits," *New York Times*, 12 February 1973; Angel Castillo, "293 from Minorities to Join City Police," *New York Times*, 31 August 1980.

50. Josh Barbanel, "City Using Single Civil Service List in Hiring for 3 Police Departments," *New York Times*, 5 February 1975. Note that those interviewed for the article did not make the logical connection to the EEOC protective order. Ralph Blumenthal, "New York's 3 Police Forces Open New Recruiting Battle," *New York Times*, 19 August 1991.

51. For manpower levels, see New York City Housing Police, *1986 Annual Report*, 5.

52. Barbanel, "City Using Single Civil Service List in Hiring for 3 Police Departments"; Norman Parnass to Alton Maddox, 29 November 1983, folder 4, box 74C4, NYCHA; Ann Morris, Maybeth Shinn, and Kimberly DuMont, "Contextual Factors Affecting the Organizational Commitment of Diverse Police Officers: A Levels of Analysis Perspective," *American Journal of Community Psychology* 27, no. 1 (1999): 75–105; see also Brian A. Reaves and Matthew J. Hickman, "Police Departments in Large Cities, 1990–2000" (Washington, DC: U.S. Dept. of Justice, Office of Justice Programs, Bureau of Justice Statistics, 2002).

53. Todd Purdum, "New Faces Revive Old Dispute on Merging 3 Police Forces," *New York Times*, 17 January 1990.

54. Peter Grymes, interview by author, 10 February 2008, tape of interview in author's possession.

55. "A Concerned Housing Police Officer" to Joseph Christian, 7 July 1983, folder 12, box 91D5, NYCHA.

56. Keeney interview; Grymes interview.

57. Wasserman Associates, "Providing a Secure Environment in NYCHA Housing Developments."

58. Howard French, "Drug Deaths after Arrests Draw Scrutiny," *New York Times*, 14 June 1989; Alphonso Pinkney, *Lest We Forget: White Hate Crimes, Howard Beach, and Other Racial Atrocities* (Chicago: Third World Press), 241–242.

59. French, "Drug Deaths after Arrests Draw Scrutiny"; Robert McFadden, "Panel Contradicts Autopsy in Death of Man in Custody," *New York Times*, 29 December 1989. Note coroner's response to the New York State investigation.

60. Don Terry, "Angry Protest Assails Police in Man's Death," *New York Times*, 24 May 1989.

61. Ibid.

62. NYCHA, "Report of Local Hearings October 1, 1966 . . . ," 16 January 1967, folder 5, box 64B7, NYCHA; "Report Local Hearings . . . ," April 1968, folder 1, box 65A6, NYCHA; "Report of Local Hearing 1970," April 1971, folder 1, box 65A6, NYCHA; Joseph Rechetnick to Albert Walsh, 8 August 1969, folder 3, box 65B1, NYCHA; "Annual Statistical Report of Local Police Department Disciplinary Hearings," 15 May 1973, folder 8, box 65B1, NYCHA; "Annual Statistical Report of Local Police Department Trial Hearings," 26 February 1974, folder 2, box 68B2, NYCHA.

63. Bernard Cohen, "The Police Internal Administration of Justice in New York City" (New York: New York City RAND Institute), 15; Norman Parnass to Alton Maddox, 29 November 1983, folder 4, box 74C4, NYCHA.

64. Jane Jacobs, *The Death and Life of Great American Cities* (New York: Random House, 1961); Glenna Lang and Marjory Wunsch, *Genius of Common Sense: Jane Jacobs and the Story of the Death and Life of Great American Cities* (Boston: David R. Godine, 2008), chapter 5; Katharine G. Bristol, "The Pruitt-Igoe Myth," *Journal of Architectural Education* 44, no. 3 (1991): 163–171; Oscar Newman, *Defensible Space; Crime Prevention through Urban Design* (New York: Collier Books, 1973). For opponents' marshaling of crime data to oppose the Forest Hills NYCHA development, see Daniel A. Wishnoff, "The Tolerance Point: Race, Public Housing and the Forest Hills Controversy, 1945–1975" (Ph.D. diss., City University of New York, 2005). For black opposition to public housing in Baisley Park, see Jim Sleeper, *The Closest of Strangers: Liberalism and the Politics of Race in New York* (New York: Norton, 1990), 151. See also "Residents Pledge Fight Against Housing," *Long Island Press*, 5 August 1971.

65. Wendell E. Pritchett, *Brownsville, Brooklyn: Blacks, Jews, and the Changing Face of the Ghetto* (Chicago: University of Chicago Press, 2002), 152; Garth Davies, *Crime, Neighborhood, and Public Housing* (New York: LFB Scholarly, 2006), 7.

66. For the problems of identifying crime data that distinguishes public housing from surrounding areas, see Harold R. Holzman, Karl Roger Kudrick, and Kenneth P. Voytek, "Measuring Crime in Public Housing Methodological Issues and Research Strategies," *Journal of Quantitative Criminology* 14, no. 4 (1998): 331–351.

67. Tamara Dumanovsky, "Examining the Neighborhood Context of NYC's Public Housing Projects" (Ph.D. diss., New York University, 1999); Terry Williams and William Kornblum, "Public Housing Projects as Successful Environments for Adolescent Development," in *The Anthropology of Lower Income Urban Enclaves: The Case of East Harlem*, ed. Judith Freidenberg (New York: New York Academy of Sciences, 1995), 160; Leo Schuerman, "Community Careers in Crime," in *Communities and Crime*, ed. Albert J. Reiss and Michael H. Tonry (Chicago: University of Chicago Press, 1986), 67–100.

68. Bloom, *Public Housing That Worked*, 148.

69. Samual Rabinove to Albert Vorspan, 22 February 1972, Forest Hills folder, 1971–1973, American Jewish Committee Archives, New York City.

70. Edward Ranzal, "Project Crime Rate Called Less Than Neighborhood's," *New York Times*, 28 December 1971.

71. Ibid.; Edward Kirkman, "Killings Start Dispute over Crime Rates," *New York Daily News*, 21 December 1971; David Shipler, "Estimate Board Rejects Housing for Lidenwood," *New York Times*, 24 November 1971; Joseph P. Fried, "Simeon's Golar's City-within-a-City," *New York Times*, 30 April 1972.

72. Kirkman, "Killings Start Dispute over Crime Rates"; "Balzano to Testify on HA Police Needs," *The Chief*, 12 April 1972. For Garelick in 1973, see Cannato, *The Ungovernable City*, 556–558.

73. "Eyewitness News Conference," 11 May 1975, folder 1, box 88B5, NYCHA.

74. NYCHA, "Press Release Comments," 20 May 1975, folder 1, box 88B5, NYCHA. For city and NYCHA crime rates in 1974 and 1975, see "Statistical Worksheet 1974 vs. 1975," April 1976, folder 4, box 89E6, NYCHA.

75. Bloom, *Public Housing That Worked*, 191.

76. Lawrence Rosen, "The Creation of the Uniform Crime Report: The Role of Social Science," *Social Science History* 19, no. 2 (1995): 215–238; Piers Beirne and James W. Messerschmidt, *Criminology* (Boulder, CO: Westview Press, 2000), 36.

77. For an example of NYCHA separating out crime against persons for reporters, see Ranzal, "Project Crime Rate Called Less Than Neighborhood's."

78. Eric C. Schneider, *Smack: Heroin and the American City* (Philadelphia: University of Pennsylvania Press, 2008), 117.

79. A number of significant publications have stemmed from this impressive empirical foundation; see Dumanovsky, "Examining the Neighborhood Context of NYC's Public Housing Projects"; Jeffrey Fagan, Jan Holland, and Garth Davies, "The Bustle of Horses on a Ship: Drug Control in New York City Public Housing," August 2005 (Columbia Law School Public Law Research Paper No. 05–89), available at SSRN: http://papers.ssrn.com/s013/papers.cfm?abstract_id=716821; Davies, *Crime, Neighborhood, and Public Housing*.

80. Williams and Kornblum, "Public Housing Projects as Successful Environments for Adolescent Development," 161; Fagan, Holland, and Davies, "The Bustle of Horses on a Ship."

81. In 1982, NYCHA estimated official records undercounted its actual resident population by 50,000 individuals, or 10 percent of its official rent rolls; in 1990 it calculated that 100,000 individuals (or 21.5 percent of its official population) had taken up residence as "ghost tenants." NYCHA has not announced a new estimate since 1990. In recalculating the crime statistics, this study assumes a 10 percent under-tally for 1982 that increased by a steady 1.5 percentage points every year after that until 1990. In the absence of new data from NYCHA, the study keeps the under-tally at 21.5 percent for the remaining years. See Rule, "17,000 Families in Public Housing Doubling Up Illegally, City Believes," and Finder, "Apartment Doubling-up Hits the Working Class."

82. Marvin Berkowitz, *The Social Costs of Human Underdevelopment: Case Study of Seven New York City Neighborhoods* (New York: Praeger, 1974), 83.

83. For dating the arrival of crack, see Roland Fryer, Paul Heaton, Steven Levitt, and Kevin Murphy, "Measuring the Impact of Crack Cocaine," in NBER Working Paper Series (Cambridge, MA: National Bureau of Economic Research, 2005).

84. Davies, *Crime, Neighborhood, and Public Housing*, 66–72. See also Bourgois, *In Search of Respect: Selling Crack in El Barrio*.

85. Jeffrey Fagan, "Drug Selling and Licit Income in Distressed Neighborhoods: The Economic Lives of Street Level Drug Users and Dealers," in *Drugs, Crime, and Social Isolation: Barriers to Urban Opportunity*, ed. Adele Harrell and George E. Peterson (Washington, DC: Urban Institute Press, 1992), 99–146; Mercer Sullivan, "Crime and the Social Fabric," in *Dual City: Restructuring New York*, ed. John H. Mollenkopf and Manuel Castells (New York: Russell Sage Foundation, 1991), 225–244.

86. Keyes, *Strategies and Saints*, 97; NYCHA, "Public Housing Drug Elimination Act Grant Application, Employee Program, 1 December 1989, folder 1, box 98A4, NYCHA. Nick Ravo, "Shakeup from Housing Police Drug Arrests," *New York Times*, 26 August 1989. Just five years earlier Irizarry had narrowly missed becoming second-in-command of the HAPD, but lost his employment discrimination case against the Authority; see *Irizarry v. New York City Housing Authority* 575 F. Supp. 571 (1983).

87. Davies, *Crime, Neighborhood, and Public Housing*, 156, 24–25; Jeffrey Fagan and Garth Davies, "Crime in Public Housing: Two-Way Diffusion Effects," in *Analyzing Crime Patterns: Frontiers of Practice*, ed. Victor Goldsmith (Thousand Oaks, CA: Sage Publications, 2000). In *Crime, Neighborhood, and Public Housing*, Davies writes (129), "in epidemiological terms, public housing crime and violence seem to "infect" adjacent neighborhoods," and (157) that "areas proximate to public housing are from a criminogenic perspective, adversely affected by its proximity." In "Crime in Public Housing," Fagan and Davies conclude that (132), "the results suggest that violence in public housing diffuse outward from the projects and increases the rates of violence in the census track generally," while for assaults there were "significant inward diffusion effects . . . for the more serious and bellwether crimes of homicide and robbery, the diffusion effects appear to be exclusively in the direction of the outlying areas."

88. Dumanovsky, "Examining the Neighborhood Context of NYC's Public Housing Projects."

89. Virginia Schomp, *New York*, 2nd ed., Celebrate the States (New York: Benchmark Books, 2005), 53.This dynamic was also at work in the LeFrak City "crisis"; see Steven Gregory, *Black Corona: Race and the Politics of Place in an Urban Community* (Princeton, NJ: Princeton University Press, 1998), chapter 5.

90. Keyes, *Strategies and Saints*, 27.

91. Newman, *Defensible Space*; Jacobs, *The Death and Life of Great American Cities*; Nathan Glazer, *From Cause to a Style: Modernist Architecture's Encounter with the American City* (Princeton, NJ: Princeton University Press, 2007), 186–187; John Robert Gold, *The Practice of Modernism: Modern Architects and Urban Transformation, 1954–1972* (London: Routledge, 2007), chapter 12. Newman had, in fact, questioned (112) Jacobs's notion that commercial facilities led to proprietorial surveillance, but the similarity of their ideas regarding informal social control and crime have been widely noted.

92. Newman's theories faced extensive critiques. Some concluded that the relationship between physical context and crime was weaker that Newman had claimed and merely displaced crime. See Charles Murray, "The Physical Environment," in *Crime*, ed. James Q. Wilson and Joan Petersilia (San Francisco: ICS Press, 1995), 349–363. Others argued that his principle of territoriality depended on the notion of outside predators, ignoring the reality that residents perpetrated much of the crime. See Rob Mawby, "Defensible Space: A Theoretical and Empirical Appraisal," *Urban Studies* 14 (1977): 169–179. Newman himself retreated from his earlier theories, eventually embracing instead one that blended the importance of social and physical elements. For the impact on NYCHA, see Bloom, *Public Housing That Worked*, 222–224, 39.

93. Robin Shulman, "Supreme Change," *Washington Post*, 16 June 2009.

94. Sidney Shchackman to J. Christian, 30 August, 1973, folder 7, box 88B2, NYCHA; Michael C. Musheno, James P Levine, and Denis J. Palumbo, "Television Surveillance and Crime Prevention: Evaluating an Attempt to Create Defensible Space in Public Housing," *Social Science Quarterly* 58 (1978): 647–656

95. Joan Shepard, "TV Screening Out Crime at City Housing Project," *New York Daily News*, 26 July 1977; NYCHA, Tenant Characteristics Tompkins Houses, 1976, folder 4, box 90A5, NYCHA; "Tompkins Liberation Center" card, folder 4, box 90A5, NYCHA; "Topics for Discussion at the Meeting to be Held . . ." 9 February 1977, folder 4, box 90A5, NYCHA; Florence Tyson, interview by author, 1 August 2007, tape of interview in author's possession.

96. Musheno, Levine, and Palumbo, "Television Surveillance and Crime Prevention"; "Arrests for Index Crime, All Projects," 1977, folder 7, box 89A3, NYCHA. Compare with arrest total from individual complexes in 1964 in box 66E1. Dean James P. Levine, interview by author, 3 August 2009.

97. Oscar Newman, "The Repercussions of Dishonesty in Research Reporting," *Social Science Quarterly* 61, no. 2 (1980): 322–325 Michael C. Levine, James P. Musheno, and Dennis J. Palumbo, "The Impact of Evaluation Research: A Reply to Newman," *Social Science Quarterly* 61, no. 2 (1980): 325–328; Charles M Bonjean, "On the Costs of Publishing Evaluation Research," *Social Science Quarterly* 61, no. 2 (1980): 329–332.

98. Davies, *Crime, Neighborhood, and Public Housing*, chapter 2.

99. Anthony Pate, "An Evaluation of the Urban Initiatives Anti-Crime Program: Final Report" (Washington, DC: Department of Housing and Urban Development, 1984), chapter 2; Keyes, *Strategies and Saints.*

100. Sylvia Velazquez quoted in Michael Massing, *The Fix* (New York: Simon & Schuster, 1998), 64.

101. Ibid., 39–46. Manuel Quintana to Rudolph Giuliani, 16 September 1987, MN 41077, roll 77, MA. 68, Koch Papers, New York City Municipal Archives.

102. Robert McCabe to Roland Diaz, 6 October 1987, folder 4, box 98B2, NYCHA. For tenant concerns about the drug trade and demands that NYCHA "do something about it," see "Cooper Park Tenant Patrol Building Captain Monthly Meeting," 14 April 1988, folder 22, box 101, National Congress of Neighborhood Women Records, Sophia Smith Collection, Smith College.

103. "The regular meeting of the NYCHA Anti-Narcotics . . ." 11 June 1987, folder 4, box 98B2, NYCHA. For a review of this legislation, see Jack Yoskowitz, "The War on the Poor: Civil Forfeiture of Public Housing," *Columbia Journal of Law and Social Problems* 25 (1991): 567–600.

104. Emmanauel Popolizio, "At Long Last, a Victory over the Drug Dealers," *New York Times*, 21 May 1988. Note that the *Times*'s byline misspelled Popolizio's first name.

105. For a retrospective analysis of Giuliani's political strategies in the 1980s, see Landon Thomas, "Giuliani Time?" *New York*, 6 May 2002: 27–29; Peter Lattman, "Breaking Down the 'Perp Walk,'" *Wall Street Journal*, 22 March 2006; John Kroger, *Convictions: A Prosecutor's Battles against Mafia Killers, Drug Kingpins, and Enron Thieves* (New York: Farrar, Straus, and Giroux, 2008), 436.

106. Manuel Quintana to Rudolph Giuliani, 31 December 1987, and Manuel Quintana to Pamela Dempsey, 31 December 1987, both in folder 4, box 98B2, NYCHA.

107. Manuel Quintana to Mr. Popolizio, "Memorandum re: Forfeiture requests," 14 January 1988, folder 4, box 98 B2, NYCHA. Note both sides.

108. Emanuel Popolizio to Rudolph Giuliani, 10 February, 1988, folder 9, box 98 B2, NYCHA; For Popolizio's friendship with Koch, see Wolfgang Saxon, "Emanuel P. Popolizio, 74, Dies; Former Housing Authority Chief," *New York Times*, 27 August 1992; Emanuel Popolizio to Rudolph Giuliani, 28 April 1988, folder 9, box 98 B2, NYCHA; Subcommittee on General Oversight, Investigations, and the Resolution of Failed Financial Institutions of the Committee on Banking, Finance, and Urban Affairs, Review of Giuliani Plan to Merge Police: Field Hearing, 103rd Congress, 2nd session, 19 September 1994, 7.

109. George James, "Officials Seize 3 Apartments in Drug Raid," *New York Times*, 2 November 1988.

110. Yoskowitz, "The War on the Poor," 569. Cranston-Gonzalez National Affordable Housing Act, Pub. L. No. 101–625, 504, 104 Stat. 4181 1990; codified as 42 ß U.S.C.A. 1437(1)(5).

111. Valerie D. White, "Modifying the *Escalera* Consent Decree: A Case Study on the Application of the *Rufo* Test," *Fordham Urban Law Journal* 23 (1996): 377–412; Gerald Lebovits and Douglass J. Seidman, "Drug Holdover Proceedings: An Overview from 'Knew,' to 'Should Have Known,' to 'Strict Liability,'" *N.Y. Real Property Law Journal N.Y. Real Property Law Journal* 35, no. 2. (Spring/Summer 2007): 16–26

112. Ross Sandler and David Schoenbrod, *Democracy by Decree: What Happens When Courts Run Government* (New Haven, CT: Yale University Press, 2003), 128–129.

113. *Doe v. New Bedford Housing Authority* 417 Mass. 273 (Mass. 1994); John Atlas, "From 'Projects' to Communities: How to Redeem Public Housing," *American Prospect*, no. 10 (Summer 1992): 74–85; Sol Stern, "The Legal Aid Follies," *City Journal* (Autumn 1995): 22–33.

114. Stern, "The Legal Aid Follies."

115. Jan Hoffman, "Amid Turmoil, Legal Aid Names New Top Executive," *New York Times*, 15 November 1994; David Rohde, "Decline Is Seen in Legal Help for City's Poor," *New York Times*, 26 August 1998.

116. Michael Rosen, interview by author, 5 May 2009, tape of interview in author's possession.

117. Sandler and Schoenbrod, *Democracy by Decree*, 129.

118. Dennis Saffran, "Public Housing Safety Versus Tenants' Rights," *The Responsive Community* 6, no. 4 (1996); Fred Siegel, "The Loss of Public Space," in *The Essential Communitarian Reader*, ed. Amitai Etzioni (Lanham, MD: Rowman & Littlefield, 1998), 187–198; Amitai Etzioni, "A New Community of Thinkers, Both Liberal and Conservative," *Wall Street Journal*, 8 October 1991.

119. *Escalera v. New York City Housing Authority*, 924 F.Supp. 1323 (S.D.N.Y. 1996).

120. Remarks announcing the "One Strike and You're Out" Initiative in Public Housing, 32 Weekly Comp. Pres. Doc. 582, 583 (28 March 1996).

121. Laurel Walker, "One-Strike-You're-Out Approach; Housing Authority Already Tough," *Milwaukee Journal Sentinel*, 1 October 1996; Adam P. Hellegers, "Reforming HUD's 'One Strike' Public Housing Evictions through Tenant Participation," *Journal of Criminal Law and Criminology* 90, no. 1 (1999): 323–362.

122. Marie Fritz, "Race and Gender in the Department of Housing and Urban Development" (paper presented to Annual Meeting of Midwestern Political Science Association, Chicago, 2008); Simon, *Governing through Crime*, 195; Parenti, *Lockdown America*, 62; Jason R. Hackworth, *The Neoliberal City: Governance, Ideology, and*

Development in American Urbanism (Ithaca, NY: Cornell University Press, 2007), 51; Gloria J. Browne-Marshall, *Race, Law, and American Society: 1607* to Present (New York: Routledge, Taylor & Francis Group, 2007), 48, 76.

123. Lebovits and Seidman, "Drug Holdover Proceedings."
124. *Department of Housing and Urban Development v. Rucker* (00–1770) 535 U.S. 125 (2002) 237 F.3d 1113. The Court's logic (and Rehnquist's theories on grammar) have come under criticism from a variety of political angles. For the liberal critique, see Michael C. Dorf, *No Litmus Test: Law versus Politics in the Twenty-First Century* (Lanham, MD: Rowman & Littlefield, 2006). For a libertarian analysis, see Roger Pilon, *Cato Supreme Court Review, 2001–2002* (Washington, DC: Center for Constitutional Studies, Cato Institute, 2002).
125. Lebovits and Seidman, "Drug Holdover Proceedings."
126. Manny Fernandez, "Barred from Public Housing, Even to See Family," *New York Times*, 1 October 2007.

CHAPTER 5 A RETURN TO ORIGINS AND THE MERGER

1. "Crime-Ravaged City Cries Out for Help: Dave, Do Something!" *New York Post*, 7 September 1990; Joe Klein, "The Real Deficit: Leadership," *New York*, 22 July 1991; Albert R. Roberts, *Critical Issues in Crime and Justice* (Thousand Oaks, CA: Sage Publications, 2003), 119–121; Steven Meyers, "Police Classes Are Postponed by Giuliani," *New York Times*, 24 August 1994. For the murder spike in 1990, see George James, "New York Killings Set a Record, While Other Crimes Fell in 1990," *New York Times*, 23 April 1991. Assistant Chief of Department Joseph Keeney, interview by author, 21 July 2009, tape of interview in author's possession.
2. Jan Holland Jeffrey Fagan, Tamara Dumanovsky, Garth Davies, "Final Report: Drug Control in Public Housing: The Impact of the Drug Elimination Program of the New York City Public Housing Authority" (Princeton, NJ: Robert Wood Johnson Foundation, 2003), digital copy of final in author's possession courtesy of Jeffrey Fagan. The discussion in these pages of NYCHA's DEP-funded efforts draws extensively from this 2003 report, and I am grateful to that study's authors for generously sharing it with me.
3. Ibid.
4. Ibid.
5. Ibid.
6. Shauna Dawns, interview by author, 12 August 2007, tape of interview in author's possession.
7. Housing Police, "Annual Report," 1991, 24, John Jay College Special Collections, NYCHA; Joseph Keeney, interview by author, 13 July 2009; "Security Partnership," n.d., folder 2, box 100B3, New York City Housing Authority Papers, La Guardia and Wagner Archives, La Guardia Community College (hereafter NYCHA); "Safe Housing Partnership," 1992, folder 2, box 100B3, NYCHA; Wasserman Associates, Inc., "Providing a Secure Environment in NYCHA Housing Developments," 15 January 1992, folder 1, box 100B3, NYCHA.
8. Harold Massey, interview by author, 17 April 2007, tape of interview in author's possession.
9. Edward Conlon, *Blue Blood* (New York: Riverhead Books, 2004), 158. Conlon became a police officer just three months after the merger of the city's three police forces, but

the institutional successor to the Housing Police, the NYPD's Housing Bureau, preserved some aspects of the DEP program's architecture until the program was eliminated by President George W. Bush in 2002.

10. Ralph Blumenthal, "New York's 3 Police Forces Open New Recruiting Battle," *New York Times*, 19 August 1991; Dennis Hevesi, "Transit and Housing Officers Sue on Transfer Law," *New York Times*, 3 October 1991; Ralph Blumenthal, "Cuomo Is Said to Be Ready to Veto Police-Drug Bill," *New York Times*, 25 July 1991; "Briefing Tours of PSA #4," 12 November 1992, folder 4, box 100B3, NYCHA.
11. Ann Morris, Maybeth Shinn, and Kimberly DuMont, "Contextual Factors Affecting the Organizational Commitment of Diverse Police Officers: A Levels of Analysis Perspective," *American Journal of Community Psychology* 27, no. 1 (1999): 77.
12. Housing Police, "Annual Report," 1991, 1992; Taylor quoted in Blumenthal, "New York's 3 Police Forces Open New Recruiting Battle"; for executive corps courses, see Housing Police, "Annual Report," 1992, 76; Massey interview; City of New York, *Driving Crime, Disorder and Fear from the Public Housing of New York* (New York: 1994), 9–10.
13. Garth Davies, Jeffrey Fagan, and Jan Holland, "The Paradox of the Drug Elimination Program in New York City Public Housing," *Georgetown Journal on Poverty Law & Policy* 13, no. 415 (2006): 26.
14. A central character of Richard Price's *Freedomland* (Santa Monica, CA: Revolution Studio, 2006) is a housing officer, but the film is set in New Jersey's public housing. For Price's background see Richard Price, "The Fonzie of Literature," *New York Times*, 25 October 1981.
15. "Merger of Police Studied by City," *New York Times*, 29 March 1962.
16. Frederick F. Siegel and Harry Siegel, *The Prince of the City: Giuliani, New York, and the Genius of American Life*, 1st ed. (San Francisco: Encounter Books, 2005), 281.
17. City of New York, "Analysis of Police Service Organizational Options for New York City," (New York: Legislative Office of Budget Review, 1980); Todd Purdum, "New Faces Revive Old Dispute on Merging 3 Police Forces," *New York Times*, 17 January 1990.
18. Val Coleman to Louis Fairlamb, 27 April 1978, folder 12, box 92D7, NYCHA.
19. Calvin Sims, "Police-Merger Fight Stalls Dispatch System," *New York Times*, 27 September 1990.
20. Purdum, "New Faces Revive Old Dispute on Merging 3 Police Forces"; Sims, "Police-Merger Fight Stalls Dispatch System"; Leonard Buder, "Housing Police Ask Merger with New York Force," *New York Times*, 16 January 1990.
21. Russ Baker, "The Rogue Police Union," *Village Voice*, 7 December 1993.
22. U.S. House, Subcommittee on General Oversight, Investigations, and the Resolution of Failed Financial Institutions of the Committee on Banking, Finance, and Urban Affairs, Review of Giuliani Plan to Merge Police: Field hearing before the Subcommittee, 103rd Cong., 2nd sess., 28 July 1994 (Washington, DC: Government Printing Office, 1994); Richard Perez-Pena, "Transit Officials Try to Prevent Withholding of Police Funds," *New York Times*, 18 January 1995.
23. Jonathan Hicks, "Housing Police Folded into Citywide Force," *New York Times*, 1 May 1995; Father Lawrence Lucas, interview by author and Nicholas Alford, 6 November 2006, tape of interview in author's possession.
24. Harry W. More, W. Fred Wegener, and Larry S. Miller, *Effective Police Supervision* (Cincinnati: Anderson Publishing, 2003), 44.
25. See, for example, Anderson Cooper, "Stop Snitchin,'" *Sixty Minutes*, CBS, 8 August 2007.

26. David Garland emphasizes this turn as primarily a response to real social changes associated with "late modernity"; see Garland, *The Culture of Control* (Chicago: University of Chicago Press, 2001), 53–73, 88–90. More recently, others have traced the new crime policies to a conservative reaction to African American progress. Vesla Weaver argues that antiblack political forces, unable to prevail against the moral power of the civil rights movement, shifted the "locus of attack" to seemingly race-neutral concerns over crime. See Vesla M. Weaver, "Dark Prison: Race, Rights, and the Politics of Punishment" (Ph.D. diss., Harvard University, 2007). "Nothing works" in rehabilitation was the seminal conclusion in Robert Martinson, "What Works? Question and Answers About Prison Reform," *Public Interest* 35 (Spring 1974): 22–54. Twenty-five years later, meta-analysis of a larger number of studies led researchers to conclude more optimistically, "most correctional treatment for adult prisoners probably have modest positive effects." See Timothy J. Flanagan Gerald G. Gaes, Laurence L. Motiuk, and Lynn Stewart, "Adult Correctional Treatment," *Crime and Justice* 26, no. Prisons (1999): 361–426.
27. Sudhir Venkatesh, *American Project: The Rise and Fall of a Modern Ghetto* (Cambridge, MA: Harvard University Press, 2000), 125. The impact of the new policies on communities is soberly reviewed in Bruce Western, *Punishment and Inequality in America* (New York: Russell Sage Foundation, 2006). The perverse manner in which as incarceration rates increase in a New York City neighborhood so too do crime rates is addressed in Jan Holland, Jeffrey Fagan, and Valerie West, "Reciprocal Effects of Crime and Incarceration in New York City Neighborhoods," *Fordham Urban Law Journal* 30 (2003).
28. Fredrich "Butch" Curtis, interview by author, 28 July 2006, tape of interview in author's possession; Artie Brown, interview by author, 15 June 2005, tape of interview in author's possession.

EPILOGUE

1. As quoted in Jan Holland Jeffrey Fagan, Tamara Dumanovsky, Garth Davies, "Final Report: Drug Control in Public Housing: The Impact of the Drug Elimination Program of the New York City Public Housing Authority" (Princeton, NJ: Robert Wood Johnson Foundation, 2003), 89–90.
2. Ibid.; Jane Schmitt, interview by author, 1 February 2008, tape of interview in author's possession.
3. Molly Wasow Park and Bernard O'Brien, "As Federal Aid Drops, City's Cost for Policing Public Housing Climbs," *IBO: Inside The Budget New York City Independent Budget Office*, no. 129 (2004); Al Baker, "New York on Track for Fewest Homicides on Record," *New York Times*, 29 December 2009; Chief Joanne Jaffee, interview by author, 25 November 2008.
4. Manny Fernandez, "Barred from Public Housing, Even to See Family," *New York Times*, 1 October 2007; see also New York Police Department, Press Affairs, "Mayor Michael R. Bloomberg Announces Operation Sage Housing to Improve Safety for Residents of Public Housing," press release, New York, 24 June 2004, www.nyc.gov.
5. Jaime Adame, "Operation Safe Housing," *Gotham Gazette*, 17 August 2004; Feinblatt quoted in New York Police Department, Press Affairs, "Mayor Michael R. Bloomberg Announces Operation Sage Housing"; Jaffee interview.
6. Al Baker and Emily Vasquez, "Number of People Stopped by New York Police Soars," *New York Times*, 3 February 2007; Erica Pearson, Frank Lombardi, and Wil Cruz, "NYPD Hands Out Informational Cards to Pedestrians Who Are Stopped and Frisked,"

New York Daily News, 30 April 2009. For stop-and-frisk numbers, see the quarterly reports archived on the American Civil Liberties Union website at http://www.nyclu.org/news/nypd-track-interrogate-record-number-of-innocent-new-yorkers-2009-new-stop-and-frisk-numbers-sh.

7. New York Lawyers for the Public Interest Community Oversight of Policing Project, "No Place Like Home: A Preliminary Report on Police Interactions with Public Housing Residents in New York City," September 2008, 1, 10, 11, http://stage.nylpi.org/pub/2008NOPLACELIKEHOMEREPORT.pdf; Hannah Rappleye, "Cops May Change Frisk Tactics" *City Limits*, 8 April 2010.
8. New York Police Department, Press Affairs, "Mayor Michael R. Bloomberg Announces Operation Sage Housing"; Victor Gonzalez, interview by author, 17 September 2008, tape of interview in author's possession; Terri Sheeps, interview by author, 7 February 2007, tape of interview in author's possession.

INDEX

ABOUT THE AUTHOR

GREG "FRITZ" UMBACH is assistant professor of history at John Jay College of Criminal Justice of the City University of New York.

Available titles in the Critical Issues in Crime and Society series:

Tammy L. Anderson, ed., *Neither Villain Nor Victim: Empowerment and Agency among Women Substance Abusers*

Scott A. Bonn, *Mass Deception: Moral Panic and the U.S. War on Iraq*

Mary Bosworth and Jeanne Flavin, eds., *Race, Gender, and Punishment: From Colonialism to the War on Terror*

Loretta Capeheart and Dragan Milovanovic, *Social Justice: Theories, Issues, and Movements*

Walter S. DeKeseredy and Martin D. Schwartz, *Dangerous Exits: Escaping Abusive Relationships in Rural America*

Patricia E. Erickson and Steven K. Erickson, *Crime, Punishment, and Mental Illness: Law and the Behavioral Sciences in Conflict*

Luis A. Fernandez, *Policing Dissent: Social Control and the Anti-Globalization Movement*

Michael J. Lynch, *Big Prisons, Big Dreams: Crime and the Failure of America's Penal System*

Raymond J. Michalowski and Ronald C. Kramer, eds., *State-Corporate Crime: Wrongdoing at the Intersection of Business and Government*

Susan L. Miller, *Victims as Offenders: The Paradox of Women's Violence in Relationships*

Torin Monahan, *Surveillance in the Time of Insecurity*

Torin Monahan and Rodolfo D. Torres, eds., *Schools Under Surveillance: Cultures of Control in Public Education*

Anthony M. Platt, *The Child Savers: The Invention of Delinquency*, 40th Anniversary Edition with an introduction and critical commentaries compiled by Miroslava Chávez-García

Susan F. Sharp, *Hidden Victims: The Effects of the Death Penalty on Families of the Accused*

Dawn L. Rothe and Christopher W. Mullins, eds., *State Crime, Current Perspectives*

Robert H. Tillman and Michael L. Indergaard, *Pump and Dump: The Rancid Rules of the New Economy*

Mariana Valverde, *Law and Order: Images, Meanings, Myths*

Michael Welch, *Crimes of Power & States of Impunity: The U.S. Response to Terror*

Michael Welch, *Scapegoats of September 11th: Hate Crimes and State Crimes in the War on Terror*